EXTENSION AND
COMPREHENSION
IN LOGIC

EXTENSION AND COMPREHENSION IN LOGIC

by

JOSEPH C. FRISCH, Ph.D., S.T.L.

PHILOSOPHICAL LIBRARY

New York

Dedicated to my Parents,
George and Elizabeth Frisch
of
Winona, Minnesota

FOREWORD

In the authentic Peripatetic tradition, philosophical analogy in its splendor as a tool must be analyzed in logic before it can be utilized to full effect in philosophy. Indeed Aristotle treated of it at the beginning of his *Categories*. Analogy implies the inescapable, human fact that quite often one word is used in different situations with subtle but systematically useful changes of meaning. Curious it is to discover how, for example, many in the neo-Thomistic school of philosophical thought, purporting to deliver the best and the profoundest of Aristotelian research to the twentieth century, have missed an essential point of Aristotle's understanding of man and have erected analogy into a self-destroying metaphysical labyrinth. Yet Aristotle's position is clear: man is a thinking animal, who, precisely because he is thinking, must speak in order to clarify his thought by systematic name-reference of less easily known objects to better known ones.

In other words, analogy is an integral and an integrating part of human language and thought for three correlated reasons. The most general principle is the body-soul relationship whose proper comprehension is essential to an adequate communication theory. Human individuals know and experience reality before constructing a language interpretation of it because they are unities possessing forms and matters as principles (i.e. instruments) of their activity. Consequently, just as an individual occupies a certain space at a certain time, so too a language in its use suffers the restrictions and advantages of space and time.

A more proximate but still common principle is the relationship in which the human reasoning power depends on the imagination (in fact, on all the internal senses) and the five external senses. As the user of any instrument must respect the conditions of his tools in order to achieve his goal in the best possible way, the thinking animal must also realize that he is conditioned by, and must therefore respect, the activity and the working limitations of the imagination.

The third and proper principle controlling language and analogy is the special attribute of the imagination by which it presents objects to the intellect as if they were quantities or the properties of quantity. Though the principle is operative in language both on the phonetic and grammatical levels, it controls the nature of analogy as a semantic problem. The role of the imagination in the formation of the meaning of words may be stated in this way. Words either in their etymology or their historically first meanings refer to material things insofar as they possesss quantity and sensible properties; consequently, from the properties of sensible quantitative realities the human intellect transfers names to all the things that it knows with some degree of clarity. The point can be formulated in another way: all the material realities known or imagined to exist can and must be named by words whose primary uses are to be traced back to some aspect of material things. It is not necessary to point out at length that this principle is not some pejorative anthropomorphism but rather a psychological statement about the human way of knowing and naming.

As the tool of human science, as a tool aiding man in his acquisition of certitude about conclusions, logic is oriented towards an adequate understanding of the relationships involved in the activities of thinking and speaking needed to reach conclusions. Through the course of centuries logicians weighted down or freed from the inhibiting prejudices proper to their own time have achieved some success in understanding the intricate nature of the syllogistic process and its two necessary prerequisite operations: that of grasping realities in tidbits (simple apprehension or incomplete comprehension) and that of attempting to compose these tidbits in an affirmative way or of dividing them in a negative manner (composition and division or, according to an inadequate jargon, judgment).

The tradition started by Aristotle's research on thinking and language continued, it would seem, to be able to revitalize itself from generation to generation as long as logicians retained an adequate grasp of the utility of the necessary instrument of the proportional names of things. Yet the historical research presented in this book by Joseph C. Frisch contains ample evidence that something strange had been going on between the late Middle Ages and the period which produced the Port Royal Logic (1662). For in this work the French words *comprehénsion* and *extension* received new values which found their way back into the Latin manuals written after 1700. (How strange in the light of the assertion of many modern Scholastics that Latin words never change!) A symptomatic parallel with these new twists of meanings in the Port Royal Logic is a strange depreciation of the place and role of the five Porphyrean predicables. Consequent to all this is the development of much of our modern logical jargon. It would appear by way of diagnosis that the underlying cause of this luxurious junglelike proliferation was a misunderstanding of the need of the analogical use of words. Rooted in the late Middle Ages, it still appears in such up-to-date observations as 'one word for every meaning and one meaning for every word.'

Nevertheless, as nature always takes it revenge on those whose neglect to respect its impositions, quantity has taken its revenge on those moderns who have misunderstood its role in the total nature of language. Words have a first meaning related to quantitative and sensible aspects of reality; these meanings are only *starting points* from which the intellect is obliged to move elsewhere. Because of the necessity of quantity as a tool of knowledge and a refusal to move from it systematically, there has appeared a modern dilemma, namely that of the identification of logic with mathematics, a modern problem still needing proper solution. Is modern symbolic logic a continuation or a destruction of the traditional Occidental, Aristotelian logic considered in its totality? The efforts of Father Frisch toward a doctrinal interpretation of 'extension' and 'comprehension' in logic based on careful historical research is a step that may help in the solution of this problem. His conclusion may fall strangely on the ears of certain modern logicians. But, in an age of dialogue, his words should not fall on deaf ears. It may be noted in passing that strangeness gives an impression, not a proof, of falsity. The main contentions of his book will grow in strength for all those who take time to reflect on his careful steps in working out the main analogies of the words 'extension' and 'comprehension': how they refer first to the physical quantitative activities of 'grasping completely' and 'stretching out'; secondly, to the emotional and volitional activities of 'clinging to' and 'going out toward' desired goods; and, finally but surely, to the activities and relationships of the senses and the intellect of 'attaining' individual objects under a certain community of knowledge named as a 'grasping'.

Father Frisch did not produce this work alone. He has worked within an oral tradition—within the sort of tradition that Alfred

North Whitehead knew how to appreciate when he wrote the following eulogy of Socrates:

> It must not be supposed that the output of a university in the form of original ideas is solely to be measured by printed papers and books labeled with the names of their authors. Mankind is as individual in its mode of output as in the substance of its thoughts. For some of the most fertile minds composition in writing, or in a form reducible to writing, seems to be an impossibility. In every faculty you will find that some of the more brilliant teachers are not among those who publish. Their originality requires for its expression direct intercourse with their pupils in the form of lectures, or of personal discussion. Such men exercise an immense influence; and yet, after the generation of their pupils has passed away, they sleep among the innumerable unthanked benefactors of humanity. Fortunately, one of them is immortal— Socrates. (Alfred North Whitehead in *The Aims of Education*, pp. 98-99. New York. A Mentor Book, 1949).

Father Frisch has had the privilege of working within the oral tradition of one of the great logicians of the twentieth century, Maurice Dionne, who, relatively unknown, leads the life of a man busy about the more important things: personal research, the formation of pupils in the classroom and in personal discussion—too busy to consign his oral teaching to writing. The onerous task of writing in order to perpetuate his research falls on those who have benefited from it. These students have learned with profit to shy away from certain basic errors in the logic of John of Saint Thomas, to appreciate the extraordinary grasp of logical doctrine possessed by Albert the Great and Boethius, and to see the need to undertake patiently the study of the great Greek commentators on Aristotle.

Monsignor Dionne has worked assiduously and obstinately in the anonymity of the classroom and private discussion for the past thirty years. His presence and force as a member of the staff of Laval University accounts for the references in a certain philosophical literature to the opinions of Gilson, Maritain and that of Laval. Reading and commenting on the texts of a selected few of the great philosophers and refusing to allow students to wallow complacently in the prejudices of their own century has been a part of

x

his oral tradition. That Father Frisch's book be historical in large part is understandable in our times, but that it contain a dense but intelligible doctrinal essay of an important logical problem is extraordinary. A proof indeed of the fecundity of the oral tradition whose life nurtured by those who do not write needs to be sustained nevertheless by the permanency of the word carefully written.

John R. Gallup,
Laval University,
Quebec, P.Q., Canada.
November 8, 1968.

CONTENTS

INTRODUCTION

The purpose of this work is to analyze what has been frequently described by logicians as the extension and comprehension of concepts. Even if there is a justification for extension and comprehension in logic, it may be questioned whether there are any concomitant dangers since one historian of logic claims that this distinction has done more harm than good. Can it be said that the importance of extension and comprehension has been magnified out of proportion to the other parts of logic? Would it be more advantageous to correlate extension and comprehension with the predicables, or would it be better to try to eliminate the distinction altogether?

It is the aim of this study to explore the distinction existing between extension and comprehension, to ascertain whether such distinction is justifiable, where it should be placed in a treatise on logic, and how it should be presented. These are questions which should be answered if one intends to have a thorough grasp of logic.

This treatise will be divided into two parts. The first part will be subdivided into two chapters. Chapter I will examine the writings of modern logicians starting from 1662. Chapter II will treat of the works of classical and ancient authors in a reverse order of time starting from 1658. The second part will present an evaluation of extension and comprehension as a doctrine of logic.

It might be stated briefly here that the conclusion of this treatise hopes to present as probable the following declarations: (1) Extension and comprehension are basically an Aristotelian distinction. (2) Extension and comprehension are closely allied with the predicables. A logician cannot have a proper understanding of the former without a thorough understanding of the latter. (3) Any well-organized treatise on logic should begin with a study of the predicables.

The method of the first part which will be employed in this research is the empirical, or *a posteriori,* method. This particular mode is characteristic of all historical research. On the other hand, the deductive, or *a priori*, method is unsound because it would oblige one to posit a principle according to which all subsequent facts ought to correspond. There is a constant danger associated with such procedure, namely, the tendency to misstate or distort historical facts for the sake of preserving a methodic balance. However, inasmuch as the second part involves an evaluation, both the *a posteriori* and *a priori* methods will be utilized.

Perhaps it will seem strange to the reader to discover that in the initial historical research, the philosophical works of modern logicians will be examined in a chronological order, whereas, when attention is turned to the classical and ancient authors, the order of time will be reversed for this historical research. This mode of procedure was not adopted in any haphazard manner, nor was it introduced merely for the sake of adding variety to the presentation of the study. Inasmuch as the historical evidence on the distinction of extension and comprehension is limited and oftentimes confusing, it was not deemed feasible to begin the investigation at the very moment when the reality underlying the distinction was first discovered and introduced into logic so as to trace its development in one chronological direction. Instead it seemed more reasonable to select one source of information to which many modern authors had recourse and by which they were greatly influenced. It was not difficult to make such a choice. The text which was cited most frequently and which influenced modern logicians was none other than the *Port Royal Logic* (1662).

While making a general survey of this distinction between extension and comprehension, it was difficult to procure the first editions published by every author and to analyze the different positions taken by each author in subsequent editions. In each instance the earliest edition available was usually consulted. Almost all of the logic books cited in this study are to be found in the New York Public Library, the Library of Congress, Washington, D.C., the Union Theological Seminary Library of New York, the University of Chicago Library, the University of Laval Library, and the Franciscan Library of Quebec.

EXTENSION AND
COMPREHENSION
IN LOGIC

PART I: HISTORICAL SURVEY

CHAPTER I: MODERN LOGICIANS (1662-1966)

Two things will be considered while tracing the origin and development of the so-called distinction between extension and comprehension in logic: first, the vocabulary used by logicians; and, secondly, the reality which these words represent. In the course of this survey, it will be observed that some logicians express the same reality in different terminology, while other logicians employ the same terminology to designate a different reality.

Preliminary research seemed to indicate that the distinction between extension and comprehension is a modern innovation. Many of the textbooks which discuss this topic credit the *Port Royal Logic* as being the major source for the original presentation of this distinction. For example, one author says:

> It was therein, for the first time in modern philosophy, taken and applied by Arnauld, with whom it was doubtless again original. It passed thence into most of the subsequent works on Logic. In Germany the doctrine was developed, but in England nothing beyond Arnauld's exposition was attempted until Hamilton expounded and applied it, borrowing largely from Krug, Esser, and other German writers, as an integral part of the science.[1]

This same opinion is reiterated by another author when he declares:

> Where the Logic of Port-Royal offers something original, as in the theory of the scope and content of concepts which appears here for the first time, it has done more harm than good.[2]

Further examination of this question also inclines one to believe that this distinction is one of recent origin because

1

the logicians, until our own day, have considered the *extent* of a term as the only object of logic, under the name of the *logical whole*: the *intent* was called by them the *metaphysical whole*, and was excluded from logic. In our own time the English logical writers, and Sir William Hamilton among the foremost, have contended for the introduction of the distinction into logic, under the names of *extension* and *comprehension*.[3]

After consulting many different texts on logic, it was decided to initiate the study of this problem in the seventeenth century. Though frequently divisions of thought are made according to great historical events, or according to geographical and national distinctions, the decision to inaugurate this survey in the middle of the seventeenth century was not prompted by a so-called important event recorded in history, but rather by the publication of a book known as *The Port Royal Logic*. This treatise, published in 1662, is quoted by people today as the common source for the distinction of extension and comprehension. *The Port Royal Logic* is also regarded as a source which seems to be independent of all prior tradition. The usual historical account of extension and comprehension is provided by Baynes in his introduction to the translation of this logical treatise.

This distinction, though taken in general terms by Aristotle, and explicitly enounced with scientific precision by one, at least, of his Greek commentators, had escaped the marvellous acuteness of the schoolmen, and remained totally overlooked and forgotten till the publication of the Port-Royal Logic. It was there, for the first time in modern philosophy, taken up by Arnauld, and is, it cannot reasonably be doubted, due to his own acuteness, since there is no evidence or likelihood of his having been at all acquainted with the Greek commentators on Aristotle, from whom alone it could have been derived.[4]

It will be seen later in the development of this study that the distinction between extension and comprehension did not escape the scrutiny of the Medieval scholars inasmuch as it is substantially contained as a doctrine in Porphyry's *Isagoge*. Those schoolmen were very familiar with that treatise. Furthermore, the Medievalists neither overlooked nor forgot the distinction, they often expressed it in a different vocabulary.[5] However, it is true that once the distinction was made, great confusion has arisen. Dr. Whately employs the words 'extension' and 'comprehension' as if they were synonymous and convertible.[6] Yet he did not escape being severely criticized by Hamilton for neglecting to explain this cardinal distinction in logic.[7] Another logician Beardsley has also identified the two words: "The comprehension of a term is sometimes called its 'extension' — the class of things over which the term, so to speak, extends."[8]

Now is the time to examine carefully a passage taken from the *Port Royal Logic* which expounds this doctrine of extension and comprehension.

But when we speak here of general terms, we understand the univocal terms which are joined to universal and general ideas. Now, in these universal ideas, there are two things which it is very important to distinguish well — *comprehension and extension*.

I call the *comprehension* of the idea those attributes which it contains in itself, and which cannot be taken away from it without destroying it; as the comprehension of the idea of 'triangle' includes extension, figure, three lines, three angles, and the equality of these three angles to two right angles, etc.

I call the *extension* of the idea those subjects to which that idea is suitable [applies]; which are also called the inferiors of a general term, which, in regard to them, is called superior; as the idea of a triangle in general extends to all the diverse species of triangle.

But, although the general idea extends indistinctly to all those subjects to which it is proper, — that is to say, to all its inferiors, and the common names express them all, — there is, nevertheless, this difference between the attributes which it comprehends and the subjects to which it extends, that none of its attributes can be taken away without destroying it, as we have already said; instead we can restrict it as to its extension by applying it only to some of those subjects to which it is suitable, without destroying it by so doing.[9]

It is to be noted that the Port Royalists define 'comprehension' as "those attributes which an idea contains in itself, and which cannot be taken away from it without destroying it".

3

It will be recalled from the study of logic that the attributes of an idea or concept can be divided into the necessary and the accidental; and that the necessary attributes can be subdivided into those which are strictly essential, that is, contained in the definition, and those which are called proper. Thus the essential attribute of a triangle is to possess three angles or three sides; it is a proper attribute 'to have three angles equal to two right angles'; and it is an accidental attribute 'to be explained by Euclid.'

According to the definition of the Port Royalists, comprehension includes all necessary attributes, that is, both essential and proper. It will be observed later in the development of this study that some modern logicians include even the accidental attributes in their definition of comprehension.

The Port Royalists define 'extension' as "those subjects to which the idea applies; which are also called the inferiors of a general term". Although it is not indicated, it seems that extension as defined in that manner would include fictional subjects as well as real ones.

Arnauld and Nicole have been criticized for their ambiguous use of the word 'inferior' when they define 'extension'.[10] They neglect to mention whether 'inferior' refers to species or individuals. Such clarification is important if we are to avoid comparing genus to species as if it were a relation of universal to individual.[11] As an example, the following two propositions are useful to illustrate such ambiguity: "Aristotle is a philosopher" and "a deer is an animal". The inferior word 'Aristotle' is not related to the superior word 'philosopher' in the same manner as 'deer' is related to 'animal'. Both 'Aristotle' and 'deer' might be called extensions of universal predicates. Yet their relation to the predicate is not identical. Whereas 'Aristotle' is an individual of which the universal word 'philosopher' is predicated, 'deer' is a universal word of which still another universal word is predicated, namely, 'animal'. Some logicians attempt to avoid this confusion by substituting the word 'denotation' for 'extension' when individual instances are meant.[12]

When the Port Royalists attempt to elaborate on their definitions of comprehension and extension, they appear to contradict themselves. They state that "the idea of a triangle in general extends to all the diverse species of triangle". But then in the following paragraph

4

they contrast comprehension with extension by saying that none of the attributes of the former can be taken away without destroying the comprehension of the idea, while the extension of an idea can be restricted without destroying it. This statement is not true if the subjects to which an idea applies are species contained in a genus. For example, one cannot talk about animals and deny simultaneously that animality extends to rationality.

There is another aspect in the Port Royalists' definition of extension which should be noted. They employ extension in a passive sense by applying the idea to suitable subjects. This use of extension in the passive rather than active sense may not seem significant here and now. Yet when an attempt is made to determine whether extension and comprehension belong to an active or passive mode of predication, this question will assume great importance. If extension and comprehension are linked to the passive mode of predication, it will be explained in the final chapter of this study why they would become immediate properties of the predicaments. On the other hand, if extension and comprehension are considered proper to the active mode of predicating, they must belong to the predicables.[13]

Even with its lack of precision, the Port Royal text is an important document in the sense that from it the majority of logicians in succeeding centuries derived a doctrine concerning extension and comprehension. Though all of these logicians may not have been directly acquainted with the *Port Royal Logic,* they still owe a debt to Arnauld and Nicole, because all subsequent logic books either refer to that classical text, or else repeat what other authors have previously borrowed from the *Port Royal Logic.* Even if, as it will be seen, Arnauld and Nicole did not originate this distinction between extension and comprehension, their book is one of major historical importance in the study of that doctrine because they originated its modern vocabulary.

One English author,[14] Crakanthorpe, may possibly be referring to extension when he considers the predicables in his so-called *Five Books Of Logic.* He says that *"genus is a universal which is predicated essentially* (by act or aptitude) *of things different specifically in nature*: as animal is predicated of man and brute; and as color is predicated of white and black".[15] In these examples,

5

the genera 'animal' and 'color' are *extended* to their respective species.

He makes a second reference to extension when he states that the *"species is a universal which is placed under the genus*: as man, brute, white. . . ."[16] It will be observed that later logicians will refer to extension in this same manner when they speak of the genus containing 'under it' the species.

Wallis alludes to extension when he mentions that genus is wider (*amplior, latior*) than the species. He speaks of the lowest species (*species specialissima*) as being one of the least extent (*minimae amplitudinis*), and of the highest genus (*Summum genus seu genus Generalissimum*) as being the widest of all (*omnium Amplissimum*).[17] Subsequently, he talks about extension when he mentions subjective parts (*partes subjectivae*), and then cites 'Peter' and 'Paul' as examples of subjective parts which are contained under 'man' and 'animal'.[18]

Du Hamel describes species in two different ways. He employs the adjective *subjicibilis* (meaning that which can be placed under) when species is compared to genus, and the adjective *praedicabilis* (meaning that which can be predicated of) when the species is compared to individuals.[19]

He asserts that "genus is accustomed to be defined as a universal which is predicated essentially but incompletely of many things specifically different in essence".[20] And he defines the lowest species as "that which is predicated completely of many things numerically different in essence".[21] In these two definitions, the author is considering the extension of genus and species in relation to those objects which are 'contained under' them.

The distinction between extension and comprehension was familiar to an eighteenth century philosophical writer. John Norris (1657-1711) speaks of enlarging thought — making it more 'extensive' — by means of abstraction. One should note the key phrases used by him, v. g., 'contains in it' (a reference to comprehension) and 'contains under it' (a reference to extension).

Besides, as Abstraction serves to the greater clearness and distinctness of Thought, so also the greater *inlargement* of it, as rendring our Ideas more general and *extensive*. Which is

6

a great help to us in thinking; for things as they are being all singular, and singulars being in a manner infinite, we should find our narrow Faculties strangely incumber'd, nay even oppress'd in the consideration of them, if we did not abbreviate and contract them by ranging them into certain general Orders or Sorts; that is, if we had not certain abstract Ideas, in which a great many of them agree, and so may be said to be contain'd under them. As for instance, when we consider an equilateral Triangle, only as a Triangle, or a Triangle as a Figure, &c. In all which kind of Abstractions this is to be observ'd, that tho' the inferiour degree contains the superior *in* it, with some further determination of its own, yet the superior contains the inferior *under* it; so that tho' the inferior contains actually more, yet the superior, as being less determin'd, *represents* more, and so contributes to the greater inlargement and extensiveness of Thought; the further consideration of which Matter I leave to the *Logicians*.[22]

Regius conserved the tradition when he wrote that the "entire nature of the genus is in the species, but the entire nature of the species is not in the genus".[23] His statement will be better understood if one illustrates it by saying "man is an animal". In this example, the entire nature of 'animal' is 'contained in' (comprehension) the species 'man'. Of course, the entire nature of 'man' is not contained in 'animal' inasmuch as man contains a specific difference (rationality) which is not part of the concept 'animal'. But he is more explicit in his reference to quantity or extension, while retaining the Porphyrian formula, when he declares "it is evident that genus is wider than species".[24]

The notion of placing something under another and that of containing something in itself is expressed by Oldfield when he turns to the subject of extension and comprehension.

Thus the universal Idea may be considered as to its *Extension,* or the Reference it has to all the Kinds, Sorts, and Individuals, subjected or plac'd under such general Head; but it may be yet otherwise considered in respect to its *Comprehension,* or of what such Idea contains in it, which is always less than what is contain'd in the Adequate Idea, or any Kind or Sort next under it, and this again contains less than the Idea

7

of a yet lower Sort. as this does finally less than that of an Individual under it. . . .[25]

The author is indicating in this passage that each subordinate idea contains more attributes, marks or characteristics than the idea above it. Of course, as each subordinate idea increases in comprehension, it diminishes at the same time in extension inasmuch as its application is restricted by virtue of the added notes or marks which constitute its comprehension.

Purchotius puts the Port Royal doctrine into eighteenth century Latin and uses explicitly the words 'comprehension' and 'extension' when he tries to explain how they are distinguished from each other. He says.

> by the *comprehension* of an idea are understood *those attributes which in the notion of any thing are so contained, so that the idea of that thing cannot stand without those attributes:* v.g., to be *composed of mind and body* is thus contained in the idea of man, so that man cannot be otherwise understood. Thus to be *round* is included in the idea of a circle, so that without this attribute a circle cannot be comprehended.
>
> By the *extension* of an idea are understood the *subjects to which that idea can be proper,* as the idea of man corresponds to Socrates, Aristotle, and others; the idea of a circle to any circle; the idea of a triangle can be applied to any triangle.[26]

From other research it was discovered that Purchotius is the first author to use the Latin words *extensio* and *comprehensio* in this particular context.

Crousaz follows the same trend of thought exemplified by the other logicians of the eighteenth century. He too speaks of genus containing under it (extension) and species containing in it (comprehension).

> When a general idea is indifferently applied to others, which are also general, it is called *Genus;* and those to which it is applied, are called *Species* of that *Genus.* . . .
>
> The same Idea, which is *Species,* as being contained under a more general Idea, becomes *Genus,* when it is applied to other Ideas somewhat less general.
>
> Whatever is contained in the Idea of *Genus,* is also to be found in the Idea of *Species;* but each *Species* has some Attri-

8

butes more than the Idea of *Genus;* and among those Attributes which the *Species* has above the *Genus,* that which is the first, the chief and the Ground of the others, is called *Difference.*[27]

In passing it is to be noted that this author confuses the notion of genus with the notion of univocity.

Without employing the words 'extension' and 'comprehension', Crousaz in still another book refers to these two properties of genus and species when he states:

> We have some general Ideas, that is to say, some Ideas applicable to a great number of things. When these things to which is applied a general Idea are different among themselves, they are called *species* in relation to this general idea which is applied to them, and which in turn is called *genus.* One finds equally in each one of the species all that this general idea includes, and, besides that, something else. Thus I have a general Idea which corresponds to the world of Figure. I apply this Idea to a closed surface of *curved* lines. I have then a *rectilinear figure,* and *curvilinear figure.* Each one of these species is a figure as much as the other: but in each one I find something which I do not find in the other. There is in some way a *genus* distinguished into its species, and in some way each Species contains the Genus with something else.[28]

In this passage the idea of extension can be understood when the author talks about applying general ideas to many other things; and the idea of comprehension can be found in the statement that "each Species contains the Genus". The 'something else', of course, refers to the specific difference.

The Englishman Watts upholds the Port Royal definition of comprehension when he includes all the essential and proper attributes in his own definition. Unlike the Port Royalists, he is more explicit in his definition of extension because he applies extension to individuals as well as to species.

> In universal Ideas it is proper to consider their *Comprehension* and their *Extension.*
> The *Comprehension* of an Idea regards all the essential Modes and Properties of it: So Body, in its *Comprehension* takes in *Solidity, Figure, Quantity, Mobility,* etc. So a *Bowl* in its *Comprehension* includes *Roundness, Volubility,* etc.

9

The *Extension* of an universal Idea regards all the particular Kinds and single Beings that are contained under it. So a *Body* in its *Extension* includes *Sun, Moon, Star, Wood, Iron, Plant, Animal,* etc. which are several *Species* or *Individuals,* under the general Name of *Body. . . .*[29]

In his second definition, Watts views extension in the active sense. Here again he differs from the Port Royalists who consider extension in the passive sense.[30]

The idea of comprehension, although perhaps not intended by Musschembroek, can be found in his explanation of the formation of a species. He says that

> *species* is a universal idea formed again from those ways in which individuals agree; for example, Paul and Titus agree in that they are lawyers, or learned, or born in the same region, or of the same religion, or endowed with rationality and body; whence is formed a certain universal idea of persons skilled in law, of learned ones, of citizens, of brothers, of man.[31]

In other words, the idea can be said to 'comprehend' the attributes, because the idea is composed of those attributes in which individuals agree.

The words 'comprehend', 'extension', and 'intension' are found in Meyerson's text when he quotes Leibniz, *Nouveau Essais,* IV, ch. 17, §8:

> Animal comprehends more individuals than man, but man comprehends more ideas or more forms; one has more examples, the other more degrees of reality; one has more extension, the other more intension.[32]

While expounding the *Logic of Leibniz,* Couturat also resorts to the words 'extension' and 'comprehension'.[33] He mentions

> one can say, roughly speaking, that from the point of extension, the subject is contained in the predicate, whereas from the point of view of comprehension, the subject contains it. In other words, the predicate is at the same time more general and more abstract than the subject.[34]

This passage at first glance may seem difficult to understand, that is, until one distinguishes the first and second operations of the intellect. Inasmuch as extension and comprehension are related to the predicables of genus and species (which belong to the first operation of the mind), they should not be correlated with judgment which involves the affirmation of a subject by its predicate. If, instead of identifying extension and comprehension with the second operation of the intellect, or with a single concept, one would identify them with genus and species, a great deal of confusion and error could be avoided.

Hutcheson speaks of extension in relation to division, and of comprehension in relation to definition. He says that the "Logical Whole or extension of an idea is declared by Division, which is 'the enumeration of several things that are contained in the extension of a common idea or name' ".[35] In the following chapter he asserts that the "Metaphysical Whole, or comprehension of a complex idea, is declared by Definition, which is a 'mode of speech explaining more simple ideas, which are joined in the ensemble' ".[36]

Although, as will be seen later on, the Medievalists considered extension and comprehension as 'properties' of the genus and species, Hutcheson, on the other hand, identifies genus with extension because he says the "Logical Whole or extension of an idea". He likewise identifies species with comprehension because he states the "Metaphysical Whole, or comprehension of a complex idea". Such usage goes contrary to the tradition of the Middle Ages.

Hutcheson mistakenly considers division to be the "enumeration of several things" (parts). Instead, the whole is first divided into parts, and only then are the parts enumerated.

His conception of definition runs counter to what is involved in the process of defining. In definition, one proceeds from the parts to the whole, whereas Hutcheson proceeds from the whole to its parts because he says that definition is a "mode of speech explaining more simple ideas" (parts). He is correct, however, when he advances from the Logical Whole to several things (parts) by means of division.

He proclaims that the "comprehension of a complex idea is declared by Definition". This statement is not true because a definition declares the nature of a thing by stating its genus and its difference; and neither the nature, the genus, nor the difference is identical with comprehension.

11

In the explanation of the Logical Whole and Metaphysical Whole, Hutcheson confuses what Aristotle propounds in his second and fourth definitions of the word 'part'. Commenting on this second definition, St. Thomas remarks that

> *in the second manner,* those things are said to be parts into which something is divided without quantity; and it is in this way that species are said to be parts of a genus. For a genus is divided into species, but not as a quantity is divided into quantitative parts. For a whole quantity is not in each one of its parts. But a genus is in each one of its species.[37]

Explaining the fourth Aristotelian definition of 'part', St. Thomas points out that *"in the fourth sense,* they are said to be parts which are placed in the definition of anything, which are parts of reason just as animal and two-footed are parts of man".[38] According to this fourth definition, genus is considered to be a part of the species; but, according to the second definition, species is a part of the genus in a different sense. In the latter case, species is a subjective part placed under the logical or universal whole (genus) ; in the former case, genus is an integral part which constitutes the definition of the metaphysical or formal whole (species).

Repeating the language of Purchotius, Angeloni also has recourse to the words 'comprehension' and 'extension'.

> *Comprehension* and *extension* should be considered in universal ideas. The comprehension of an idea is an aggregate of all things which are contained in the idea itself. Thus the comprehension of the idea of a body is to be extended, solid, divisible, mobile, etc.. which are comprehended in the body; the comprehension of an idea of a triangle is to have three sides comprehending space. The extension of the idea is an aggregate of all subjects to which that idea belongs. Thus the extension of the idea of a body is every body; the extension of the idea of a triangle is every triangle. Comprehension is always referred to those things which the idea itself contains; extension, however. is referred to the objects to which the idea is understood to belong.[39]

This logician does not make precise enough the definition of comprehension. It is left to the reader to decide whether comprehension embraces all accidental characteristics as well as essential and proper ones. On the other hand, he identifies extension with the individual.

Baumgarten employs footnotes in German to explain his Latin text. When he speaks of 'comprehension' (*comprehendit*), he refers to it with the word *inhalt;* and, when he speaks of 'extension' (*ambitus*), he uses the word *umfang.* Here is what this author has to say:

> The NOTION represents something common to several things (§51.) : hence the note of several things (§54.) : hence it enters into other concepts, and is contained in others (§55.). Those which the notion enters into, or in which it is contained, IT CONTAINS THEM UNDER ITSELF (it embraces, it comprehends). Concepts contained under the notion are referred to the same notion.
>
> The CONCEPT containing another under itself is SUPERIOR in respect to it (transcendental). The CONCEPT contained under another is INFERIOR in respect to it. Therefore, every notion in respect to some concepts is a superior concept (§56.). The sum total of inferior concepts contained under this notion is the extension of that concept.[40]

An unknown author of the eighteenth century explains what other authors call extension by such words as 'including', 'agreeing' and 'comprehending'. He says that

> a *general* idea, or *genus,* is one *common nature* which includes several others. Thus animal is a *genus,* because it includes *man, horse, elephant, fly,* etc., which are also *common natures:* And *bird* is a *genus,* as comprehending *eagle, crow, sparrow, lark,* etc. A *special* idea, or *species,* is one *common nature* agreeing to several *individuals.* Thus man is a *species* as agreeing to *William, Peter, John,* etc., and city is a *species,* as agreeing to *London, Paris, Constantinople,* etc.[41]

In the case of genus, one universal is extended to other universals; while in the case of species, the universal is applied only to individuals.

It will be noted later in this chapter that the word 'comprehend' may have several meanings. Sometimes it will be used in reference

13

to extension; but more often it will apply only to comprehension or intension.

Unlike the unknown English author of *Logic, Ontology And The Art Of Poetry*, the Italian Genovesi uses the word 'comprehend' to signify that ideas embrace certain attributes which are common to or contained in individuals.

> Therefore, *species* signify ideas which comprehend common things in individuals: genera signify ideas which embrace common things in species. But if there would be several genera having certain common properties, then these common properties are included in the more general idea and name.[42]

Elsewhere he employs the same terminology when he declares that "genus is a notion especially common which comprehends other less common notions begotten by it, and that common notion is said of these less common notions".[43]

Speaking of the comprehension of a term, Best asserts that it is

> the aggregate of all the simple ideas, which make up the complex idea, which, the term signifies. Thus, the comprehension of an *artificial Globe,* is made up of the simple ideas, *Round, Hard, Variegated body,* together, with all the different materials, which enter into the composition, both, internally (as the wood and paper of which it is made) and externally (as a delineation of the different parts of the earth), for such is the complex idea, that we have of an artificial globe, and is therefore it's comprehension.[44]

He says that the extension of a term is an

> aggregate, of all the individuals, which belong to that name, as, the extension of an artificial globe, not only includes one, but all the artificial globes, in the world: The extension of the term *Man,* not only includes one individual, but all the men in the world.[45]

The thought of Porphyry seems to echo in Best's explanation of genus and species:

> The Genus has less comprehension, because there must be some idea left out of the Species, to make, the remaining ones constitute the Genus; Thus, to make, the Species *Man,* cor-

14

respond in every respect, with *Animal,* the idea meant by rationality, or reasoning faculty, must be left out, and then, the remaining part of the comprehension, agrees with *Brute,* as well as with *Man.*[46]

Then inquiring which has the greater extension, genus or species, he replies:

> The Genus, for there must be some of the ideas constituting the Species left out, to make the remaining ones constitute the Genus, and of course, those remaining ones must extend to a greater number of individuals, by which, the extension is increased; . . . the idea represented by the term *animal,* has greater extension, than the idea represented by the term *Man.*[47]

In the year 1800, Immanuel Kant published his *Logic.* For his lectures on logic, Kant made use of a compendium which was compiled by Meier, a disciple of the Wolffian school.

Just as the early philosophers viewed concepts from the viewpoint of quantity, so Kant speaks of cognition as being quantitative:

> The Quantity of a cognition may be taken in a twofold sense, either as *extensive* or as *intensive.* The former refers to the *extent* of the cognition, and accordingly consists in the number and variety of its contents, the latter refers to its intrinsic value, which concerns the logical importance and fruitfulness of a cognition considered as the ground of many and important consequences *(non multa sed multum)* .[48]

Although Kant enumerates here a twofold quantity, his 'intensive quantity' of knowledge does not mean that each cognition contains in it several attributes or characters, but rather, by its very nature, each cognition is the source of many other cognitions. In other words, the intensive aspect of cognition is treated as a principle instead of a quantity.

In 1801, an American published a compendium of logic in which he makes a brief reference to the words 'comprehension' and 'extension' while discussing the various divisions of idea. He declares that

15

the idea of a bird, considered as a compound idea, includes life, sense, spontaneous motion, a covering of wings, feathers, &c.: but, as a general idea, it denotes the several species of the feathered creation, the hawk, the eagle, the lark, &c; to all which it extends with equal propriety. In the former case, the several parts of the compound idea are called its COMPRE-HENSION; in the latter, the genera, the species, and the individuals, to which the universal idea may be applied, are called its EXTENSION.[49]

In the following year, another American author refers to the same distinction by saying:

> This way of considering things according to the number of their parts and properties, is called by logicians the *comprehension* of an idea. . . .
> Individuals, to which the universal idea is applied, are called its *extension*.[50]

Inasmuch as comprehension and extension are related to the predicables, it is interesting to observe that an English author does not mention either comprehension or extension when he discusses the predicables. It seems that he misunderstands the traditional explanation of the nature of the predicables. Since Reid did not see that a predicable refers to the manner in which a predicate may be said of the subject, he comes to the conclusion that there are more than five predicables. Referring to Burgersdick, Thomas Reid says:

> Those things only, says he [Burgersdick], are to be accounted predicables, which may be affirmed of *many individuals, truly, properly,* and *immediately.* The consequence of putting such limitations upon the word *predicable* is, that in many propositions, perhaps in most, the predicate is not a predicable. But, admitting all his limitations, the enumeration will still be very incomplete; for of many things we may affirm truly, properly, and immediately, their existence, their end, their cause, their effect, and various relations which they bear to other things. These, and perhaps many more, are predicables in the strict sense of the word, no less than the five which have been so long famous.[51]

16

This same basic misunderstanding allows Reid to accept and mention in passing what Locke maintains in his *Essay on the Human Understanding,* Book 4, Chap. 1, that all our knowledge consists in perceiving certain agreements and disagreements between our ideas. Locke reduces these agreements and disagreements to four titles: (1) Identity and diversity; (2) Relation; (3) Coexistence; and (4) Real existence.[52] These four predicables are given as a complete enumeration without mentioning any of the ancient predicables.

An English writer mentions the distinction, but he substitutes the word 'denotation' for 'extension'. According to him, things are denoted and properties are comprehended. In the comprehension of a word, he includes the obvious as well as the less obvious and relative properties of a word.[53]

It is interesting to note that the German philosopher, Georg Wilhelm Friedrich Hegel (1770-1831) gave some consideration to the quantitative aspects of spiritual facts (such as a concept is) without referring directly to the 'comprehension' or 'extension' of concepts. In his text on *Logic* (1816) he declares:

> Quantity, of course, is a stage of the Idea: and as such it must have its due, first as a logical category, and then in the world of objects, natural as well as spiritual. Still even so, there soon emerges the different importance attaching to the category of quantity according as its objects belong to the natural or to the spiritual world. For in Nature, where the form of the Idea is to be other than, and at the same time outside, itself, greater importance is for that very reason attached to quantity than in the spiritual world, the world of free inwardness. No doubt we regard even spiritual facts under a quantitative point of view. . . .[54]

But then he tempers his statement by issuing the following warning:

> After all that has been said, we cannot but hold it in the interest of exact and thorough knowledge, one of the most hurtful prejudices, to seek all distinction and determinateness of objects merely in quantitative considerations.[55]

Levi Hedge introduces in his logical work the distinction between comprehension and extension by dividing things into genera and species. According to him, *"species denotes a sort or class, including only individuals; and genus, a class including under it two or more species. . . ."*[56]

After presenting several examples of genera and species, he states:

In the distribution of things into genera and species, regard is had to the *comprehension* and *extension* of general terms. By the *comprehension of a term is meant the aggregate of all the known properties of that thing, or class of things*, to which it is applied. Thus, *gold* includes in its comprehension a material substance, a yellow colour, superior weight, ductility, fusibility, and every other known property of that body. The *extension of a term regards the number of individual subjects, to which it may be applied*. So the term *gold* includes in its extension every separate parcel of that metal. *Man* includes in its extension every individual of the human race.[57]

Hence, according to Hedge, comprehension means the sum of all the known properties of a thing, while extension refers to the individual subjects.

Reiffenberg points out that Latinists refer to extension by employing the word *omnis*, and to comprehension by the word *totus*.

Extension is the number of all those individuals to which the idea is proper. Extensive totality is the *omnis* of the Latinists.

Comprehension is the sum total of all the particular ideas which compose the idea in which it is applied. The comprehensive totality is expressed in Latin by the word *totus*.[58]

One English philosopher, who profoundly influenced other logicians, deserves special attention in any dissertation on this subject. He presents the distinction between comprehension and extension in the following manner:

As a concept, or notion, is a thought in which an indefinite plurality of characters is bound up into a unity of consciousness, and applicable to an indefinite plurality of objects, a concept is, therefore, necessarily a quantity, and a quantity varying in amount according to the greater or smaller number of characters of which it is the complement, and the greater or smaller number of things of which it may be said. This quantity is thus of two kinds; as it is either Intensive or Extensive. The Internal or Intensive Quantity of a concept is determined by the greater or smaller number of constituent characters contained in it. The External or Extensive Quantity of a concept is determined by the greater or smaller number of classified concepts or realities contained under it. The former (the Intensive Quantity) is called by some later Greek logicians depth, *(Bathos);* by the Latin logical writers *comprehension, (comprehensio, quantitas comprehensionis, complexus,* or *quantitas complexus).* The latter (the Extensive Quantity) is called by the same later Greek Logicians the *breadth, (platos);* . . . by the logical writers of the western or Latin world, the *extension* or *circuit, (extensio, quantitas extensionis, ambitus, quantitas ambitus)* and likewise the *domain* or *sphere* of a notion, *(regio, sphaera).*[59]

According to Hamilton, if the concept is considered internally it contains within itself a certain quantity of attributes or marks. These attributes are referred to as the comprehension or depth of a concept. For example, the concept 'animal' contains within it the attributes or partial concepts of 'sentient' and 'living being'. Now each of these partial concepts are also wholes composed of other partial concepts. 'Living being' is constituted by the concepts 'animate' and 'body'. The concept 'animal' also contains the partial concepts of 'animate' and 'body' because

when one thing is predicated of another, all that which is predicable of the predicate will be predicable also of the subject. Thus 'man' is predicated of the individual man; but 'animal' is predicated of 'man'; it will, therefore, be predicable of the individual man also: for the individual man is both 'man' and 'animal'.[60]

After citing this passage, Hamilton summarizes it in a single Latin sentence: *Praedicatum praedicati est praedicatum subjecti* (the predicate of the predicate is a predicate of the subject).[61] Aristotle's explanation can also be paraphrased in the form of a general principle that "whatever is of the part, is also part of the whole".[62]

On the other hand, if the concept is considered externally, it contains under it certain attributes or characteristics. These attributes are known as the extension or breadth of a concept. Thus the concepts 'biology', 'zoology' and 'botany' are contained under the more general concept 'science'. These concepts, which are subordinate to the more general concept 'science', can also be considered as wholes which in turn contain other subordinate concepts. Here again the general principle holds true, namely, "whatever is of the part, is also part of the whole".

It should be noticed that since the middle of the nineteenth century, English writers have generally followed Sir William Hamilton in substituting the word 'intension' for the word 'comprehension.'[63] However, many modern authors prefer 'comprehension' to 'intension' because students of logic often mistake 'intension' for 'intention'.[64]

W. Stanley Jevons disagrees with Hamilton when the latter distinguishes between an extensive syllogism and an intensive syllogism by employing the words 'contained under' and 'contains in it'. Jevons cites from Hamilton's *Lectures on Logic* the following syllogisms:

Extensive Syllogism:	Intensive Syllogism:
All man is mortal; But Caius is a man, Therefore, Caius is mortal.	Caius is a man; But all man is mortal; Therefore, Caius is mortal.[65]

For Jevons, these two syllogisms are the same; only the major and minor premises are transposed.

Quoting at length from Hamilton's text, he says:

The Major term Caius contains in it the Middle term man; But the Middle term man contains in it the Minor term mortal; Therefore, the Major term Caius contains in it the Minor term mortal.[66]

He regards Hamilton's statement of a syllogism in the intensive form as a clumsy explanation because the author neglects to mention that

20

it is individual things which are *contained under* in the extensive sense, and qualities, or attributes, which are contained in the other sense. Is it not absurd to say that Caius contains man, without explaining that *man* is here taken intensively? A thing does not contain any of its qualities in the same way that the class of man, extensively regarded, contains one of its members or significates, namely, Caius.[67]

There are two important points which Jevons disregards when he criticizes Hamilton's intensive syllogism. First of all, one should not syllogize from the universal to the singular because science is concerned only with universals. There is always a possibility of encountering an exception when the syllogism is resolved with the individual. Secondly, when concepts are described extensively as 'containing under' (extension) and intensively as 'containing in themselves' (comprehension), the relation existing between concepts is one of universal to universal, and not of universal to individual. This particular aspect of the problem concerning extension and comprehension will be discussed in the final chapter of this work when extension is correlated with the predicable *genus,* and comprehension is correlated with the predicable *species.*

It is interesting to observe that when Hamilton considers the distinction between extension and comprehension, he refers to sources which predate the *Port Royal Logic.* Such sources vociferously oppose the opinion that the distinction originated with the Port Royalists.

During the same year that Hamilton was delivering his *Lectures on Logic,* an American was defining comprehension and extension as follows: by

the comprehension of a term is meant the aggregate of all the known properties of a genus, species or class to which it is applied.

The extension of a term regards the number of species into which a genus, or the number of individuals into which a species is divided.[68]

Solly employs the word 'matter' to designate 'comprehension' — a word which is rarely found in other texts on logic. Here is what he has to say on this subject:

21

The matter of a conception consists of the various representations contained in it.

The sphere of a conception consists of the things that come under it, or answer its conditions.

The conception of a horse has more matter than the conception of an animal: for the former conception must contain all that is contained in the latter conception, and something more besides. But the sphere of the conception of a horse is less than the sphere of the conception of an animal; as there are many more things that answer the conditions of the latter than the conditions of the former conception.[69]

It will be noticed especially that when he speaks of comprehension, he talks about representations 'contained in' a conception; and when he discusses extension, he mentions things 'contained under' a conception.

In 1843, J. S. Mill offered this account of connotation and denotation to describe the intensional and extensional properties of a concept:

A non-connotative term is one which signifies a subject only, or an attribute only. A connotative term is one which denotes a subject, and implies an attribute. By a subject is here meant anything which possesses attributes. Thus John, or London, or England, are names which signify a subject only. Whiteness, length, virtue, signify an attribute only. None of these names, therefore, are connotative. But *white, long, virtuous,* are connotative. The word white denotes all white things, as snow, paper, the foam of the sea, etc., and implies, or, in the language of the schoolmen, *connotes* the attribute *whiteness.* The word white is not predicated of the attribute, but of the subjects, snow, etc.; but when we predicate it of them, we convey the meaning that the attribute whiteness belongs to them. . . .

All concrete general names are connotative. The word *man,* for example, denotes Peter, Jane, John, and an indefinite number of other individuals, of whom, taken as a class, it is the name. But it is applied to them because they possess, and to signify that they possess, certain attributes. . . . The word *man,* therefore, signifies all these attributes, and all subjects which possess these attributes. But it can be predicated only

22

of the subjects. . . . The name, therefore, is said to signify the subjects *directly*, the attributes *indirectly;* it *denotes* the subjects, and implies, or involves. or indicates, or as we shall say henceforth *connotes*, the attributes. It is a connotative name. . . . Even abstract names, though the names only of attributes, may in some instances be justly considered as connotative; for attributes themselves may have attributes ascribed to them: and a word which denotes attributes may connote an attribute of those attributes. Of this description, for example. is such a word as *fault;* equivalent to *bad* or *hurtful quality*. This word is a name common to many attributes, and connotes hurtfulness, an attribute of those various attributes. . . .

Proper names are not connotative: they denote the individuals who are called by them; but they do not indicate or imply any attributes as belonging to those individuals.[70]

In his exposition of connotation and denotation, Mill distinguishes three different types of connotative terms: (1) attributive terms such as white, long and virtuous; (2) concrete general names such as man; and (3) abstract terms such as fault, that is, when they are considered as a genus in relation to other attributes. He also differentiates two types of non-connotative terms: (1) proper names such as John, London and England — these only signify a subject; and (2) abstract terms such as whiteness, length and virtue — these only signify an attribute.

Now what does Mill mean by the word 'denotation'? He explains his meaning by saying that "the word white denotes all white things, as snow, paper, the foam of the sea, etc." Thus denotation means the subjects of which a term (v.g., white) can be predicated. And what does he mean by the word 'connotation'? Using the same example, Mill declares "but when we predicate it (white) of them (subjects such as snow), we convey the meaning that the attribute whiteness belongs to them". Hence connotation is a character or attribute which is indicated as possessed by the subject. When it is stated that white "*connotes* the attribute *whiteness*," it is also stated that objects such as snow and paper, which are denoted by white, possess the attribute of whiteness.

If a term possesses both traits, namely, "denotes a subject, and

23

implies an attribute," it is connotative. But if the term "signifies a subject only, or an attribute only," it is non-connotative.

Many modern logicians have accepted these two meanings. They understand denotation to signify the individual subjects to which a term is applicable, and connotation to signify the characteristics possessed by the term. Bradley, however, is one logician who objects vehemently to Mill's use of the words 'connote' and 'denote'. He insists that these words

> serve no useful purpose in logic. They are unnecessary and objectionable. They have no advantage over the terms in general use, and they have in addition a positive vice. To "connote" is to "imply"; and the meaning of a word is not its implication.[71]

Joseph concurs with Bradley when the latter maintains that the connotation of a term is not its meaning.[72]

Stebbing contests Mill's definition of a connotative term as "one which denotes a subject, and implies an attribute".

> Mill so defined "connotative name" that it follows that if a name is connotative it *must apply* to something — which is what Mill meant by *denoting*. But . . . a descriptive phrase which is, of course, connotative may have no application, e. g. 'glass mountain', 'circular square', 'consistent philosopher,' 'impeccable statesman'. It is clear, then, that "connotation" cannot be defined as Mill defined it.[73]

On one point Mill feels that he is in complete agreement with the Scholastic view when he says that "the word white denotes all white things, as snow, paper, the foam of the sea, etc., and implies, or, in the *language of the schoolmen, connotes* the attribute whiteness". In other words, he agrees with the Scholastics as regards attributive terms. But he goes a step further and applies the distinction of connotation and denotation to what was not considered by the Scholastics, namely, concrete general names, proper names and abstract terms. This fact is mentioned by Minto while discussing the history of the distinction between connotation and denotation.

What Mill did was not to invert Scholastic usage but to revive the distinction, and extend the word connotative to general names on the ground that they also imported the possession of attributes. The word has been as fruitful of meticulous discussion as it was in the Renaissance of Logic, though the ground has changed. The point of Mill's innovation was, premising that general names are not absolute but are applied in virtue of a meaning, to put emphasis on this meaning as the cardinal consideration.[74]

Joseph summarizes the entire discussion on the history of this particular distinction by noting that 'connotation' and 'denotation' were not originally equivalent to 'intension' and 'extension', even though treated by many modern logicians as such. He reminds us that the Scholastics contrasted connotative terms with absolute terms, and "their function of connoting was distinguished from that of standing for something".[75]

A great deal of criticism is levied against Mill because he maintains that proper names have no connotation and are to be regarded as unmeaning marks.[76] Inasmuch as this particular aspect of the problem does not affect an understanding of Mill's doctrine on connotation and denotation, there is no reason why such criticism should be discussed in this treatise.

It may be well to mention here that the word 'connotative' is found in the *Port Royal Logic*.

The names which signify things as modified, denoting first and directly the thing, though more confusedly, and indirectly the mode, although more distinctly, are called *adjectives* or *connotatives;* as round, hard, just, prudent.[77]

There seems to be no justification for the use of the words 'denotation' and 'connotation' in reference to the problem of extension and comprehension. J. S. Mill employs the two words in contradistinction to the Medievalist usage. According to the Medievalists, the distinction between denotation and connotation is strictly a grammatical one which the logician is obliged to borrow and exploit. J. S. Mill offers no evidence whatsoever that he is aware of such grammatical structure. In the Middle Ages, 'denotation' referred to the signification of a word, while 'connotation' referred

25

to a certain mode of signifying a grammatical value. The Medievalists regarded a connotative word as one which connotes a subject grammatically and denotes an attribute semantically. Consequently, in accord with J. S. Mill's example, the word 'white' connotes all white things, and denotes the attribute 'whiteness'; whereas, according to Mill's phraseology, the word 'white' denotes all white things, and connotes the attribute 'whiteness'.

Rattier considers the comprehension of an idea as existing in the confines of space and time.

> The ensemble of parts of a *complex* constitutes what logicians called the *comprehension* of the idea. The idea is more or less comprehensive according as its object includes a greater or lesser number of elements united or implied in each other, that is to say, existing at the same point of space and time.[78]

His designation of extension is applied to classes formed from a group of species or a group of individuals.

> The number of beings whose being grouped together forms a *class* determines what one calls the *extension* of the idea. The idea becomes more extensive as the genus contains more species, and as the species contains more individuals.[79]

When the English writer William Thomson treats of extension and comprehension, he presents another point which is closely allied with the subject of extension and comprehension, inasmuch as it is also founded on a conception of a word as a whole composed of parts — that is, the distinction of clear and distinct.

First of all, he speaks of extension:

> When we compare a vague and general conception with a narrower and more definite one, we find that the former contains far more objects in it than the latter. Comparing plant with geranium, for example, we see that plant includes ten thousand times more objects, since the oak, the fir, the lichen, the rose, and countless others, including geranium itself, are implied in it. This capacity of a conception we call its extension. The extension of *plant* is greater than that of *geranium*, because it includes more objects.[80]

Then he alludes to intension:

But conceptions have another capacity. While plant has more objects under it than geranium, it has fewer marks in it. I can describe the leaves, petals, stamina, and pistils of geranium; but of plant no such description is possible. I cannot say that every plant has a stem, for there are the lichens to contradict me; nor a flower, for ferns have none, and so on. I can say little more about plant, than that all plants have growth and vegetable life. The logical expression of this defect is, that its intension is very limited.[81]

This same author mentions that other logicians express the distinction between extension and intension (comprehension) by such words as "the sphere (breadth) and matter (depth) of the conception, *magnitudo et vis conceptus*".[82] It should be observed here that *magnitudo* means breadth or extension and *vis* signifies depth or comprehension.

Sir William Hamilton likewise calls our attention to the corresponding difference between clear and distinct which was cited by William Thomson. He tells us that

we owe the discrimination of Distinct and Indistinct from Clear and Obscure notions to the acuteness of the great Leibnitz. By the Cartesians the distinction had not been taken; though the authors of the *Port Royal Logic* come so near, that we may well marvel how they failed explicitly to enounce it.[83]

Then he elaborates on this passage by saying: "the difference between a clear and a distinct knowledge: ... a distinct knowledge lies in the knowledge of the constituent parts; while a clear knowledge is only of the constituted whole."[84]

A young man may retain a clear image of the house in which he spent his boyhood days. He can also distinguish that house from other houses in the same neighborhood. But, unlike the artist who can reproduce that house in detail on a canvas, this young man does not necessarily have both a clear and distinct knowledge of that house.

A classic example which illustrates the contrast existing between clear and distinct knowledge can be found in the writings of St. Augustine. "What, then, is time? If no one asks me, I know; if I want to explain it to someone who does ask me, I do not know."[85]

In other words, St. Augustine confesses that he has a clear, but not a distinct notion of time.

The Port Royalists distinguish similar characteristics in an idea.

In an idea, one can oppose clearness to distinction, and obscurity to confusion; for it can be said that an idea is clear to us when it strikes us vividly, though it is not distinct, as the idea of pain strikes us very vividly, and, according to that, can be called clear. Nevertheless, it is rather confused, inasmuch as it represents to us pain as in an injured hand, though this pain exists only in our mind.[86]

All that the Port Royalists say about this subject has been copied from Descartes. Unfortunately, their presentation of this distinction tends only to confuse what in Descartes is lucid and precise. Here are two concise Cartesian principles which treat of clear and distinct notions:

What is a clear and distinct perception. That it can be clear without being distinct, but not vice versa.[87]

If, as it has already been stated, a clear notion is only knowledge of the whole, whereas a distinct notion is knowledge of the parts constituting the whole, then it is understandable why Descartes expounds as a philosophical principle that clear knowledge can exist without distinct knowledge, but distinct knowledge cannot exist without clear knowledge. A child, for example, might be said to have a clear idea of man when he recognizes him at first sight, and yet not be said to know precisely that man is a rational animal (distinct idea). But once he acquires this distinct knowledge, he will still continue to retain his clear idea of man.

Leibniz expressly mentions that the distinction described by Descartes is the same as his own. His explanation is even more luminous than Descartes'.

I have the habit of following here the language of Descartes, according to whom an idea will be clear and confused at the same time: and such are the ideas of sensible qualities experienced by the organs, as that of color or pain. They are clear because they are recognized and discerned easily, one from the other; but they are not distinct because it is not distinguished what they include.[88]

28

According to what has been said, clear knowledge considers an object as separated from all those things which are outside of it. Such a knowledge implies a movement from the outside to the inside. Here the *terminus a quo* is the larger whole of the world of ideas and the *terminus ad quem* is the smaller whole of one particular idea. For example, one can progress from a larger whole (a knowledge of the universe) to a smaller whole (a knowledge of the moon). Although this knowledge of the lesser whole is clear, it is still characterized by a confused knowledge of the parts. In the case of distinct knowledge, the *terminus a quo* is a knowledge of the smaller whole and the *terminus ad quem* is a distinct knowledge of the parts of the same whole. In both clear and distinct knowledge, there is a movement from lesser clarity to greater clarity. Yet, unlike clear knowledge which boasts only a single clarity of the whole, distinct knowledge has a double clarity, namely, a clarity of the whole and a clarity of the parts. Thus, until the astronauts will have made their first historic landing on the moon, men today possess only a clear knowledge of the moon. They are able to distinguish the moon from other celestial planets. But once the moon has been explored and studied in detail, mankind will possess a distinct knowledge of its parts. Such progress will conform to man's process of knowing, namely, a movement from a clear knowledge of the whole to a distinct knowledge of its parts.

Although the discrimination of clear and distinct pertains to the qualitative aspects of a concept in contradistinction to the quantitative aspects of a concept, it is still intimately linked with extension and comprehension. Whether one considers the extension or comprehension of a concept, that very concept will be either clear or distinct. Just as it is impossible to abstract the qualitative characters from the quantitative characters in a real apple, so it is similarly inconceivable to abstract the qualities of a concept actually existing in the mind from its so-called quantities of comprehension and extension. For this reason, it seemed imperative to consider briefly the distinction of clear and distinct while presenting the Port Royal doctrine of extension and comprehension.

Barron, referring to extension and intension in one of his footnotes, discusses this distinction in relation to genus and species. He says that a genus contains only the few properties which are common to the several species which it includes, and which are not nearly so numerous as those that belong to each species. The species, again, contains the properties which are common to all the individuals it includes, and which are not so numerous as those that pertain to each individual. The *genus* animal, for instance, includes few properties, life, shape, color, motion, growth, decay. The *species* man contains all these properties of the genus, besides those of the species, namely, power of speech, thinking, acting with design, and many others.[89]

In 1860, De Morgan substituted the words 'scope' and 'force' for the conventional words 'extension' and 'comprehension'.[90] For example, if one declares that "every man is an animal", the word 'man' will be used in all its scope (extension), but not in all its force (intension). On the other hand, 'animal' will be employed in all its force, and not in all its scope. According to everyday language, 'scope' means extension, but De Morgan's use of the word 'force' does not express the idea of comprehension as much as the power of producing a vivid image or representation in the mind. In his *Syllabus,* De Morgan speaks of the extension of classes and the comprehension of real external attributes.[91]

De Morgan reveals a keen insight into the relation of internal and external quantities when he makes the following declaration:

> The logicians who have recently introduced the distinction of extension and comprehension, have altogether missed this opposition of the quantities, and have imagined that the quantities remain the same. Thus, according to Sir W. Hamilton 'All X is some Y' is a proposition of comprehension, but 'Some Y is all X' is a proposition of extension. In this the logicians have abandoned both Aristotle and the laws of thought from which he drew the few clear words of his dictum: 'the genus is said to be part of the species; but in another point of view (*allos*) the species is part of the genus'. *All animal* is in man, notion in notion: *all man in animal,* class in class. In the first, all the notion *animal* part of the notion *man:* in the second: all the class *man* part of the class *animal.* Here is the opposition of the Quantities.[92]

That same year, an American was speaking of logical concepts with such words as 'generalization' and 'specification' from which are deduced two characteristics of all concepts, that is, 'extension' and 'comprehension'. He explained that

> every notion, . . . as a condition of its conceivability, must contain a plurality of attributes, in consequence of which it is capable of subordination to a higher notion; and it must contain a limited number only of attributes, in consequence of which lower notions may be subordinated to it.[93]

The notion of quantity, that is, the notion of one concept containing in it certain attributes (comprehension), and also containing under it other concepts (extension) reiterates here what has already been distinguished by Hamilton as an internal quantity and extensive quantity.

Leechman mentions extension and comprehension when he refers to the predicables. He declares:

> Of these predicables some are more universal than others; and this gave rise to what is taught in Logic respecting the *extension* and the *comprehension* of a term. By the former is meant the number of individuals of which the term may be predicated. The later signifies all the simple ideas which united constitute what the term denotes.[94]

Shedden applies 'extension' and 'comprehension' to the difference between 'denotation' and 'connotation'.[95] He claims that 'quantity' of a concept is constituted by its extension and comprehension.[96] He also says that

> *general names* vary in their *comprehension* and *extension.* Their comprehension depends on the number of qualities which form the group which they represent; their extension, on the number of individuals or objects to which those qualities apply.[97]

This author, like several other English authors, applies comprehension to the sum of real external attributes.

In 1865, another Englishman considered a concept as being a magnitude or quantity.

31

This quantity is twofold. First, it has a number of Marks, which are reduced to unity in Thought, because they are conceived as inhering in one object or thing. This is its Quantity of Intension. Secondly, it denotes a number of objects, which are reduced to unity in Thought as one class or species, because each of them possesses all these Marks. This is its Quantity of Extension.[98]

To facilitate the recognition of various ways in which logicians express the distinction of quantity of concepts, this same author enumerates in two separate columns the different forms of expression:

Logical or Universal whole has	Metaphysical or Formal whole has
Extension,	Intension,
Breadth,	Depth,
Sphere,	Comprehension,
Contains under it,	Contains in it,
denotes,	connotes,
Objects,	Marks,
Things.	Attributes.[99]

Subsequently, Bowen explains how the twofold quantity of concepts enables one to understand that the subject of a proposition is in the Predicate, and the Predicate is in a subject.

With reference to the Quantity of Intension, the Predicate is in the Subject, inasmuch as it is but one of several Marks which make up our Notion of the Subject. Thus, *man is animal; animal* may be regarded as a part of *man,* because it is a part of the meaning of the word; and, when taken in connection with the other parts, *living, two-handed, rational,* makes up the whole Intension of the Concept *man.* But in respect to the Quantity of Extension, man is contained under animal, — the Subject in the Predicate, — since he is but one out of many kinds, all denoted by this one General Term, or contained under this one concept, animal.[100]

This notion of the 'Subject' containing within itself not only the marks or attributes which constitute the 'Predicate' but also other characteristics is discussed by still another Englishman. He refers to this type of comprehensiveness as the 'intension' of a term. For him, inasmuch as a term of 'extension' embraces a greater number of objects than a term of 'intension', the former term may be predicated of the latter one.[101]

The same viewpoint is presented by an American who comments on the doctrine of comprehension and extension as expounded by Hamilton. Concepts are regarded as quantities because they either contain *in* themselves attributes, or contain *under* themselves objects.[102]

Jevons speaks of the 'extent' of the meaning of a term, that is, the number of objects denoted, and the 'intent' of meaning, that is, the number of qualities implied.[103] Instead of comparing concepts in the Hamiltonian manner (as external and internal quantities), he speaks of the meaning of one general term being included in the meaning of another and vice versa.[104] For him the reality of intent and extent is 'meaning', and intent is understood as embracing "the whole infinite series of qualities and circumstances, which a thing possesses".[105] He is cautious to avoid the confusion which arises when the universal term is compared to the individual term. His comparisons are always relations of the universal term to another universal term.

One cannot find fault with Jevons when in 1874 he distinguished between the 'extent' of meaning and the 'intent' of meaning. But when he published another book in 1877, Jevons used the same distinction without naming it explicitly. Speakinw of species having a narrower extension than the genus, he explains:

> In one way it has less meaning than the genus, because there are fewer objects called brick-dwelling houses, than those which may be called dwelling-houses. But in another point of view there is more meaning in the species than in the genus, because we know more about the things.[106]

He could have mentioned that in the first instance, 'meaning' referred to 'extension', whereas, in the second instance, 'meaning' referred to 'intension' (comprehension).

Jevons is criticized by Eaton because he failed to distinguish between two different relations, namely, class-membership and class-inclusion. For example, he presents as examples of the extension of 'metal', iron, gold, silver, etc.; and he offers as examples of the extension of 'steamship', the Great Eastern, the Persia, the Himalaya, etc.

Consider the distinction between the statements, "the Mauretania is a steamship" and "steamships are ships". In the one case we are asserting that a certain entity, the Mauretania, is a *member* of the class of steamships; in the other, that the class of steamships is *included* (subsumed under) the class of ships. Obviously, steamships taken in their unity as a class are not a member of the class of ships, for the class of ships is composed of ships — vessels that can sail the sea — and not of classes. A ship is the sort of thing of which it can be said in the genuine sense of attribution that it can sail the sea, and this is sheer nonsense as asserted of a class. Now, the items comprised in the extension of a general term are all those which are *members* of the class determined by that general term; and these are all the items of which the term can be predicated in the genuine sense of attribution. No genus is ever predicated of its species in the genuine sense of attribution. Though the propositions, "men are animals", "steamships are ships", are loosely said to predicate something of a subject, they really state relations of formal implication, or of class-inclusion. They certainly do not assert that "the class of men is an animal" or that "the class of steamships is a ship". Therefore, the species are not *members* of the class determined by the genus and do not constitute the extension of the genus. The species are subclasses included in the genus. In the same way, the extension of a relation is the pairs, triads, tetrads, etc. which the relation genuinely relates. Thus, the extension of "x loves y" is composed of the pairs of persons who love one another, not of the different varieties of love-filial, brotherly, etc.[107]

Willcox reflects the thought of Porphyry when he mentions that genus has a wider extension than species. According to him,

> *genus* is broader than species, simply by having fewer attributes, but having greater *extension* of numbers. *Species* is narrower than *genus* by being more restricted in *extension,* but more complex in the *comprehension* of attributes. *Extension* is said of numbers of individuals; and *comprehension* is said of numbers of attributes.[108]

34

Pieralisi explains comprehension and extension in the following manner:

> By the *comprehension* of an idea, one wishes to indicate the number of ideas or of simple notes which concur to constitute its being, and into which, if they are numerous, it could be resolved mentally. The diversity of these notes makes the idea even different from other ideas. Their diverse number makes the idea of comprehension greater or smaller. It is from the diversity of this number that the ideas take a diverse denomination in relation to their comprehension.
> By *extension,* width, or sphere of an idea, one wishes to denote the number of individuals represented by it. Thus are represented by one idea these individual beings (not collectively, but each one by itself) that have in their being all these forms, notes or reasons represented by the simple notions concurring to form the comprehension of this idea.[109]

Both comprehension and extension are presented by Prisco in the following paragraphs:

> As a result, between the concepts of genus, species and the individual, there is an opposed and reciprocal containing. The genus contains the species, and the species contains the individual, as the superior contains the inferior. But, on the other hand, the individual includes the content of the specific and generic concept. For example, in the human individual is found humanity, and in humanity is found animality. This opposed and reciprocal containing of concepts gives place to *comprehension* and *extension.*
> We understand by the *comprehension* of a concept the totality of elements which it contains *in itself;* and by *extension,* the totality of subjects which it contains *under itself.*[110]

Speaking of the inverse ratio which exists between comprehension and extension, Sanseverino declares:

Now the comprehension and the circuit [sphere, extension] of a notion are related to each other contrarily, because the greater its comprehension, the less its circuit; and contrariwise, the greater its circuit, the less its comprehension. "In any genus," says St. Thomas, "as much as something is first, the more simple it is, and it consists in fewer principles." [Ia-IIae,

35

q.19, a.2c.]. The reason for this fact . . . is that the difference, because it constitutes the species by perfecting the essence inchoate in the genus, divides the genus itself. As a result any of the species into which the genus is divided possesses something which is not present in the genus, namely the difference, but it does not encompass the contrary species as does the genus. Hence in any species something is present which is not present in the genus, namely the difference, but any species has fewer individuals subordinated to it than the genus. For example, the comprehension of man is greater than the comprehension of animal, because in man there is animal perfected by reason, but the circuit is less because animal embraces not only the notion of man, but also the notion of beast.[111]

In this text one does not find the words *comprehensio* and *extensio* but rather the Latin words *complexus* and *ambitus*. The latter words are not in the tradition of the vocabulary employed by the Port Royalists whom Purchotius followed.

J. H. Gilmore discusses at some length the twofold quantity of concepts and how the subject can be in the predicate, and how the predicate, at the same time, can be in the subject. He tells us that

logically, the species is in the genus; metaphysically, the genus is in the species. That is: so far as our conceptions are concerned, the individual, or the lower class, exists in the class above it; so far as actual existence is concerned, the higher class exists only in the lower, the lower only in the individual.[112]

He employs this example to show that the subject and predicate of a proposition have two values: an extensive value and an intensive value. The following proposition illustrates these two values: "man is an animal". From the viewpoint of extension, the species and subject 'man' is in the genus and predicate 'animal' because the predicate contains *under* it more objects than the subject. But, from the viewpoint of intension, the predicate 'animal' is in the subject 'man' because the subject contains *in* itself more attributes than the predicate. The former case is an example of conceptual existence, while the latter case is an example of what Gilmore might have called actual existence.

36

The use of the word 'metaphysically' by Gilmore is in bad taste because the science of metaphysics studies first intentions while logic treats of second intentions. Since genus and species are second intentions, they are not proper to the domain of metaphysics as such.

This notion of one concept containing another is also mentioned by a nineteenth century Jesuit philosopher.

In any universal idea *extension* and *comprehension* must be considered. The latter is a collection of properties which the universal idea embraces in itself; the former is a multitude of objects or individuals of which that idea can be predicated. These objects are called *inferior* ideas or *subjects.* Thus the idea of "man" embraces the attributes of living, sentient and rational substance; this is its comprehension. But the individuals of which this idea can be predicated, as "Peter", "Paul", constitute its extension.[113]

Bain defines extension or denotation as the individuals to which the term applies, and comprehension or connotation as the community of attributes, or points of agreement, making up the characters or definition of a term.[114] The idea of unity is stressed in his definition of comprehension.

J. H. Gilmore's assertion that a predicate has a twofold value (extensive and intensive) is further developed by Noah K. Davis (1880) when he declares that we can think of a predicate as a mark (intension) or as a class (extension). He designates the one as thinking in the intensive quantity and the other as thinking in the extensive quantity. Davis maintains that we cannot think one without thinking the other. However, according to him, one form of thinking usually predominates in the individual. He believes that

thinking in intension is more usual with cultivated, and in extension with uncultivated, persons. Compare the scholarly synonyms of mark, — *quality, property, attribute, characteristic,* etc., — with the vulgar synonyms of species, — *class, sort, kind* or *kin, group, variety, set, lot,* etc. Children, too, seem to prefer extension; and hence pupils in Logic usually find more difficulty in understanding the theory relative to intension, this quantity being less familiar. Also, it seems that the literature of thought, from the early days of Greek philosophy until modern times, shows a strong inclination to the extensive

37

quantity, describing things by classes; and that the tendency of modern thought is to the intensive quantity, describing things by attributes. Certainly, the literature of Logic, from Aristotle to Arnauld, treats exclusively of extension. Again, this appears in rude languages as compared with the refined, as might be presumed; since a language, in its early stages, gives common names to things in groups, as sorts or kinds; but as it progresses. adjectives multiply, largely derived from the substantive nouns.[115]

Davis' statement that "the literature of Logic, from Aristotle to Arnauld, treats exclusively of extension" is false. Aristotle presented both intension (comprehension) and extension in proper proportion; otherwise, he would never have written the sentence that "the genus is called a part of the species" (*Metaph.* V. c. 25, 1023b24-25). In the following chapter, it will be indicated that intension and extension were discussed by many logicians from the time of Aristotle to the time of Petrus Gassendus (1658).

Zigliara divides ideas into singular and universal ideas. Concerning the latter, he says that there are

inferior and *subordinated* things in which is a universal idea. — It is evident, however, that each *universal* nature has both *inferiors* of this kind in itself and *certain other things.* Whence the universal is more powerful in *extension* than its inferiors; but the latter are more powerful in *comprehension* than the universal itself.[116]

Bradley declares that intension or comprehension means to consider an idea in its content, that is, in abstraction from its reference.[117] At the same time, he considers the extension of an idea in two different senses: actual or ideal instances. He explains his own meaning of 'actual' and 'ideal' in the following footnote:

'Ideal or actual'. By 'actual' I meant here 'existing in our real world'. But the 'ideal' instance, though not in this sense 'real', must be taken as an individual or particular. The extension always means the particular object or objects to which the meaning is applicable.[118]

Bosanquet remarks that an observation made by Aristotle is the basis for the development of the difference between the intension and extension of a concept. According to Aristotle, in one sense, a genus contains its species; in another sense, every species must contain its genus.[119]

Intension and extension are identified with connotation and denotation respectively by this English author. For him, extension designates 'individual things' while intension designates 'relations'.

> To think in denotation (extension) only, would be to think of individual things without knowing what we are thinking of; to think in connotation (intension) would be to think of relations without knowing what subjects are determined by them.[120]

Bosanquet criticizes Bradley who confines extension strictly to actual objects which exist only at the present moment.

> I can see no justification for the limitation of extension to actual objects in the sense of objects existing in present time; as extension seems to me to be simply an element in intension, the element which when made precise takes the shape of number.[121]

Although some logicians regard 'comprehension' and 'connotation' as synonymous with 'intension', and 'denotation' as synonymous with 'extension', Keynes differentiates the meanings of these terms. He admits that "the force of the terms 'extension' and 'intension' in the most general sense might perhaps also be expressed by the pair of terms 'application' and 'implication.' "[122]

Inasmuch as language plays an important role as an instrument of thought, Dr. Keynes prefers to speak first of names rather than of concepts. He says that "the 'extension' of a name then consists of objects of which the name can be predicated; its intension consists of properties which can be predicated of it".[123]

Many of the controversies and misunderstandings which arise from the problem of the connotation of names are due, according to Keynes, to a lack of discrimination. Hence he distinguishes three different kinds of intension: (1) 'Conventional intension' which embraces all those qualities essential to a name. Any individual lacking one of these qualities could not be designated by that specific name. (2) 'Subjective intension' which comprises those qualities of a name by which a person recognizes or identifies an object.

39

This type of intension does not exhaust the essential qualities of a general name; in fact, it may include some nonessential qualities. Since this kind of intension is subjective, the qualities belonging to the name may vary from person to person, and may even vary for the same person on different occasions. (3) 'Objective intension' which includes all the qualities of the two preceding types, and often many others besides.[124]

Keynes identifies 'conventional intension' with 'connotation'. He claims that John Stuart Mill employed connotation in this sense, namely, that connotation does not mean all the qualities possessed by a name, nor those qualities mentally associated with a name, but only those which are essential to a name. For example, he says,

> although all equilateral triangles are equiangular, equiangularity is not . . . included in the connotation of equilateral triangle, since it is not a property upon which the classification of triangles into equilateral and non-equilateral is based.[125]

Keynes mentions that there are some logicians who identify connotation with subjective intension and objective intension. He himself limits connotation to conventional intension.

After considering 'connotation' as equivalent to 'conventional intension', he proceeds to identify 'comprehension' with 'objective intension'.[126] He also prefers to employ 'denotation' in the sense of 'objective extension' in order to exclude all fictitious or conceptual beings.[127]

Keynes agrees with Mill by maintaining that proper names have no connotation (conventional intension), but he insists that they do possess subjective intension and objective intension (comprehension).[128]

In view of the different distinctions made by Keynes, one might apply connotation to the name or term, subjective intension to the mental representation, and comprehension to the thing objectively considered.[129]

Maritain voices disapproval because Keynes distinguishes connotation from comprehension in the strict sense. In this case, as already explained, connotation signifies those qualities which define the object of a name or concept, while comprehension refers to the

40

object's recognizable qualities or attributes. After claiming that this distinction has no meaning, Maritain adds:

This distinction is defective . . . for it does not oppose the *properties* to the *essence* or to the characteristics which define the object of a concept in *itself*, but rather does it oppose these properties to the characteristics which define it *for us*, which are of use to us in defining it, and which, in the case of descriptive definitions, are not constitutive elements of the essence, but are precisely properties.[130]

And Stebbing objects to Keynes' terminology as not helpful when the latter speaks of 'subjective intension'.[131]

In spite of these criticisms, one German writer has lavish praise for Keynes. He says that "John Neville Keynes' *Studies and Exercises in Formal Logic* is the most perfect presentation of classical formal logic in general."[132]

Tigert associates intension with marks and extension with objects to which the marks are ascribed. He asserts that

intension may be defined as the sum-total of the Marks or properties which any object must possess . . . to admission to a given class, or designation by a given common name.

Extension may be defined as the number of individuals possessing the Marks which entitle them to admission to a given class or designation by a given common name.[133]

After presenting these definitions, the author lists some of the synonyms commonly employed by logicians to indicate extension and intension.

In general, Extension has for synonyms, Extent, Breadth, Sphere, Denotation, Extensive or External Quantity, Circuit, Domain, Application; while the synonyms of Intension are Intent, Depth, Comprehension, Connotation, Intensive or Internal Quantity, Content, Implication. Extension always, in the last analysis, is to Objects, and Intension to Marks.[134]

The more traditional words of 'comprehension' and 'extension' are employed by Veitch and Coppens to express this distinction of concepts. Veitch observes that

41

every concept has a double or twofold side. As embodying the idea of an attribute or attributes, it has a meaning, content, or comprehension *(Inhalt)*. As through the attribute or attributes applicable to several objects, it has a compass, breadth, or extension *(Umfang)*. It takes in objects or classes: in the former aspect it indicates attributes, in the latter it denotes objects.[135]

According to Coppens,

comprehension means the total signification, all the notes comprehended or contained in an idea; thus, the concept 'man' comprehends the notes 'animal' and 'rational'. . . .
Extension means the total number of individuals to which the idea extends or applies; the extension of the concept 'man' is all men.[136]

Lotze, when discussing the comprehension and extension of concepts, offers this explanation:

It is said that the content *(materia)* of the higher general concept *(genus)* is 'contained' in the content of the lower *(species);* that is, that all the marks which are essential to the genus occur also in the species. But, conversely, the content of the species is not entirely contained in that of the genus: but the former possesses, besides the particular marks of the latter, certain ones peculiar to it as species. . . .[137]

Thus, inasmuch as attributes or contents are concerned, the species exceed the genus in comprehension or intension. But, inasmuch as objects are concerned, the genus surpasses the species in extension. Lotze substitutes the words 'extent' and *ambitus* for 'extension'. It will be recalled that Sr. William Hamilton was already familiar with the word *ambitus.*

An American Jesuit refers to Lotze's distinction in somewhat different language.

We may think of an object of thought under two different aspects, either as an *idea,* comprising a number of simpler ideas, or as a *class* containing a number of smaller classes; or, to use a nomenclature already familiar to our readers, as a whole of *comprehension,* or a whole of *extension.*[138]

Here again is found the distinction in an expression of a twofold quantity, namely, internal and external quantity.

Another Jesuit defines the comprehension of an idea or concept as the "combination of distinguishing marks which shine out in the idea", and extension as "the multitude of subjects of which any idea can be enunciated".[139]

Hyslop, who admits that he is indebted to Jevons for both the matter and method used in the presentation of his book, defines 'extension' and 'intension' in the following fashion:

> Extension is the *quantitative power of terms or concepts,* and so indicates their numerical application. It may refer to individual-or class-wholes, whether substantive or attributive, real or conceptual.
>
> Intension is the *qualitative power of terms or concepts,* and so indicates their denotation of qualities. It may refer to a single quality, a group of qualities in an individual-whole, or the common quality or qualities of a class-whole, whether substantive or attributive, real or conceptual.[140]

Thus, according to Hyslop, extension may apply to individuals or to classes which exist either in reality or in the mind. At the same time, these individuals may be substances or attributes. Intension, on the other hand, refers to one or several qualities possessed by an individual or a class. These qualities may also be real or conceptual, substances or attributes.

This author remarks in the course of his discussion that genus differs from species 'quantitatively'; but genus differs from differentia 'qualitatively'. He declares that all generic concepts have a twofold capacity: mathematical and logical.[141]

Sidgwick, influenced by J. S. Mill, speaks of 'connotation' and 'denotation'. "The connotation of a name", he says, "may be explained as the *conditions under which that name is intended to be applicable* — applicable as a predicate to any subject." And he adds, "by the denotation of a name, on the other hand, is meant *the things or cases to which it is intended to be applied.*"[142]

Minto claims that the relation of individuals and attributes to a general name can be designated by various words. He refers to such individuals considered jointly as the "*denotation,* or *extension* or

43

scope of the name"; and the "common attributes as its *connotation, intension, comprehension,* or *ground.*"[143] For him, the entire 'denotation' is the 'class', while the entire 'connotation' is the 'concept'.

Blanc explains extension and comprehension by means of the relation between genus and species.

> The genus contains the species and reciprocally, depending on the point of view that one takes. The genus is extended to more individuals than the species; but it comprehends less notes or elements. Thus the idea of animal (genus) is extended to men and to beasts; but it is less rich than the idea of man (species) if one analyzes it, since man possesses all the attributes of animality, and even more those of reason. In a word, the genus has more *extension* than the species, but it has less *comprehension.*[144]

Considering the essence of a universal term in relation to its content and in relation to its application, Brother Louis of Poissy distinguishes between the comprehension and extension of terms.

> *Universal terms have two properties: comprehension and extension, which are in inverse ratio to each other.* — The essence represented by a universal term is made up of one or of many elements; thus, the essence of man consists of "animality and rationality"; the *comprehension* or *intension* of a universal term is the sum of the elements which it contains. The essence represented by a universal term is found in a greater or less number of subjects; thus, the essence of man is found in every man; the *extension* of a universal term is the number of beings to which it applies.[145]

When Fowler discusses 'connotation' and 'denotation', he refers to terms. "A term is said to 'denote' individuals, or groups of individuals, and 'connote' attributes, or groups of attributes."[146] Thus, according to his understanding of connotation, terms refer to attributes in a secondary manner, whereas, according to the Scholastics, terms refer to attributes primarily and to subjects secondarily. Fowler considers 'connotation' to be the sum total of real external attributes.

Sigwart speaks of the extension of a concept as "the sum-total of lower concepts which are subordinated to it".[147] He upholds the opinion that 'comprehension' includes all necessary and accidental attributes of a 'name'. The Port Royalists, by way of contrast, restricted comprehension solely to necessary (essential and proper) attributes.

Sigwart distinguishes between the 'logical extension of a concept' and the 'empirical extension of a name'. He illustrates his distinction by saying: "Two footed unfeathered animal is a different concept from that of man; only when used as names do they denote the same beings."[148] It is a matter of chance that these two concepts of different intension designate the same reality.

Smith construes the meaning of a term as embracing both its denotation (which he identifies with signification) and its connotation. He also regards meaning as equivalent to a notion or concept. And, like many other modern logicians, he considers connotation to be synonymous with intension, and denotation with extension.[149]

Rickaby presents the distinction between extension and comprehension (or intension) from the viewpoint of something containing and being contained. Thus, if the predicate is represented as containing the subject, the predicate may be regarded in extension. But if the subject is viewed as containing the predicate, the subject is considered in intension.[150] This viewpoint reflects the thinking of J. H. Gilmore (1879) who has already been quoted in this study.

When Mercier treats of comprehension and extension, he refers to the concept as a metaphysical whole and as a logical whole. The "metaphysical whole, which comprises corporeity, life, sensibility, reason . . .", applies to the intension of a concept, and the logical whole, "which embraces all men of the past, present, and future, or even simply possible men . . .",[151] applies to the extension of a concept. This distinction between the metaphysical whole and logical whole in relation to intension and extension has already been mentioned by Francis Bowen (1865).

Rabier asserts that comprehension and extension exist in a reciprocal relationship between ideas according as certain elements are included or excluded from ideas.

The relations of inclusion or exclusion among ideas result from the reciprocal comprehension and extension of ideas.

45

The *comprehension* of an idea is the *sum total of characters* which the idea includes. The *extension* of an idea is the *sum total of beings* in which this sum total of notes is found realized. The comprehension of an idea is thus the ensemble of attributes of which it is the subject (v. g., man is an animal, two-handed, rational, etc.); the extension of an idea is the ensemble of subjects of which it is the attribute (v. g., the Europeans, Africans, Oceanians, Americans are men).

Comprehension is the proper *matter* of the concept; extension is the *circumscription* or the sphere of application of the concept.[152]

Aikins describes connotative terms as having a double function: they point out an object of thought and they describe it. He states:

When we say that a man came to the house we not only tell the hearer that one or other of a certain large group of things came to the house, but we incidentally describe that thing, implying that it has all the qualities and other relations of a man; and when we say that John is a man we not only describe him but incidentally we tell that he is one of a certain group. Terms which perform this double function are called connotative; those which do not, nonconnotative.[153]

Denotation is identified with extension, and connotation with intension in this same text.

Hibben notes that some writers apply the words 'extension' and 'intension' to concepts, and 'denotation' as well as 'connotation' to terms. He calls terms the "language symbols of concepts".[154] He also remarks that extension and intension are used interchangeably with denotation and connotation in everyday usage.

Venn makes an interesting observation on this subject of denotation and connotation. Denotation is something real to him while connotation is something notional or conceptual. "The denotation we may be said to find; the connotation we must be said to make."[155] Hence, according to him, denotation exists in reality and is perceived directly, while connotation exists in the mind and is perceived indirectly.

Gibson reminds his readers that definition provides the connotation, and division the denotation. He is the only logician encountered in the course of this research who declares that intension is equal to connotation plus denotation.[156] For him intension signifies the full relevant development of the meaning of a concept by means of definition and division. He defines denotation and extension in a unique manner: "denotation we define as differentiation of meaning, to be interpreted disjunctively. . . . Extension we define as application of meaning to individual objects, to be interpreted conjunctively."[157]

Gredt asserts that the "comprehension of a concept is the sum total of notes which constitute a concept; extension is the sum total of all objects whose image is the concept".[158] According to this author, the notes or attributes of a concept, which constitute its comprehension, are always conceptual; but the objects comprising the extension of that concept are always real.

Dewey claims that confusion was introduced into the domain of logic when logicians abandoned the ontological basis for the distinction between extension and intension. If extension and intension are not regarded as existential, and if denotation and connotation are not regarded as conceptual, then there is a danger of identifying extension with denotation and intension with connotation.[159] He seems to complicate things and create even more confusion. For him, comprehension is not a sign of intension when he says "the two pairs, *extension* and *intension* for use in connection with denotative terms — and *comprehension* and definition (for use with connotative terms) meet the needs of clarity and completeness".[160]

"Intension," says Dewey, "is meaning as a principle of identifying particulars; extension is the groups of particulars identified and distinguished."[161] In other words, meaning, as a principle of recognizing the nature of a particular in isolation, may be called intension. And, when the individual things have been recognized, they can be counted up to form a group. This counting up is called extension.

The Italian Monaco defines comprehension as the *"sum total of perfections* (or *notes,* as they say) *to which the term refers in regard to the thing signified".*[162] And he defines extension as the "number of things or subjects to which the term can be ascribed".[163] Monaco mentions that these two fundamental properties of terms, namely, comprehension and extension, are based on the fact that one thing may possess several perfections (comprehension), or several things may have the same perfection (extension).[164]

Turner insists that the meaning of terms can be viewed in two directions: *horizontally*, the term is viewed in its extension because it extends in one direction to individuals or groups of individuals; *vertically*, the term is viewed in comprehension because it descends to include certain attributes or qualities.[165] The visualization of concepts in two directions brings to mind the reference made by Hamilton where it was observed that some Greek logicians designated extension by the term breadth *(platos)* and comprehension by the term depth *(bathos)*.

Turner also presents a list of synonymous words arranged in two separate columns to illustrate the varied terminology employed by logicians when discussing extension and comprehension.

Extension	Comprehension
Extent	Intent
Denotation	Intension
Sphere	Connotation
Breadth	Depth
Application	Implication
Scope	Force[166]

Turner prefers to use the words 'extension' and 'comprehension'. Denotation and connotation are his second choice.

Adamson considers the distinction between connotation and denotation to be a grammatical and not a logical problem.[167] He thinks that the word 'connotation' has introduced itself into logic without any reason to justify its presence. He remarks that today 'connotation' conveys a meaning which is at variance with its earlier usage. His reference to the grammatical meaning of 'connotation' recalls a similar usage employed in the Middle Ages.

Schiller employs the words 'denotation' and 'connotation' as well as 'extension' and 'intension'. While criticizing the law that extension and intension vary inversely, he says

it is true that though the qualities stated in the definition of a more extensive class or genus are fewer and less determinate than those stated in the definition of its species, yet the qualities *possessed* are more. For a genus must have the qualities of all its species.[168]

Hence he considers it false to conclude that the qualities diminish as you increase the extension of a class or genus. It will be explained later that, according to St. Albert, the genus contains the qualities of the species in power (*in potestate*), but not in act (*in actu*) or in potency (*in potentia*). The expression *in potestate* implies an active power to do something rather than a passive power to receive something as in potency (*in potentia*).

In contradistinction to other logicians who associate comprehension with genus and species, Levesque restricts it exclusively to difference, property and accident.

> All human conceptions are reduced to three groups: substances, modes and relations. *Porphyry* first classified universals or general ideas and he reduced them to five by considering them either from the point of view of extension (which gives the genus and species), or from the point of view of comprehension (whence result the difference, property and accident).[169]

L'Abbé Robert pursues traditional lines when he defines the comprehension or content of an idea as *"the ensemble of elements which comprises or contains an idea,"* and the extension of an idea as *"the ensemble of individuals to which the idea is ascribable".*[170] He upholds that the extension of a term embraces all present, past and future objects designated by that term.

According to Pesch,

> the collection of those notes, which the concept of a thing contains, is called the ensemble or *comprehension* of a concept. From which comprehension is distinguished the *circuit* or *extension* of a concept, which is a greater or lesser number of subjects to which some concept can be applied.[171]

Here is one of the first texts where a Scholastic philosopher writing in Latin identifies the word *extensio* employed by the Port Royalists and Purchotius with the Latin word *ambitus* as used by the classical Medieval scholars.

Willems identifies the word 'comprehension' with the formal object of cognition and the word 'extension' with the material object of cognition. He considers extension to be proper to logic and comprehension proper to ontology. In other words, he makes extension a subject of primary importance for logic and comprehension as a part of a background — in the sense that it belongs to the remote foundation of genus. By the word 'ontology', Willems is not referring to the science of metaphysics; he is referring only to first intentions. Here is his explanation:

> Put in motion by simple apprehension, the mind can turn back on its act by *psychological, ontological* or *logical reflection:* the first considers the act subjectively, that is, as an affection of the mind, its nature and its origin, whence it pertains to psychology; the second considers the very *object* of cognition, and I mean the formal object, that is, the comprehension of a concept; finally, logical reflection considers directly the *mode* of cognition, its material object, that is, it regards the extension of a concept.
>
> 1. If we talk about *comprehension,* (a) a concept which is first of all confused and obscure is made clear and distinct by ontological reflection, just as an object seen at a distance becomes better known the closer we come to look at it; (b) the notes constituting the concept are distinguished as essential and accidental, so that the concept, at first confused, becomes distinct and is raised to the perfection of a scientific definition.
>
> 2. But if the *material object* or *extension* is considered, it becomes apparent through logical reflection that the concept is not only suitable to express some object immediately, but because it is universal, it can manifest an infinite number of individuals of the same nature, whence the concept formed from a sensible thing by means of direct abstraction, already a universal *in itself or in potency* (direct universal), through an ontological reflection of the mind or rather logical reflection is *actually* extended and made a *reflex universal.*[172]

Joseph introduces the subject of 'intension' and 'extension' in his logic book by explaining a passage from the writings of Aristotle. That passage, which he does not quote verbatim, reads as follows: "As man is in animal, and as usually we say the species is in the genus. In another way, as the genus is in the species, and a part of the species is wholly in the definition of the species."[173] In the beginning of that third chapter, Aristotle lists eight different ways in which one thing can be said to be in another. The third and fourth ways are quoted in the preceding citation. When Aristotle mentions "as genus is in the species," he means that genus is a part of the definition of the species just as the specific difference is also a part of that definition. Consequently, the genus and differentia can be said to be in the species as parts are in a whole.[174]

Commenting on the Aristotelian reference, Joseph says:

'Animal' is in 'man', in the sense that you cannot be a man without being an animal, so that being animal is included in being man. 'Man' is in 'animal', in the sense that among the forms of animal nature, man is included.

In the technical language of later Logic, this distinction may be expressed by saying that in intension the species includes the genus, in extension is included in it.[175]

He defines intension and extension in this manner:

The *intension* of a term is what we *intend* by it, or what we mean by it when predicating it of any subject; the *extension* is all that stands subordinated to it as to a genus, the variety of kinds over which the predication of the term may *extend*.[176]

Notice that according to this definition extension is more prominent in the subject while intension is more prominent in the predicate, because he adds to his definition of intension the phrase "when predicating it of any subject". And, lest the reader will not understand his definition, Joseph redefines those same two terms: "the extension is the variety of species in which a common character is exhibited, the intension the common character exhibited in this variety".[177]

When he wishes to distinguish between the individuals and species to which a term extends, Joseph employs the word 'denotation' in reference to individuals, and 'extension' in reference to species.[178] Hence the extension of 'animal' would be 'man' and 'brute', but the denotation of 'man' would be 'Socrates', 'Plato', 'Aristotle', etc.

Sellars distinguishes between the 'meaning' of a term and its 'connotation'. He declares in the first place, the distinction between denotation and connotation comes out clearly only for class terms; in the second place, the meaning of a class term includes both its denotation and its connotation. We mean the objects we think of as well as the qualities they have in common.[179]

In this instance, meaning is regarded as a generic concept in relation to denotation and connotation.

Munzi, without citing the exact source, says that the "comprehension of a term in general is what we receive from the definition of Aristotle: namely, intelligibility contained in that in which a proposition is resolved; extension, all that which can perform the function of subject or predicate in any proposition".[180] As an example, the comprehension of man, for Munzi, is contained in a 'rational animal'. Individuals of which man is predicated would constitute man's extension.

Goblot does not accept the distinction of the comprehension and connotation of concepts as presented by Dr. Keynes. The latter logician identified only conventional intension with connotation. Therefore, connotation would embrace only those qualities which are essential to a name, and not all those qualities possessed by a name, nor those mentally associated with a name. On the other hand, in his definition of comprehension, Goblot includes not only all the properties derived from the essence, but all the concepts contained in a particular generic or specific concept as species or sub-species, and all other properties implied by the latter.[181] Thus the comprehension of 'animal' would not only include such characteristics as sentient, living, bodily substance, but also such concepts as dog and its sub-species of Golden Retriever, St. Bernard, Collie, etc., as well as individual dogs of each breed. In other words, the extension of a concept would form a part of the comprehension of that concept.

Here is Goblot's definition of extension and comprehension:

The extension or denotation of a term is the number of individuals contained in the genus, that is to say, some possible judgments of which it is the attribute; its comprehension or connotation is the number of qualities common to the in-

52

dividuals of the genus, that is to say, some possible judgments of which it is the subject. If a term is general, that is to say, a concept, its denotation is infinite; if it is singular, its connotation is infinite.[182]

Goblot considers all the characteristics possessed by different species and sub-species as existing within the power of their respective genus. He says that "a vertebrate is not an animal with neither fur, feathers nor scales, but an animal whose tegumentary appendages *may have* the forms, fur, feathers, or scales".[183] For, it may be commented here, these characteristics are contained only 'in potency' by the genus and not 'in act'. The genus 'animal' is potentially richer than the species 'man'; but in act, the opposite is true. The species 'man' contains 'rationality' in act, whereas the genus 'animal' contains 'irrationality' within its power. St. Albert expresses this thought succinctly when he says "a specific difference is not in the genus, but is within its power".[184]

Goblot would have us believe that comprehension includes not only all essential attributes but also all accidental ones which a concept contains even potentially. Such a notion of comprehension is altogether confusing. "If by the comprehension of the idea we understand all that may truthfully be affirmed of this idea",[185] then the comprehension of the concept 'man' should contain attributes as walking, talking, sleeping, eating, working, scientist, teacher, husband, father, living in New York, etc. No longer would comprehension be understood strictly as a logical property of a concept. If one employs Dr. Keynes' terminology, it can be said that Goblot identifies comprehension with subjective intension.[186] However, since his notion of comprehension is much more embracing than that of Jevons, he prefers to refer to total comprehension under the title of connotation.[187]

While speaking about the essential properties of an idea, Uccello remarks:

> But the ensemble or sum total of notes, of which any idea is composed, is said to be its COMPREHENSION. . . . However, the sum total or ensemble of beings, which can be manifested by any idea, is said to be the EXTENSION of this idea.

The comprehension and extension of an idea truly pertain to its nature because:

(a) Comprehension is something intrinsic to the idea; in fact, if from the idea "man" you take away the note "rationality", you will destroy the essence of man.

(b) Extension, although it is something extrinsic to the idea, for the idea would remain the same even if it would exist only in one subject to which it would belong, nevertheless it indicates a capacity or aptitude per se towards its extension, with the sole exception of the idea "God" which can belong only to one being.[188]

According to Johnson, "extension stands for a set of substantives, intension stands for a set of adjectives".[189] He looks upon these two notions of extension and intension as more general than denotation and connotation.

Joyce refers to those characteristics or attributes which are expressed by a common concept as the intension or comprehension of a term. And he calls the individuals to which a term is applicable the extension of that term.[190]

When he discusses connotation, he states that "the only satisfactory account of connotation is that which takes it to signify the fundamental characteristics, which determine the application of the term".[191] He stresses this fact in opposition to those logicians who maintain that connotation must signify everything that we know about a thing at the present time. According to Joyce, the "connotation must concern the thing as it is known, not the thing in its objective reality".[192] On the other hand, denotation for him refers to real objects expressed by concepts.[193]

Cunningham employs connotation with reference to attributes or qualities, and denotation with reference to things.[194] He also uses connotation as synonymous with intension, and denotation with extension. He remarks that denotation is demonstrative inasmuch as it points out an object, while connotation is descriptive inasmuch as it reveals something about an object.

Toohey makes a unique distinction between 'explicit' and 'implicit' comprehension.

The *comprehension* of an idea is the sum-total of notes or attributes which the idea explicitly represents in the object. The sum-total of notes which are not explicitly represented by

54

the idea, but which may be determined by an analysis of the formal object of the idea, may be called the *implicit comprehension* of the idea.

The *extension* of an idea is the sum-total of individuals or objects which are severally represented by the idea; that is, it is the sum-total of individuals of which the idea can be predicated when they are taken one by one. These objects or individuals are called the *Inferiors* of the idea.[195]

It should be noted here that in the third edition of his text,[196] he uses primarily the words 'connotation' and 'denotation' and secondarily the words 'comprehension' and 'extension'.

It is noteworthy to observe that De Mandato associates the word *amplitudo* with extension when he defines the latter word: *"the extension of a term* is its amplitude [width] in relation to those things concerning which it can be predicated".[197] The use of the word *amplitudo* bears a resemblance to such words as *ambitus* or width (employed by Latin logicians) and *platos* or breadth (employed by Greek logicians). At the same time, De Mandato says that the *"comprehension of a term* is the sum total of notes to which the term refers concerning the thing signified".[198]

The German Jesuit Frick has recourse to similar terminology when he refers to extension as *ambitus* (width) and *amplitudo* (amplitude or width) and defines it as "the capacity of an idea representing several or fewer objects".[199] And the comprehension of an idea is "the sum total of notes which are expressed by the subjective idea and constitute the objective idea".[200]

McClure discusses intension and extension when he refers to meaning. He considers meanings to be mental. In contrast to physical data which constitute the realm of 'existence', meanings constitute the realm of 'essence'.[201] "Meaning", he says, "is an intrinsic quality, an immediate value, a resident attribute of thinghood. . . . Once the meaning is acquired it is subsequently intuited. . . ."[202] "Intuition of intrinsic meaning is in no sense a cognition. . . . When we are dealing with intrinsic meanings we are dealing with thinghood, not with knowledge or cognition."[203]

Then speaking of extension, the author adds, "the thing meaning has an extrinsic reference, it mediates, it points to something beyond itself".[204]

Crumley reverts to 'implication' and 'application' of terms when he speaks about intension and extension. He claims that this

> distinction is based upon the twofold function of conception which not only takes out of experience the common qualities that form an essence, but which also puts these qualities back into experience by pointing out the things that possess them.[205]

Of course, the "common qualities" mentioned here constitute the intension of a term, while "the things that possess them" comprise the extension of a term.

Adler notes that denotation can serve as a check on an "infinite regressus in the use of other terms".[206] Thus if an object is indicated by a definition, there is no need to define still further the words which comprise the definition. "But," he adds, "if the definition of a word is attempted through connotation, the other words evoked themselves need definition."[207] According to Adler, denotative meanings of words are names which refer to objects, while connotative meanings are notational entities.

Latta and Macbeath stress the notion of unity as essential to the connotation and denotation of a term. They declare that

> the connotation of a term is not its reference to a mere aggregate of independent qualities, but to a system of qualities related to one another so as to form a unity. Similarly the denotation is the reference of the term to one or more such systems, each considered as a unity. Connotation and denotation are thus inseparable aspects of the term. If the term connotes qualities, it must connote them as elements within the unity of a system, and so far as the term refers to such a system as one thing it is denotative.[208]

Forbes and Hird identify extension with denotation, and intension with connotation. They say that

> Genus and Species are considered in intension (connotation) when they are predicables and mean *attributes* of classes. In this sense they are explained by *definition.*
>
> Genus and Species are considered in extension (denotation) when, as in ordinary language, they mean *classes.* In this sense they are explained by *division.*[209]

They also mention that the genus includes the species in extension and the species includes the genus in intension. For example, the concept 'animal' includes the concept 'man' because 'animal' is predicated of and extended to 'man'; but, in another sense, the concept 'man' includes the concept 'animal' because its intension embraces certain intelligible notes which are also contained in the concept 'animal' (v.g., sentient, living, body, substance).

Enriques affirms "that the real meaning of a concept is to be found in its 'comprehension' or 'connotation' . . ." and this meaning "attaches itself instead to 'extension' or 'denotation'".[210] He opposes his definition of comprehension to nominalism which denies the reality of universals.

Meyerson quotes Aristotle's *Pr. Anal.*, I, c. 1, 24b27-28, concerning the two ways in which one can conceive the signification of a proposition: "That one term should be included in another as in a whole is the same as for the other to be predicated of all of the first."[211] This passage can be illustrated by saying that the term 'man' is included in the term 'animal' (considered as a whole). It is an example of extension inasmuch as the term 'animal' can be predicated of all subjects included in the term 'man'.

Jorgensen declares that the German logician Frege made a distinction comparable to that of Mill's denotation and connotation.

> Frege distinguished first of all between the symbol itself *("das Zeichen")*, its indication or denotation *("Bedeutung")*, its meaning *("Sinn")* and its associated ideas *("Vorstellungen")*. The symbol itself is the written, spoken or otherwise produced physical phenomenon to which the three other elements are attached. The indication is the object indicated by the symbol. meaning being the idea which the symbol expresses. Frege's distinction between these two terms corresponds in some respects to J. S. Mill's distinction between "Denotation" and "Connotation". And the ideas are the subjective psychological elements of knowledge associated with the symbol. The indication — i. e. the object — is objective, and exists independently of the person's thinking and speaking; the meaning — i. e. the concept — must be the same in the minds of the person's thinking; the idea, on the other

hand may differ very greatly as between different individuals. The meaning of the word "horse" is the same for all who know the meaning of the word, but one may form the idea of roan, another that of an Arab, another that of a dappled grey. So also the indication of the symbol is different from its *"Sinn"*. Thus for instance the words "morning star" and "evening star" have the same indication, as indicating one and the same celestial body; the meaning, however, is different, in that the former term expresses the idea of a star visible in the morning, whereas the latter expresses the idea of a star visible in the evening.[212]

Although Jorgensen insists that Frege's distinction between denotation and connotation "corresponds in some respects to J. S. Mill's distinction", there is actually more contrast than similarity between these two positions. According to Mill, denotation and connotation are opposed as primary meaning and secondary meaning. Both denotation and connotation 'exist within the mind'. On the other hand, according to Frege, indication (denotation) is opposed to meaning as something 'outside the mind' is opposed to something inside the mind. This is a radical departure from all prior uses of the word 'denotation' inasmuch as everybody else believes that denotation refers to meaning as something in the mind, whereas in this case denotation is suddenly transformed into a word designating the object existing independently of any person's thinking.

It should be remembered that meaning is always in the mind and not in the object. In other words, our knowledge of things is in the mind, but we can denominate the object in relation to the intelligibility of that same object.

Frege maintains that the spoken or written word 'horse' constitutes its symbol. The individual horse existing outside the mind is the indication or denotation of 'horse'. The meaning would be a quadruped, herbivorous animal. And the connotation or associated ideas would embrace 'a dappled grey', ' roan', or 'an Arabian' horse. Denotatively, 'horse' is the object upon which everyone agrees. Connotatively, 'horse' is used according to the imagery or interpretation which each person brings to that word.

Jorgensen also mentions that "several German logicians (Sigwart, Erdmann, Drobisch, A. Riehl) define the extension *(Umfang)* of a term as the class, or collection of its subordinate term".[213] From this definition, Jorgensen concludes that an individual term (which cannot be subdivided into subordinate terms) would have no extension.

He lists five different sorts of properties which some logicians insist must be included in determining the intension of a term:

(a) the 'essential' qualities of the objects concerned,
(b) those qualities which are necessary and sufficient to distinguish the objects concerned from all other objects,
(c) all the qualities of the objects concerned known to some person or other,
(d) all the qualities of the objects concerned known to a certain person, and
(e) all existing (known and unknown) qualities of the objects concerned.[214]

In a corresponding manner, extension will have different meanings such as all objects which contain the properties enumerated under (a) or (b) or (c), etc.

Eaton discusses extension and intension in connection with terms. He identifies extension with denotation, and intension with connotation.[215] He claims that the contrast between the extension and intension of terms is founded on the logical distinction between a universal and its instances. He says "a universal taken in abstraction from its instances *is* an intension; but a universal might have instances in the actual world, and these would constitute its extension".[216] Thus a particular object is an example of extension, while the qualities or attributes abstracted from that object are an example of intension.

Eaton believes that adjectival and relative terms such as 'white' and 'father' refer primarily to intension and secondarily to extension. On the other hand, he considers proper names and singular terms to be primarily extensional and secondarily intensional.[217]

When Shaw thinks of the extension of a concept, he thinks of an assortment of nouns; but when he considers the intension of a concept, he thinks of a variety of adjectives.[218] He is convinced that the logical distinction between extension and intension can be presented more effectively with the words 'denotation' and 'connotation'. To Shaw, the latter words seem to make a concept more active and alive. He says that "we may speak of a connotative term as one which expresses the essence of an idea, whereas a denotative term is confined to its exemplification in individual things".[219]

He regards connotation as being more enduring than denotation. "Long after denotation has succumbed and every member of the concept class has become extinct, connotation is still extant and is, as it were, as fresh as ever. The marks of the concept persist where the members pass away."[220] He exemplifies this assertion by the dodo bird which is now extinct in ornithology, but still extant in logic.

Maritain defines both comprehension and extension in reference to breadth.

> The comprehension of a concept is its breadth in relation to its characteristic notes. The extension of a concept is its breadth in relation to the individuals (or more generally to the objects of thought) in which it is realized, and which it groups in its unity.[221]

These so-called notes, which constitute the comprehension of a concept, include essential notes and also properties (v.g., risibility in the case of man) which are contained implicitly in the concept, even if they are unknown to us. In reference to extension, Maritain is very precise when he states "the extension of a concept includes both the individuals and the objective concepts (universal but of less extension than itself) in which it is realized".[222] He cites as an example of extension the concepts 'man' and 'beast' which are contained in the extension of the concept 'animal', and, therefore, 'this man', 'this dog', etc., are also contained in the extension of that same concept. At the same time, he emphasizes the fact that a concept is definitely not a collection of individuals, but a nature found in each one of them. This emphasis is made in opposition to nominalism which confuses extension with a collection of individuals.

Grenier defines the comprehension of a concept as "the collection of notes which constitute the concept," and the extension of a concept as "the collection of individuals and objects in general to which a universal concept belongs".[223] His definition reflects the thinking of many other modern scholastics on this subject of comprehension and extension.

In his treatise on logic, Gonseth quotes the definitions of comprehension and extension as found in the *Port Royal Logic*.[224] He does not add any new insights to this distinction.

Evans and Gamertsfelder associate denotation and connotation with extension and intension. They assert that "denotation refers to the 'thingness', the individuality, the peculiar and distinctive character which everything that can be named at all must have. . . . Connotation refers to the characteristics, the descriptive features, and the constituent elements of a thing, idea, or person."[225] They mention that denotation as a function of terms is useful for classification, while connotation is important for definition.

Coffey credits his expose of the extension and intension of concepts and terms to Dr. Keynes.[226] He reminds us that "comprehension . . . includes more than connotation: it includes all the attributes which are *de facto* common to all members of the class. It therefore includes all attributes necessarily involved in, or connected with, the connotation."[227] Or to phrase it in Keynes' terminology, comprehension includes more than connotation because, known as 'objective intension', it embraces all the qualities of conventional intension and subjective intension as well as many others besides. On the other hand, connotation or conventional intension comprises only those qualities essential to a name.

Smith speaks of genus and species as having a twofold meaning: extension and intension. He declares "the individual things to which the term applies, comprise its meaning in 'extension' (extent, breadth, or denotation). The qualities that serve to define the term comprise its meaning in 'intension' (intent, depth, or connotation)."[228] He considers genus to be a subdivision of class, and, of course, he regards species as a subdivision of genus.

Frye and Levi distinguish, first of all, between the logical connotation and the psychological connotation.

> Customarily the word "connotation" is used in the latter sense to signify what we think of, or what is suggested to us, upon hearing any word, or even the fringes of meaning which the word possesses. . . . But when the logician speaks of the connotation of a name, he is not referring to whatever idea

comes into an individual's mind when the name is mentioned, but to the idea or concept or quality represented by the name.[229]

They consider any name ambiguous if it possesses more than one denotation or connotation. To them, connotative ambiguity is a more serious obstacle to communication than denotative ambiguity because the former is less discernible.

Bittle calls comprehension and extension the logical qualities of an idea. He considers these qualities important to measure the value of judgments and inferences. These qualities are defined by him in the following manner:

> By the *comprehension* of an idea we understand its meaning, signification, thought-content; and we define the comprehension of an idea *as the sum total of all the attributes or thought-elements which constitute the idea* in its representation of a thing.
>
> .. ..
>
> While the comprehension gives the content of an idea, the *extension* expresses the *application* of this content to the individuals and groups in which it is found. The extension of an idea is therefore defined as the *sum total of all the individuals and groups to which an idea can be applied.*[230]

Bittle allows the beings represented by an idea to have either an actual or an imaginary existence. He cites examples of certain ideas whose extension includes only one individual: v.g., 'the tallest mountain', the 'largest building', etc.

Before distinguishing between connotation, denotation, intension and extension, Stebbing reminds the reader that words have a twofold reference: a reference to thought and a reference to fact. An individual and its attributes can be separated in thought but not in fact. Then she states that

> the *connotation of a term* is the characteristic, or set of characteristics, which anything must have if the term can be correctly applied to it. What the term applies to is the members of the class determined by the characteristic, simple or complex. This constitutes what is called the denotation of the term.[231]

Stebbing differentiates connotation from intension by dividing the latter into three separate groups which Dr. Keynes has already designated as conventional intension, subjective intension, and objective intension. Only conventional intension can be identified with connotation.

She also distinguishes between extension and denotation. "Extension, therefore, are classes, not individuals; the denotation is *the membership of the classes, not the classes.*"[232] This difference is clarified by the example of a 'centaur' which lacks denotation since such creature does not exist, but which has extension such as 'wise-centaurs' and 'foolish centaurs'.[233]

In another textbook by Stebbing, extension is used in two different senses. It is said to mean:

(1) The relation of a class to the subclasses it includes; (2) the relation of a class to the individual members which compose the class, these individuals being understood to be *either* (a) all those which may be said to *exist,* in the ordinary meaning of the word "exist," or (b) all individuals real and imaginary.

Neither (1) nor (2) corresponds exactly to what Mill meant by denotation but (2a) approximates to it.[234]

Castell applies the name 'extension' to things and 'intension' to properties possessed by those things.[235] Inasmuch as names have this twofold reference, there are two kinds of definitions:

An *extensive definition* is one which aims to fix the meaning of a term by citing instances of which it is the name. . . . A definition of *fruit* in terms of *apples, pears, plums,* etc., would be an extensive definition.

An *intensive definition* is one which aims to fix the meaning of a term by citing the property or properties common to the instances of which it is the name. . . . David Hume's definition of *miracle, A violation of the laws of nature, though* perhaps inadequate, is an attempt to define that term intensively.[236]

Black states that denotation includes all the individuals which exist or have existed, while connotation includes all those properties which an individual must possess in order to be what it is.[237] For example, all individual chimpanzees are 'denoted' by the word 'chimpanzee'. At the same time, this word 'chimpanzee' 'connotes' those properties which an individual must have in common with other chimpanzees in order to be classified as a chimpanzee.

Cohen and Nagel view the three elements of a proposition (subject, predicate and copula) in two ways:

> Either as a class of objects (which may have only one member), or as a set of attributes or characteristics which determine the objects. The first phase or aspect is called the *denotation* or *extension* of the term, while the second is called the *connotation* or *intension*.[238]

These logicians employ Dr. Keynes' vocabulary and divide intension into three groups, namely, conventional (connotation), subjective, and objective (comprehension) intension.

In an earlier published book, Cohen did not distinguish between the extension and intension of concepts. He regarded concepts as verbal signs instead of mental signs, and he called verbal meaning the denotation of words. For him 'denotation' in the broad sense includes what Mill calls 'connotation'.[239]

When McCall defines the comprehension of an idea, he refers to the sum total of notes that constitute the essence. Thus he says that "the comprehension is the sum of the intelligible aspects, or elements, or notes of a concept".[240] And when he defines the extension of an idea, he says that it is the "sum of real things (both actual and possible) to which this essence can be applied".[241] Therefore, the extension of 'man' would be 'all possible men'.

Just as Dr. Keynes distinguishes several different kinds of intension, so Hartman differentiates four types of comprehension and three kinds of extension.

> 1. *The essential comprehension* of a universal concept includes all the essential notes of the corresponding class of objects . . . . (v. g., man: substance, material, living, sentient, rational).
> 2. *The distinctive comprehension* of a universal concept includes the logically proximate genus and the properties of the pertinent class of objects . . . . (v. g., a mammal is a vertebrate characterized by mammary glands, a diaphragm, and hair).
> 3. *The complete comprehension* of a universal concept

64

includes the proximate genus, the specific difference, and the properties of the class of objects represented . . . . (v. g., man is a rational animal, endowed with free will and the gift of speech, capable of being educated, fitted for the pursuit of political and religious activities, etc.).

4. *Singular comprehension,* or the comprehension of a singular concept, includes all the notes of one identified object or collective unit . . . . (v. g., George Washington is the first president of the United States).

The extension of a universal concept is the class of objects which it represents. The extension (a) may be without expressed limitations and embrace all the present, past, and future members of the class; (b) it may be limited by place, time, or some other restriction; (c) it may also be viewed as the sum of the subclasses that make up the class.[242]

Gilby makes some interesting observations on the quality and quantity of ideas when he discusses the doctrine of extension and comprehension. He refers to extension by such words as 'area', 'range', 'span' and 'sweep'; and to comprehension by the words 'intensity', 'force', 'depth', 'fullness' and 'penetration'. Before quoting him, it may be well to consider a reference cited by Gilby in one of his footnotes concerning quantity applied analogically to quality.

However, similarity and dissimilarity are considered not only according to the same or diverse quality, but also according to the same or diverse mode of participation. For it is not only black that is unlike white, but also less white is unlike more white; for there is also movement from less white to more white, as from one opposite to another opposite, as is stated in V *Phys.*[243]

According to Gilby,

ideas and notions are qualities that can vary according to area and intensity, conditions of quantity applied by analogy to quality. Area is measured by the number of units comprised, thus we speak of acres more or less wide, of fleets more or less large, of ideas more or less embracing. Intensity is measured by the penetration effected, by the degree of possession or domination over the material, thus we speak of colour more or less bright, of sounds more or less loud, of ideas more or less exhaustive. Both measurements may be used when qualities are compared; we can say that there is more white in the cliffs of Dover than in this page, meaning that there is a greater extent of whiteness, but that this page is whiter, meaning that there is a greater intensity of whiteness: similarly as regards love, for benevolence may be judged both by its range and by its localization and force. So also knowledge may be rated according to span and to depth, by sweep and fullness, extent and penetration, or, to use scholastic terminology, by *extensio* and *comprehensio.*

The area or extent of an idea is judged by the number of objects contained.

The intensity or penetration of an idea depends on its completeness as the representation of an object, on its ability to express the special characteristics as well as the general features.[244]

Extensio and *comprehensio* cannot be considered as scholastic terminology. This sort of phraseology was introduced by the Port Royalists in French and by Purchotius in Latin. It would be better to classify those two words as pseudo-scholastic terminology.

According to one group of logicians, extension is meaning applied to the actual world, that is, if the proposition which contains the word is true. If the proposition is false, extension does not apply to anything. Intension, on the contrary, is meaning independent of the extensional property of the truth or falsity of any proposition.[245]

Parker and Veatch ascribe a double meaning to concepts: primarily, a certain 'what' or essence (comprehension); secondarily, the individuals that have such a 'what' (extension).[246] They, unlike another group of logicians (Paul Henle et al.), insist that extension as an aspect of conceptual meaning includes only possibilities because

concepts are blind to all existential distinctions. To see once again that extension cannot mean the actual, real existence of instances of the comprehended nature—though actual instances are included as possible, since everything that is actual is also possible — one need only note that if this were the case every concept would be true, since what every concept intended would actually exist as intended, and error and falsehood would then be impossible.[247]

66

Quine believes that Aristotle's notion of essence was the fore-runner to the modern notion of intension or meaning. He remarks that while things have essences, only linguistic forms possess meanings. "Meaning", he says, "is what essence becomes when it is divorced from the object of reference and wedded to the word."[248]

Johnstone regards extension as embracing class-objects and intension as comprising meaningful qualities. He insists that the "extension of a term is the class of all objects to which the term applies . . . . the intension of a term consists of all the qualities which could be meaningfully ascribed to it."[249]

Before enumerating and explaining Dr. Keynes' three types of intension or connotation, Searles states that

the *denotation* of a term is all *actual things* to which the term applies; the class of such things constitutes its extension. . . . The *connotation* of a term is that *set of characteristics*, attributes, or qualities common to the members of a class and by which a criterion is provided for judging when the term is correctly applied.[250]

It may be noted here that one modern historian of logic is rather critical of the Port Royalists and their *Port Royal Logic.*

One dominant feature of *The Port-Royal Logic* is its lack of enthusiasm for the logical theory of the scholastics. It pays a tribute to Aristotle by acknowledging his "very vast and comprehensive mind,". . . . The Port Royalists say "there is, in fact, no author from whom we have borrowed more in this Logic than from Aristotle" *(The Port-Royal Logic,* 8th. ed., by Thomas Spencer Baynes, trans., p. 21). But the borrowings of the Port-Royalists from Aristotle are not always complimentary. Here and there they cite Aristotle's definitions and reasonings as examples of things to avoid (Baynes, pp. 168-169, 252). . . . They place little value on the ten categories which they consider to be man-made conventions rather than ultimate truths, and which lead men to be satisfied with verbal formulations rather than with a distinct knowledge of things.

They devote a brief perfunctory chapter to another great concept of scholastic logic, the five predicables, saying as they dismiss them. "This is more than sufficient touching the five universals. which are treated at such length in the schools" (Baynes, p. 55).[251]

Hepp refers to the classical distinction between comprehension and extension by the words 'signification' and 'application'. He speaks of names as having two dimensions of cognitive meaning: a name either signifies a set of characteristics which anything must possess before that name can be applied to anything, or a name applies to cases or instances which have these characteristics. This author claims that logicians often refer to signification as connotation, while he himself identifies the application of a name with denotation or extension.[252] In a footnote, he also distinguishes the present or 'actual' application (all cases now existing) from the 'total' application (all cases whether past, present or future).[253]

After explaining extensional (denotative) meaning and intensional (connotative) meaning, Schipper and Schuh differentiate two types of intension which are not mentioned in other logic texts. They remarks that intension may be

> *personal intension,* or the connotation of a term as used by a given individual, and *social intension,* or the meaning of a term common to a group of people, in virtue of which they are able to communicate among themselves.
>
> Personal intension may be more or less specific than social intension, since some individuals use language with greater or less precision than do others. However, . . . the *utility* of a person's vocabulary depends upon how closely the personal intension of his language approximates the social intension of language used by friends, associates, writers, and others with whom he comes in contact.[254]

Smith reminds us that comprehension and extension do not have any counterpart in reality. They are simply logical forms or relations and add nothing real to a concept. With this thought in mind, he defines the comprehension or intension of a concept as "the number of characteristics or qualifications which determine the content of a concept", and the extension of a concept as "the number of inferiors to which the concept applies".[255]

After defining the comprehension of a term as "the sum total of the intelligible elements of the quiddity signified by the term (or concept) ",[256] Bachhuber adds this comment:

> The comprehension of a term is not limited to what we explicitly think of when we grasp the meaning of a term; nor does it include only those implications that we actually deduce from a quiddity. Comprehension is not subjective but objective. It includes all the intelligible elements objectively contained in a quiddity, whether we actually think of them or not. The comprehension of a term usually contains many notes of which we have no explicit knowledge at all.[257]

This author agrees with Dr. Keynes when he equates comprehension with objective elements.

Bachhuber introduces a distinction not found in other treatises on logic. Differentiating between absolute extension and functional extension, he declares:

> *The absolute extension of a term and concept is the sum total of the subjects — of the actual subjects as well as the possible subjects — whose quiddity (essence, or nature) is signified by the term and concept.*
>
> .. ..
> *The functional extension of a term or concept includes only those subjects that it actually sets before the mind when it is used in discourse.*[258]

Hence actual extension includes all those subjects which exist or can exist, while functional extension comprises those subjects which exist. For example, a man of the future or a mythical hero could only be classified under actual extension.

Blyth distinguishes three modes of meaning which he calls respectively 'denotation', 'signification' and 'connotation'.

> Denotation is the relation between a word and the objects named or called by that word. Signification is the relation between a word and the properties of objects called by that word. Connotation is a relation between a word and other words.[259]

Then he gives examples of each mode of meaning. In the case of denotation, there is a relation which exists between the word 'woodchuck' and the animals which are properly called woodchucks. In signification, there is a relation between the word 'woodchuck' and the characteristics or properties of certain animals which are called woodchucks. And, finally, in connotation, the word 'woodchuck' has a meaning relation to other words. It can be substituted for 'ground hog' but not for 'porcupine'.

Creighton and Smart choose the words 'refer' and 'describe' when they discuss extension and intension.

> Terms are used to *refer* to things, to name and identify them. Thus 'man' refers to the different individual men, John Smith, Thomas Brown, etc., as well as to the various classes of men, Caucasians, Indians, Mongolians, etc., ... But words are also used to *describe* as well as to name. That is, they represent the qualities or attributes belonging to things for which they stand.[260]

These twentieth century authors consider extension, denotation, depth and range as synonymous, and intension, connotation, breadth and comprehension as synonymous.[261] The majority of authors identify depth with intension, and breadth with extension. Therefore, it seems strange to observe with what fluidity some modern logicians employ words without justifying their use by previous tradition. If the word 'breadth' translates the same reality as the Latin word *extensio,* one wonders how any logician can associate 'breadth' with intension. Furthermore, if extension proceeds in a lateral or horizontal direction, how can it be associated with 'depth' which proceeds in a vertical direction? Surely Creighton and Smart are not using breadth and depth in their first imposition of meaning when they oppose the traditional trend of usage for these words.

Beardsley employs the word 'comprehension' as convertible with the word 'extension'. Here is what he has to say:

> The comprehension of a term is sometimes called its "extension" — the class of things over which the term, so to speak, extends. And the signification is sometimes called its "intension". Or you could contrast the *implication* of a term with its *application:* the comprehension consists of those things that the term applies to; and the signification consists of those characteristics that the term implies *about,* or attributes to, the thing it comprehends.[262]

In an earlier treatise, Beardsley employs the words 'denotation' and 'designation'. The former word refers to a class or group of things, while the latter is used synonymously with connotation, that is, it designates the characteristics of things.[263]

Inasmuch as Beardsley uses the words 'comprehension' and 'extension' as synonymous, the reader is put in contact with a tradition prior to the Port Royal Logic. St. Thomas offers an example of such earlier tradition, which will be studied in the following chapter, when he declares that

> comprehension is said to be twofold: in one manner, according as something is included in the one comprehending. . . . In another sense, comprehension designates nothing other than the attainment of something which is presently possessed; just as someone attaining anyone is said to comprehend him.[264]

Wuellner reiterates the twofold meaning of 'comprehension' propounded by St. Thomas. But he adds that comprehension can also mean:

> (1) the essence represented in a concept; the sum total of notes actually represented in a concept. (2) the intension of a term.[265]

When logicians ignore one or the other of these meanings, ambiguity will prevail. Hence, it is all important to understand the total analogy of these words in order to know which meaning is intended in the domain of logic.[266]

Molesworth is rather critical of those logicians who follow in the footsteps of J. S. Mill. He says

> the controversy as to which names are connotative and which are not, and as to the limits which ought or ought not to be imposed on connotation, is not, however, the concern of logicians. Their interest is in things named, and insofar as the followers of Mill focus their attention on names, they have abandoned the theory of logic for the theory of language.[267]

Copi considers the value of subjective, objective and conventional connotation or intension in relation to definition. He claims that the notion of *subjective connotation* is inconvenient for purposes of definition because it varies not merely from individual but even from time to time for the same individual, as he acquires new beliefs or abandons old ones. . . . The concept of *objective connotation* is inconvenient for reasons of its own. Even in those rare cases where the complete extension of a term is known, it would require omniscience to know *all* of the characteristics shared by the objects in that extension. . . . The *conventional connotation* of a term is its most important aspect for purposes of definition and communication, since it is both public and can be known by people who are not omniscient.[268]

Bochenski maintains that the idea underlying the distinction between comprehension and extension is presupposed in Porphyry's *Isagoge*,[269] and that this distinction has its counterpart in the scholastic doctrine of simple and personal supposition.[270] He observes that although Leibniz was aware of this distinction, the German philosopher did not refer to it in traditional terminology. Quoting from Leibniz' *De forma logicae comprobatione per linearum ductus,* Bochenski states that

up to now we have assessed the quantities in respect of *(ex)* the individuals. And when it was said: 'every man is an animal', it was meant *(consideratum est)* that all human individuals form a part of the individuals that fall under 'animal' *(esse partem individuorum animalis)*. But in respect of *(secundum)* ideas, the assessment proceeds just conversely. For while men are a part of the animals, conversely the notion of animal is a part of the notion applying to man, since man is a rational animal.[271]

Without employing the words explicitly in this particular passage, Leibniz seems to refer to extension when he speaks of 'man' as part of the notion 'animal', and he seems to refer to comprehension when he speaks of 'animal' as a part of the notion 'man'.

Clark and Welsh explain denotation and connotation by a word. They claim that "a word denotes the objects to which it correctly applies; what it connotes are the properties or traits which the object or entity must have to be an object of the kind to which the word applies".[272]

72

Mourant maintains that comprehension comprises the essential characteristics or attributes, while extension embraces individual instances or subjects.[273] He states that "comprehension is the meaning of a term and extension the relation of that meaning to the things it can mean".[274] He is also of the opinion that "the term 'comprehension' would seem to have a more determinate relation to the terms 'denotation' or 'extension' than does the term 'intension' with its subjective aspects".[275]

After defining comprehension as the "essential content of the concept", and extension as the "applicability of concept to the range of objects it stands for",[276] Sullivan notes that comprehension and extension can never be understood as completely exclusive of each other. Irrespective of the richness of the concept's comprehension, that concept will refer necessarily to some aspect of reality and hence possess some extension. The author reminds us, however, that the concept's extension need not refer to something which is in actual existence.

Browne mentions that the denotation of a term "refers to that thing",[277] while the intension of a term "consists of all the attributes that a thing must possess in order to be denoted by that term".[278] It will be noted that both of these definitions lack precision.

Before concluding this chapter, one should consider some of the German logicians who developed a doctrine of comprehension and extension based upon the *Port Royal Logic*. Although Sir William Hamilton and other members of the English school were influenced by members of the German school, it seeems advisable that the German logicians should be treated separately in order to present more vividly the similarities and differences which characterize their opinions on this particular doctrine. Krug, for example, asserts that every concept is a quantity *(quantum, grösse)* inasmuch as each concept includes a multiplicity of representations or ideas *(vorstellungen)*. This multitude of representations or ideas, is, as it were, joined together or interrelated in such a way as to constitute the interior *(intensiva)* quantity *(grösse)*. The Latinists would refer to this interior quantity or content of the concept as *quantitas complexus.*[279]

On the other hand, if one considers the multiplicity of representations or ideas found 'under' a concept, attention is then focused

73

on the quantity *(grösse)* of the sphere which was known to the Latinists as *quantitas ambitus.*[280] Therefore, in judging the quantity of a concept, one must look to its 'sphere' as well as to its 'content'. The former designation is sometimes referred to as the area or the circle of the content *(regio s. sphaera notionis).*[281]

Schulze speaks of a concept *(begriff)* as containing matter *(stoff, materia)* and form. The matter (that which is conceived can be simple or multiple. The form is the generality of a concept, namely, that attribute by which is conceived only what is common to several things *(dinge).*

This author refers to comprehension and extension when he presents the concept as the notion of a single thing which can contain *(begreifen)* multiples in it *(in sich)*, but not under it *(unter sich).*[282] The concept which contains multiple representations or ideas *(vorstellungen)* 'in it' is an example of comprehension, while the concept which would contain multiple representations or ideas 'under it' is an example of extension.

Fries considers concepts by means of projections. Each concept contains partial projections which are identical with its content (comprehension). The totality of a concept's projections is called the sphere *(umfang,* extension) of a concept.[283] This relationship of content and sphere, which is the essence of concepts, gives rise to the classification and subdivision of concepts by genus, species, kind, subkind, etc.

According to Reinhold, the individual ideas belonging to one category form the extension *(umfang)* or sphere of a concept. The magnitude or quantity *(grösse)* of the extension varies with different concepts. Such magnitude is called the extensive quantity of the concept *(extensiva quantität).* The extension of the concept may also be known as the content of the category *(fach).*

On the other hand, the content *(inhalt)* of the concept *(begriff)* is nothing else but the concept itself. This concept is thought by us through the medium of a grammatical idea and designated by a word which is common to the individual. Thus the grammatical designation joined to the designated object in one unit is called a concept. And that which is designated as a differentiation from the grammatical designation is called the content of the concept.[284]

Esser also dwells on the aspect of multiplicity when he discusses the quantity of concepts. He states that the multiple ideas *(vorstel-lungen)* connected to a whole by the concept are called the magnitude or quantity *(grösse)* of the concept. This quantity is either internal, that is, quantity of content *(quantitas interna, intensiva, sive complexus)*; or it is external, that is, quantity of extension *(umfang, quantitas externa, extensiva, ambitus)*. The inner quantity, or content, consists of those differentiating characteristics which are connected to a whole by the concept; the external quantity, or extension, consists in the number of objects or things to which the concept can be applied.[285]

Fischer maintains that the inner development of the general concept causes a sequence of specific concepts in which each superior concept is the unity and truth of all those concepts which are inferior to it. The true definition of a concept enlarges its contents *(inhalt)* as well as its extension *(umfang)*. Therefore, the concept which is most common or comprehensive in its extension is by that very fact the most definite and complete as an idea *(gedanke)*.[286]

Ritter claims that, inasmuch as each individual concept must unite in itself the meaning of many phenomena, there should be assigned to that concept an extension, or sphere *(sphäere)*, or area *(gebeit)*, or amplitude *(weite)* to which it gives particularly its whole meaning.[287] And, inasmuch as the meaning of many phenomena are united in one individual concept, this concept must have a content. Thus one distinguishes between the extension *(umfang)* and the content *(inhalt)* of a concept. The latter is derived from the extension of the concept — it acquires its particular or characteristic meaning from its application to different phenomena.[288]

Drobisch mentions that the totality of characteristics of an object-concept is called its content *(inhalt, complexus)*; and the ordered totality of all the species of this content is called its extension *(umfang, ambitus)*. Thus the totality of that which is contained 'in' the concept is its content, whereas the totality of that which is contained 'under' the concept is its sphere.[289] He applies extension to species because he considers the sphere of a concept as the sum of its species.[290]

Dr. Ueberweg defines the comprehension of a concept in the following manner: "The sum total of the part-conceptions is the *content (complexus)* of a conception."[291] By the words 'sum total' are meant the individual attributes of an object which stand to each other and to the whole (not as a mere aggregate) in definite relations. And he explains an attribute of an object as everything in that object by which it is distinguished from other objects.

When Ueberweg defines the extension of a concept, he says: "The EXTENT *(Ambitus, Sphäera,* sometimes *extensio)* of a conception is the totality of those conceptions whose similar elements of content make up its content."[292]

Among the German authors just cited, it will be observed that Esser and Ritter identify extension with something 'outside the mind', while Krug, Schulze, Reinhold, Fischer, Drobisch and Ueberweg identify extension with something 'in the mind'. Furthermore, some of these authors restrict extension to species (v.g., Krug, Fries, Fischer, Drobisch and Ueberweg), while others limit it to individuals (v.g. Schulze, Reinhold, Esser and Ritter). It is curious to imagine how Schulze and Reinhold can apply extension to what exists in the mind and still apply it to individuals which are outside the mind. Perhaps, like Isaac Watts, they intend implicitly to apply extension to species as well as to individuals.

Of course, it is quite obvious to every reader that these same authors look upon comprehension as the content or inner quantity of a concept, or as the sum total of concepts 'contained in' a specific concept. The latter conception is opposed to those English writers who regard comprehension as the sum of real external attributes (v.g., Shedden, De Morgan, Jevons, Fowler, etc.).

If one were to summarize the work of these logicians who expressed their opinions about extension and comprehension from the time of the publication of the *Port Royal Logic* to the present era, no clear and distinct doctrine could be distilled. Each logician seems to understand quite well what he himself means or intends by the words 'extension' and 'comprehension', but oftentimes his own impositions of meaning on those two words do not coincide or harmonize with the meanings attached to them by other logicians. In fact, as one approaches the modern authors of logic, less and less agreement is found existing among them. A prudent conclusion from the evidence of this chapter might be that the science of logic is presently undergoing an unscientific order of development. In sharp contrast to the German school of logic which has been seen to display a certain coherence when it treats this question, the French, American, English, Italian and Spanish schools of thought consistently lack uniformity in their presentation of the doctrine.

In the modern era of logic, the trend toward vagueness and confusion is so great that certain logicians attach meanings to the words 'extension' and 'comprehension' without any attempt at justification. A tendency for the moderns to reject tradition and any fixity of meaning which has been imposed on extension and comprehension by the ancients has prevented many from developing with more exactitude the doctrine of extension and comprehension. This chapter seems to indicate that modern logic has fallen into a quandary of countless and needless introductions of new words and new meanings.[293] Before extricating ourselves from such a dilemma, we must turn our attention to those logical treatises which predate the *Port Royal Logic*. Perhaps there we shall discover a useful clarity and precision of thought.

CHAPTER II: MEDIEVAL AND ANCIENT LOGICIANS
(1658-530 B.C.)

Four years before the publication of the *Port Royal Logic,* Gassendus was explaining the relation of species to genus. *"Whatever belongs to the Genus,"* he said, "belongs also to the Species; so that, inasmuch as it belongs to Animal to be endowed with sensation, it also belongs to Man."[1] Here, without even mentioning the word 'comprehension', the author is stating that both the genus 'animal' and the species 'man' contain or comprehend the attribute 'sensation'.

A moment later Gassendus considers such species as prudence, justice, fortitude and temperance to be contained under the genus 'virtue'. He says that *"what belongs to all the species, belongs to the genus;* so that inasmuch as Prudence, Justice, Fortitude, Temperance are worthy of love, Virtue will be lovable".[2]

The idea of extension is found in the following passage written by Burgersdijck:

> When, however, genus is said to be predicated of *several things,* it is distinguished from individuals. When it is said to be predicated of several things *different in species,* it is distinguished from the species which are predicated of several things different in number.[3]

Then he compares the extension of genus to the extension of species: "genus is wider than its species, and species is wider than the individual. . . ."[4] The idea of comprehension is understood when he mentions that "species includes its genus, and besides the genus, the essential difference. . . ."[5]

Arriaga distinguishes between the *species subjicibilis* (that which

78

can be placed under) and the *species praedicabilis* (that which can be predicated). His definitions employ the vocabulary of Porphyry. He says *"species subjicibilis,* which is a correlative of Genus, is defined as *that which is contained under the genus".*[6] One will recall that modern logicians utilize the expression *contained under* to designate extension. And *"species praedicabilis . . .* is *that which is predicated completely of several things different in number. . . ."*[7] It was already explained in the previous chapter that the term *subjicibilis* is used when species is compared to genus (v.g., man is an animal), and the term *praedicabilis* when species is compared to individuals (v.g., John is a rational animal).

An important source which bridges the gap between the opinions of the ancients and of Antoine Arnauld and Nicole on extension and comprehension is a philosophical treatise published in 1635 by Daniel Stahl. In this work the author endeavors to present logic as a collection of rules; his expose of logic is not as lengthy and fully developed as that, for example, found in the writings of St. Albert the Great. In general the rules are direct citations from Aristotle and Porphyry. This book, conserving traditions dating back to these two men, tries to make logic as an art comprehensible to the beginner. Whereas John of St. Thomas[8] destroys almost in its entirety the order proper to the logical treatises *(Organon)* of Aristotle and neglects to treat the predicaments (categories) and predicables at the beginning of logic, Stahl, more faithful to that order, manifests a better understanding of the Aristotelian tradition.

In Chapter XII of his text, Stahl discusses the universal whole and its subjective parts, v.g., genus and species. He refers to 'genus' as the 'universal whole' in relation to species and individuals, and to 'species' as the 'universal whole' in relation to individuals. He also refers to 'species' as a 'subjective part' in relation to genus, and to the 'individual' as a 'subjective part' in relation to genus and to species.[9]

Among the sixteen doctrinal rules which he examines in that twelfth chapter, the fourth and fifth rules are the most pertinent to the problem of extension and comprehension. Before considering these rules, it may be well to state the author's first three rules.

(1) A genus is predicated of all species contained under it. . . .

(2) Whatever is predicated of a genus, is predicated also of a species. . . .

(3) A genus is prior to a species. . . .[10]

In his commentary on the first rule, Stahl offers several interesting observations of the word 'contained' which will not be dwelt upon here.[11] Such observations will be considered in the final chapter of this study.

When he articulates his fourth rule, he puts his reader in contact with the Aristotelian and Porphyrian tradition both as to doctrine and as to vocabulary. The rule enounces that "a genus is wider than a species".[12] Stahl elaborates on this rule by declaring that a genus is wider than the individual species or wider than any one species taken by itself. He offers two examples to support his contention, namely, that the genus 'animal' is wider than the species 'man', and the genus 'virtue' is wider than the species 'temperance'. On the other hand, a genus is not wider than all of the species taken simultaneously: v.g., the genus 'animal' is not wider than the species 'man' and 'brute' taken together — it is equal to them or reciprocal in its width.

Although Stahl does not employ the word 'extension' in the fourth rule, the same doctrine that the Port Royalists intended by extension is contained therein. Furthermore, the doctrine signified by the word 'comprehension', and which is implicitly contained in rule 4, becomes clear in rule 5. According to the fifth rule, "a species is collective [unitive] of many things in one nature, but a genus is still more collective. Porphyry, chapter on genus and species §37".[13] Then Stahl proceeds to explain this rule in the following manner:

> All individuals of one species unite in the nature of the species itself: as all human individuals unite in human nature. But in the nature of the genus, not only do the individuals of one species unite, but the individuals of all species of such genus unite: as all men and all brutes in the nature of animal. And hence it is that a species is spoken as collective of many things in one nature, but a genus is still more [that is, more collective].[14]

In the third paragraph of his commentary on rule 5, Stahl quotes a distinction proposed by Cajetan concerning the twofold way

80

in which one thing can be more collective of many things: first of all, intensively, the species is more collective than the genus inasmuch as it brings together those things which have already been united; secondly, extensively, the genus is more collective than the species because more things are found under its unity.[15] After making such a distinction, Cajetan compares the species to the leader of a small army well unified, and the genus to the leader of a large army of diverse factions.

Thus the two ideas enunciated in rules 4 and 5 respectively, that is, "a genus is wider than a species" *("genus est latitus specie")* and "a species is more collective" *("species magis est collectiva")*, imply the doctrine of extension and comprehension as propounded by the Port Royalists.

Interpreting the words of Stahl and his dependence on the text of Cajetan, one can say that the doctrine of extension and comprehension is found at the very heart of the predicables of genus and species. This arrangement contrasts sharply with the procedure adopted by the Port Royalists who, after treating the predicables in a desultory manner, turn their attention to analyzing concepts apart from the predicables. It is while they are analyzing concepts denuded of predicables that they discover extension and comprehension, and in this way they both destroy and maintain the Aristotelian distinction.

Unlike his contemporaries, John of St. Thomas and the Port Royalists, who ignored the value of the predicables and their close relation to extension and comprehension, Stahl upheld the ancient tradition both as to doctrine and vocabulary and clearly manifested through the medium of logical rules how extension and comprehension are linked with the predicables of genus and species. For that reason, he deserves attention in the history of logic. Though he offers little originality, he is an important witness to the past and to his contemporaries. This author merits the credit for handing on the doctrine of extension and comprehension, though the Port Royalists deserve credit for creating the new vocabulary.[16] His explicit use of Cajetan's words *extensive* and *intensive* reveals how these words served as forerunners to the modern vocabulary of 'extension' and 'intension' (comprehension). Notwithstanding the common opinion that the distinction between comprehension and extension originated with the *Port Royal Logic* (1662), Stahl's text offers incontestable evidence that this distinction had an earlier origin.

Commenting on one part of the Porphyrian definition of genus, namely, "[genus is that which is predicated] of several things different in species", John of St. Thomas (1589-1644) says that other predicables can be said 'materially' of several things specifically different, but, unlike genus, they cannot be said 'formally' of those things.[17] An implicit reference to extension can be found in this first definition of genus inasmuch as that which is predicated of several specifically different things must itself be more extensive than each individual species considered separately. If the predicate were coextensive with the subject, then it could not be predicated of other species. But, of course, a genus is predicated of several different species. Consequently, the genus is more extensive than the species. This notion of extension is reiterated when John of St. Thomas declares "that genus is compared to species as something more formal, inasmuch as it is less contracted".[18]

The greater extension of genus is emphasized when it is mentioned that genus is also predicated 'immediately' of different species as well as 'mediately' of individuals which are numerically different, whereas species is only predicated immediately of such individuals. "Consequently, genus is also predicated of several things different numerically, but not as the lowest species, which is predicated immediately of those things."[19]

An allusion to the comprehension of the species is made when he considers the genus to be a whole as well as a part. It is a whole "in the manner of conceiving" and a part "of the thing conceived and signified".[20] Thus, the genus 'animal' is a whole when it is predicated of the species 'man'. But, if one considers the thing conceived from the genus, namely, the species, then the genus becomes a part which constitutes the quiddity of such species.

An implicit reference to extension is found in the following statement: "For the species is said to be placed under, which is gathered under the assigned genus, or concerning which the genus is predicated essentially."[21]

Although John of St. Thomas refers to several definitions of difference by Porphyry, especially the one where the species exceeds the genus in comprehension ("difference is that by which the species exceeds the genus"), he does not comment on that particular definition.[22]

It is important to note at this point that no author cited in this first part of Chapter II uses explicitly the words *extensio* and *comprehensio*. That is why references are made here to the 'notion' of extension and comprehension, or to the 'allusion' of extension and comprehension.

Perhaps Du Moulin means to refer to extension when he says:

The Genus is a nature which belongeth unto many things differing in Species. As this word, animal, is a Genus signifying a nature common both to *man* and *beast:* Animal is the Genus; man and beast are the Species.[23]

The idea of extension is even more manifest when he declares that the "species is a nature comprehended under the Genus".[24] In this context, the word 'comprehended' designates 'contained under' and not 'contained in'. It should be observed in this instance that 'comprehended' is understood as being synonymous with the notion of extension.

When Du Moulin includes the nature of the genus in the nature of the species, namely, that the species 'contains in it' the genus, he is describing what the modern logicians call 'comprehension'. Thus he says:

Where the Species is, there the Genus must needs be also. For whosoever is a *man*, is also an *animal*. And whosoever saith, that *this is a lettice,* doth by consequent affirme, that *it is an herb.*[25]

Though conserving the simplicity of the vocabulary used throughout the Middle Ages, Alamannius invokes attention to the notion of extension when he points out that genus is found in more things than its species.

Moreover, animal, inasmuch as it is a genus, is wider than man and lion concerning which it is predicated; but to be wider is to bespeak and to contain the whole, which man or lion, or any other species bespeaks. Therefore, the genus contains the whole which the species bespeaks, and consequently the differences.[26]

His reference to comprehension is made when he speaks of the species exceeding or surpassing the genus.

The species is said to exceed the genus by means of the difference, even though it not be true that the latter be not contained in the genus confusedly and indistinctly, but because the species surpasses, that is, the species even exceeds in its significate that which the difference signifies explicitly.[27]

Sanseverino makes an implicit reference to extension when he discusses the first meaning of genus, namely, a collection of things.

The name of genus is accepted in a threefold sense which is accustomed to be called the threefold meaning of genus, and is taken from Aristotle, *Metaphy.* V, c. 28. First, genus is said to be a collection of many things in whatever manner they are related to one thing and to each other. . . .[28]

Although this author cites Aristotle as his reference for the definition of genus, he is really quoting from Porphyry's *Isagoge.* In Chapter 28, Aristotle does not employ the word *collectio* in any of his definitions of genus. For example, Aristotle says, "the term 'race' or 'genus' is used if generation of things which have the same form is continuous".[29] Furthermore, in this chapter, the word 'genus' is given four different meanings and not three. Porphyry in his *Isagoge* lays aside the definition of the *genus subjectum.*

The notion of extension is also found when Sanseverino discusses species: "Species, inasmuch as it is predicable, is defined as that which is predicated essentially of many things different in number."[30]

Comprehension, on the other hand, is found in this author's treatise when he states that "species is composed of genus and difference, v.g., man is composed of animal and rational. Therefore, in this manner, difference is defined as constitutive of the species".[31]

Both the notion of extension and the notion of comprehension can be found in statements enunciated by Molinaeus. He asserts that "genus contains all species in potency. The species contains the genus in act because animal is in the definition of man."[32]

It may be well to note here that the genus is usually considered as a 'whole', while the species in relation to its genus is a 'part' of the whole. However, when the genus is contained in the definition of the species, then the genus becomes a 'part' of the definition of the species which is considered as a 'whole'. For example, in the definition "man is a rational animal", the genus 'animal' is a part of the definition of the species 'man'.

Fonseca alludes to the notion of extension when he speaks of certain things being more or less universal.

> And as among universals, certain ones are less universal, as man and whiteness; certain ones more universal, as animal and color; and certain ones, to the highest degree, as substance and quality. . . .[33]

Another implicit reference to extension occurs when he comments on the one-and-many relationship between species and genus:

> Finally, so that by ascending from species to genera, and from individuals to species, we gather together one from many, so by descending from genera to species, and from species to individuals, we make many from one; for many men are one man by the participation of the species. . . .[34]

His reference to comprehension is made when he uses the words *excedit* and *amplius* while distinguishing the specific and individual difference.

> A specific difference is also said to be that by which the species exceeds the genus. In the same manner, the individual difference can be said to be that by which the individual exceeds the lowest species. Just as, therefore, 'man' in his common essence has more than does 'animal', by this fact that he is a sharer of reason; so Socrates in his singular essence surpasses this essence of the common man by the very fact that he is this singular and determined individual.[35]

The notion of a generic concept comprehending (in the sense of 'containing under it' and not 'containing in it') a specific concept is cited by Soncinas. In the following text, observe that the author is speaking in a somewhat different manner. He is not only talking about comprehension in relation to genus and species, but also about the 'comprehension of concepts'. This way of speaking resembles the vocabulary of the Port Royalists when they discuss the 'comprehension of ideas'.

85

For a specific concept, e.g., a concept of man, . . . is to comprehend all men indifferently, and by reason of this indifferent comprehension, is confused. . . . However, a generic concept has a greater confusion, because it comprehends several species indifferently.[36]

In this passage, the verb 'comprehend' *(comprehendere)* and the noun 'comprehension' *(comprehensio)* are to be understood in the sense of extension because it is a question of a greater whole containing a lesser whole or part (e.g., the genus containing the species and individuals, or the species containing the individuals). And inasmuch as the generic concept comprehends or contains more things, e.g., species as well as individuals, without distinguishing them *(comprehensio indifferens)*, the generic concept comports a more confused knowledge. However, inasmuch as the specific concept comprehends or contains fewer things (only individuals), it implies less confused knowledge.

Soncinas is using the noun 'comprehension' in a logical text in such a way that one is obliged to admit two different kinds of comprehension: *comprehensio differens* and *comprehensio indifferens*. This citation seems to mark the first time that the noun form 'comprehension' appears in a Latin logical treatise and is qualified by the adjective 'indifferent'. Since he imposes the sense of extension on the word 'comprehend' or 'comprehension', his contextual usage does not herald or envisage the meaning later applied to that same word by the Port Royalists.

Fenner employs the term 'comprehend' to designate the extension of a whole to its specific parts. He also seems to refer to the counterpart of extension, namely, comprehension, when he mentions 'living thing' containing in it 'bodily substance'.

The whole kinde or general is a whole, which giveth or conteineth the being or essence which is common to the severall or specialles, as a living thing is generall to man and beast, conteining in it a bodily substance, which hath life and sense, which is the generall being of man and beast.

A severall sort, is a part comprehended under the whole kinde or generall forme, from whence he taketh that being which is common to all the other parts or specialls, as in the 12. to the Rom. The Apostle devideth the ordinary offices of the Church into Prophetes, that Ministers occupied in the word, and other Ministers occupied in other businesse in the Church. The first sort hee devideth agayne into the Teacher who is occupied in doctrine, and the Pastor who is occupyed in exhortation. The second sorte againe into Elders, which rule the Church, and Distributors, which distribute to the poore: in which and such like examples, the first is called the moste generall, the other the undergenerall or subalternall, which in respect of the former, is the special, and in respect of that that followeth is the generall. The last, is the lowest sort, or most speciall, because it cannot be divided into moe specialles, and this devision of the causes into the effectes, is most excellent. . . .[37]

Three explicit references to comprehension and extension are contained in Toletus' *Commentary*. He also employs the distinction between 'intensive and extensive collective ability' which has already been observed in the treatise of Stahl, and which will be seen again in Cajetan's writings.

For genus is more universal since it comprehends under itself many species.[38]
. . . It is that which is more a unity which is said to be more collective intensively; and in another way, that which comprehends more things, is thus said to be more collective extensively. Moreover, understand this that the less universal is more collective intensively because the more they are a unity which belong in the less universal, than which are only in the more universal: but the more universal is more collective extensively because it contains more things under itself, and so speaks Porphyry.[39]

Those things which agree in the lesser universal are more one than those things which only in the greater universal. However, the greater universal is more collective in an extensive manner because it contains under it more things, that is to say, it is the peculiar property of the larger universal to bring things together in an extensive way. Porphyry also spoke in this manner.

Commenting on how genus and species differ, Toletus declares:

First, however, they differ because genus contains the species; but species does not contain the genus: understand this in regard to power, that is, the genus contains the species and all things which are in potency to the species, [v. g.,] individuals; but the species contains, for example, the nature of the genus, but not the power, because it does not comprehend all things which are contained under the genus: and hence it is, the genus may be predicated of more things than the species.[40]

Titelmannus alludes to comprehension when he employs the Latin word *abundare* (to exceed).

Thus animal exceeds its genus "living body" by the difference "sentient", and thus in all other things. For whatever has a genus also has its species, and beyond this whole the species has the difference in itself, as an essential part, which the genus does not possess in such a manner. Whence it follows that, by means of every constitutive difference, the species exceeds its genus.[41]

Wilson speaks of extension in terms of the 'largenesse', and 'narrownesse' of words. He also uses the word 'comprehende in' to refer to what the moderns call 'comprehension'. Here the word 'comprehension' has an analogical meaning. This usage, therefore, differs noticeably from that found in the *Port Royal Logic*.

When we go about to expounde any matter, first we must beginne with the definicion, to knowe the verrie nature of the thyng, the whiche we can not doe, except we first learne the predicables, for thei shewe the largenesse and the narrownesse of wordes, how ferre thei doe extende, and how muche thei comprehende in them. As when I see a farre of come unto me, firste I knowe that he is a man, then when he cometh nigher, I knowe whether he bae of myne acquaintaunce, or no. Likewise, when I goe about to declare what one is, and to open the nature of any thyng, I use the largest wordes, and so it must nedes bee, that I beginne with the predicables, bicause thei shew how muche, every woorde dooeth comprehende in it self, and howe large, or narrowe it is. Thei be called predicables, because some one thyng, is spoken of an other. And thei are (as a man would saie) markes or notes of woordes that are spoken of many, shewyng how and by what manner the same wordes are attributed to other.[42]

In the following passages, the author employs the word 'comprehende' to designate extension:

> . . . the Logician first and foremoste, professeth to knowe woordes, before he purposeth to knitte sentences. Neither is there any one woorde, whiche is not comprehended, under one of the five common woordes.
>
> Genus is a generall woorde, the whiche is spoken of many, that differ in their kinde. . . . Genus, is a generall worde, under the whiche, diverse kindes of sortes of thynges are comprehended, as under a livyng creature, are comprehended, men and beastes. Under Arte, are comprehended, Logike, Grammar, Rhetorike, etc.[43]
>
> Species, *seu forma*, the kinde, or sorte of any thyng (comprehended under a worde more universall) is the same of whom the general worde is spoken, when the question is asked, what it is. . . .
>
> Or Thus, Species is a common worde, that is spoken of many, whiche differ onely in nomber, as man is spoken of Socrates, Plato, Aristotle, and of every proper name belongyng to any manne.[44]

These remarks by an English author of the sixteenth century reveal an excellent understanding of Porphyry's doctrine in logic.

The idea of extension is manifest in the following explanation of a genus divided into its proper species.

> A genus is that which is predicated essentially of several things different in species: so that to one inquiring, what is a man, what is a donkey, what is a cow, it is rightly answered, a man is an animal, a donkey is an animal, a cow is an animal. Species is that into which comprehended under itself a genus is divided: as man is a species of animal. For it is comprehended under animal.[45]

In this citation, the notion of extension is found in the words *sub se comprehensam* because the species must be considered to be embraced under the total extension of the genus.

Then quoting from Cicero I, lib. *de oratore,* Agricola repeats the notion of extension whereby the genus comprehends or embraces *(complectitur)* the species. Here the idea of extension is found in the word 'communion' *(communio)* which contains within itself the meaning of extension.

> Genus, however, is that which . . . embraces two or several parts. . . . Virtue is a certain genus: for it comprehends several parts, that is, species, namely, prudence, justice, fortitude and temperance. . . . Again, animal is a genus because it comprehends two parts, man and brute, which parts, although they are specifically different, nonetheless are in a certain mutual participation of the genus itself. . . .[46]

The logic of the renowned Protestant reformer Melanchthon does not seem to contain anything illuminating on this subject.[47]

Both Sir William Hamilton and Thomas Spencer Baynes cite in their writings[48] Cajetan's most explicit reference to extension and comprehension (intension) when he considers species as collective of many things in one nature and genus as still more collective.

> To this it can be said briefly that to be more collective of many things can be understood in a twofold manner: In one way, intensively; and thus species is more collective, because it unites more closely the things which have been brought together, and the reason adduced is convincing. In another way, extensively; and thus genus is more collective. because many more things fall under its unity, than under the sphere of the species. Whence species and genus are considered as two leaders, of which one has a small army, but exceedingly unified. the other a great army, but of diverse factions. For the former collects more intensively, the latter extensively.[49]

Cajetan speaks of genus being more extensive than species when he declares:

> genus is more collective than species, inasmuch as that is greater which contains all things, which contains another and beyond that still others, as animal is greater than man; that is truly less which does not contain whatsoever the other encompasses, as man in respect to animal. . . .[50]

The notion of comprehension is brought to our attention when it is mentioned that the whole is in the parts with the added comment that the genus is a whole and the individual is a part, whereas

90

the species is both a whole and a part. Clarifying this statement of Porphyry, Cajetan remarks

that is said to be a whole in a twofold manner, namely, a universal whole and a definable whole. And likewise a part is spoken of in a twofold way, namely, subjective part and defining part. A universal whole is called superior in respect to inferiors, which are said to be its subjective parts. However, a definable whole is called that which is defined in respect to the parts of its definition, which are called defining parts.

However, to say that something is a whole or a part differs only according to one of these modes; for that which is a whole in one way, is a part of the same in another way, and vice versa. For the superior in respect to the inferior is a universal whole, because it contains in its power that and other things and is predicated of them; and it is a defining part of the same, because it is contained in act and intrinsically in the definition of that thing, and consequently, the inferior in respect to the superior is a definable whole and a subjective part.[51]

Although the distinction between comprehension and extension is obvious in the first text quoted from Cajetan, the author's final reference to comprehension is much more implicit when he explains how the species exceeds the genus, that is, not by what is contained under it, but rather what is contained in it. The cause of this excess is, of course, the specific difference which is found in the species but not in its proximate genus. Such excess is expressed by the Latin verb *abundare* which is an implicit reference to comprehension.

The species exceeds the genus through the difference, and not anything else, since the species includes nothing, which the genus lacks, except the difference; and the proximate cause why the species includes more than the genus is the difference itself. . . .[52]

Adding to this explanation of the species surpassing the genus, he says: "the species exceeds the genus, because it actually has more in itself than the genus actually has in itself. For the species has the difference in itself in act, which the genus does not possess in act. . . ."[53]

Verneus offers an interesting example of how the individual is considered to embrace several ideas when he mentions that a person comprehends a certain number of attributes or characteristics in his nature. *"Peter* comprehends more ideas than *man;* I say truly, *Peter is a man*: which means, *in Peter there are similar predicates ascribed to other men."*[54]

In an important Pseudo-Thomistic text, though the word 'extension' is not found, the synonym 'latitude' is introduced. This text reads as a paraphrase of the logical rule 'genus is wider than species' *(genus est latius specie).*[55] Inasmuch as this author speaks of a 'certain latitude' *(quamdam latitudinem)*, the word 'latitude' is used in an analogical sense and does not designate dimensive quantity. The Pseudo-Thomas states "that any form which has under it many things, that is, which is taken universally, has a certain latitude . . . ." And the basis of this observation is to be found in the definition of a universal: "for it is found in several things and it is predicated of several things."[56] This sort of latitude is explicitly applied to a genus

> according to formal grades, of which one by itself is more noble and perfect than the other; and this, as is said, is the latitude of genus, under which are diverse formal degrees specifically different.[57]

On the other hand, the idea of comprehension appears in the traditional vocabulary of *abundat* and *excedit*.

> Difference is that by which the species surpasses the genus: because the species surpasses, that is, exceeds in its significate even that which the difference signifies explicitly.[58]

Duns Scotus (1266?, 1274?-1308) notes that genus is greater (and this should be interpreted as 'more extensive') than species because it is predicated not only of different species, but also of different individuals.

> For I say that in their foundations Genus is a greater Universal than Species. Likewise, in their intensions, because it is predicated of things which are different in species and in number. Species, however, are predicated of things which are only

different in number. And so species has more things placed under it, not however actually *in exercise,* on the contrary, fewer things.[59]

When he speaks of genus possessing or containing many species, Duns Scotus distinguishes between 'act and potency' on the one hand, and 'aptitude' on the other hand. That a *"genus requires many species* can be understood in a twofold way: in one manner, in act or in potency; in another manner, in aptitude. . . ."[60] Then he explains what he means by the word 'aptitude'.

Aptitude is the inclination of something toward anything according to its nature, or rather a non-repugnance, as is obvious in man to laugh, and in a surface to whiteness. Potency, however, speaks of an order to act.[61]

The notion of comprehension is found in the following passage when the genus is regarded as 'contractible' with reference to the species:

Genus is also found in one species as potential, contractible and actual, and consequently, has less entity, and less actual and essential intelligibility than its species.[62]

"Less actual and essential intelligibility" means that the genus contains fewer intelligible notes or attributes, that is, it has less comprehension than the species.

When Duns Scotus clarifies how the species exceeds the genus in comprehension by means of the specific difference, he states that the "genus contains the differences actually potentially, that is, it contains them indeterminately, while the species contains them determinately".[63]

Although the text of Duns Scotus seems to imply extension and comprehension, his way of speaking is so different from the traditional way that the value of his explanation of genus and species is highly questionable.

In spite of the fact that the words 'extension' and 'comprehension' are employed in a goodly number of texts by St. Thomas Aquinas, their usage is rarely set in a strictly logical background relating to genus and species. Those passages which refer to the physical quantity of extension and the physical action of grasping and holding, as well as the use of these words with reference to emotions, will be studied in some detail in Chapter III.

The most explicit reference to 'extension' is found in St. Thomas' commentary on Aristotle's *Posterior Analytics*. In the following paragraphs, extension is restricted to the predicable genus:

> As to the first it is to be considered that those things which are predicated essentially must be always and universally predicated, as was stated above, and therefore, taking those things which are always predicated of each individual, he says that among them some are found which are extended in more than that individual thing in which they are; but not, nevertheless, in such a way as to be outside the genus.
>
> And he explains what it means 'to be in more', and he says that those things are said to be in more whichever are universally in something, but not in it alone, but also in something other. By this we are given to understand that there is another opposite member, namely that there is something which is extended in more, and is outside the genus.[64]

This quotation seems to indicate that perhaps the problem of extension is rooted in the third operation of the intellect inasmuch as the treatise, from which this passage is drawn, studies the demonstrative syllogism, namely, an effect of the third operation. Furthermore, in this particular section, Aristotle is analyzing the art of discovering definitions which comprise the middle terms of syllogisms.

Although one is able to find the expressions *esse in plus* and *extendere in plus* in the Latin translation of the Aristotelian text, such important identification of vocabulary is not contained in Porphyry's *Isagoge* or Aristotle's *Categories*.

Even though St. Thomas did not use the noun *extensio* historically in logic, still there is ample evidence to prove that the words *extendere in plus, esse in plus* and *excedere* are synonymous. Quoting briefly from two consecutive paragraphs, one finds the following excerpts:

Non ergo oportet quod differentia sit in plus quam species.

. . . .

Videtur igitur quod differentia ultima non excedat speciem.[65]

In this citation, *esse in plus* is employed synonymously with *excedere*. And, of course, it has already been seen in the text previously quoted (n. 529) that *extendere in plus* is identified with *esse in plus*. A similar identification of these three expressions is also found in still another lesson in St. Thomas' commentary as well as in the Latin text of Aristotle's treatise.[66]

In St. Thomas' *Commentary On The Sentences*, the notion of extension is revealed implicitly from a negative viewpoint when the denials of species and genus are predicated of other things.

> For according as man is in fewer things than animal, so much the more is the negation of animal predicated of fewer things than the negation of man.[67]

In other words, the contradictory of a less extensive concept will include more than the contradictory of a more extensive concept. This premise, used in an objection but not denied in the response, reveals that St. Thomas would have accepted the law of inverse ratio as enunciated by modern logicians.

> The comprehension and extension of concepts are in inverse ratio to each other: in other words the greater the comprehension, the less the extension; and, the less the comprehension, the greater the extension.[68]

Thus one finds in St. Thomas a vivid application of this law of inverse ratio.

In his treatise *On Truth*, St. Thomas uses the word 'comprehension' with reference to logic when he says: "A thing is comprehended whose definition is known, if nevertheless the definition itself is comprehended."[69] If the definition implies the comprehension of a thing, then it seems safe to argue that the elements of comprehension (namely, genus, difference and species) have their own comprehension.

Both extension and comprehension are found implicitly in the word 'contained' as one reads the following citation from St. Thomas' *Commentary On The Metaphysics*:

> Now the truth is that universals are principles, namely, of knowing; and thus genera are principles to a greater degree because they are simpler. The reason why they are divided

into more members than species is that they contain more members potentially. But species contain more members actually. Hence they are divisible to a greater degree by the method of dissolving a composite into simple things.[70]

The idea of extension occurs when it is mentioned that the genus contains (that is, 'contains under it') more members in potency than does the species. But the species 'contains in it' (implicit reference to comprehension) more members in act than does the genus.

Historically speaking, it is certain that St. Thomas never employed the nouns 'extension' and 'comprehension' in such an explicit way as found in the *Port Royal Logic* and the modern Latin Thomistic manuals. However, the foundations of the development of such vocabulary have been indicated particularly with the verb *extendo, extendere.* Concerning the doctrinal basis for the development of this vocabulary, much remains to be seen, and such observations will be made in Chapter III of this treatise.

A contemporary of St. Thomas Aquinas and St. Albert who influenced many Medieval and modern logicians was Peter of Spain. In spite of his great influence, he cannot be utilized to shed any additional light on the problem of extension and comprehension.[71]

One does not find the vocabulary of extension and comprehension in the commentaries written by St. Albert (1193-1280). However, this commentator utilizes expressions which can be adequately translated by the words 'extension' and 'comprehension'. Here is a sampling of what to expect from this author: In his *Commentary On The Predicables,* he compares genus to species.

> Indeed the genera surpass the species by reason of their containing those species which are under the genus: because according to the sphere of the community the species do not contain the genera. On the other hand, the constituted species surpass the genera by reason of their containing the proper differences by which they are constituted. . . .[72]

In this passage, St. Albert is speaking about two kinds of containing: (1) There is a containing by the genus of those species according to the sphere of the community *(secundum ambitum communitatis).* This kind of containing is an obvious reference to extension. (2) There is also a containing by the species of the proper differences whereby the species surpass the genera. This type of containing refers to comprehension.

In his *Commentary On The Posterior Analytics,* once again he discusses extension when he speaks of the community and sphere of predication, and of substantial predicates being extended in more things.

Of those things which are present in any one thing as substantial predicates, some are extended in more things according to the community and sphere of their predication than is the community of the subject or species which must be defined: . . . .[73]

Extension is likewise considered when St. Albert describes genus as possessing a certain aptitude *(aptitudo)* to be divided by opposite differences.[74]

Both comprehension and extension are couched in terms of quality and quantity respectively when this philosopher, using the *qualitas differentiae* in a twofold way, speaks of species possessing a greater qualitative value while genus possesses a greater quantitative value.

For both species and genus are determined by the quality which is the difference, but genus is determined by its quality in order to signify more than the species; because genus by its quality determines for itself subjects different in species and number, but the quality which determines the community of the species, does not determine the species except inasmuch as it [the species] may contain those things which differ only numerically.[75]

An allusion to extension and comprehension is contained in the following passage:

However, genus is more collective and unitive than species, in this that it collects more things than the species collects, although the species is also more one according to intention than the form of the genus: for those things which are one in species differ less from each other, and are more one, than those things which are one in genus, since genus unites more things in itself and combines more than the species: for it unites and

97

collects many species and all those things which are collected in the species.[76]

When St. Albert declares that the genus "collects more things than the species", he is pointing to an external collection (extension), whereas when he asserts that the species "unites more things in itself", he is referring to an internal collection (comprehension). Although St. Albert discusses here the same distinction propounded by Cajetan, namely, that genus is more collective in one sense and species is more collective in another sense, he seems to give, unlike Cajetan, greater prestige to the extensive unitive capacity of the genus than to the intensive unitive power of the species. This will be seen again in the commentary of Ammonius.

It may be well to note what St. Albert means by saying that genus is collective and unitive. He explains that the two words are the same in substance, yet they differ according to reason:

For the activity of gathering together presupposes many things and is terminated in a certain unity; the activity of unifying presupposes a unity and many elements are brought together within this unity.[77]

Hence, according to a distinction of reason, the activity of gathering or collecting begins with 'many things' and terminates in 'one', while the activity of unifying begins with 'one' and terminates with 'many' joined in a unified whole.

It is evident that, even though St. Albert does not employ the Port Royalist vocabulary of 'extension' and 'comprehension', he does mention this distinction repeatedly in his own characteristic phraseology: v.g., *secundum ambitum communitatis, extenditur in plus, aptitudo, qualitas differentiae, genus est magis collectivum, species uniat plura in se,* etc. Such references offer additional evidence that, contrary to the statement uttered by Thomas Spencer Baynes,[78] this doctrine was not overlooked by the Medievalists. Indeed, the scholastics taught this doctrine, though they presented it in a language that is not familiar to the modern logician.

St. Bonaventure has not written any explicit philosophical treatise on the subject of logic. Whenever he discusses genus and species in his theological texts, his manner of speaking does not seem to differ from the vocabulary common to St. Albert and St. Thomas.[79]

An attempt to compose a logic according to the mind of St. Bonaventure does not appear to provide any important material falling within the scope of this study.[80]

Nicephorus Blemmida alludes to comprehension when he mentions that the 'species surpasses the genus'.

The difference is that by which the species surpasses the genus. For man surpasses animal by means of 'rational'. For animal is neither rational nor irrational in act; since opposites revolve about a common element. Nevertheless, animal exists potentially both as rational and irrational, and has all (constituted) differences under itself.[81]

Whatever has been iterated by Blemmida reflects no original thinking, new interpretation, or even a new vocabulary. He presents what has already been found in the prior and subsequent writings of logicians.

John of Salisbury touches extension and comprehension only in a remote way when he discusses common nouns and universals. He states an important principle by declaring that things, as they exist in nature, are distinct and separated from each other by reason of their properties; yet, in the intelligence of man, these same things exist in a less distinct manner. Consequently, in the process of naming, individuals are brought together under a common signification. At the same time as their name becomes more common or universal, their extension is increased and their comprehension is decreased. And concomitant to this increase and diminution, the knowledge of such things becomes confused and vague. One should note particularly in the following passage that John of Salisbury indicates a correlation between the process of naming (nominare), that is, referring to individuals, and the process of signifying (significare), that is, the community of meaning under which the individual is to be brought. Using the name by application to individuals is proper to the second operation of the intellect, while the process of signifying the community of meaning under which the individual is to be brought is proper to the first operation of the intellect.

Likewise in his *Elenchi* [Aristotle, *Soph. El.,* c. 22, 178b, 37ff.]: "Common names, such as the word 'man' and all common nouns, do not signify the individual, but rather a certain kind of thing, or a thing in some sort of relation to something, or its manner, or something like this." A little later he says [Aristotle, *ibid.*, 179a, 8ff.]: "It is evident that a general universal predicate is not to be understood as some particular individual, but rather as signifying quality, relation, quantity, or something of the sort." . . . Things existing in nature have definite limits, and they are separated from one another by their properties, but knowledge of them is frequently less definite and the concept of them is in a certain way vague. The celebrated principle that what common nouns mean and what they name are not identical does not militate against what has just been said. For singulars are named by them, but universals are signified by them.[82]

This whole discussion is a commentary of Aristotle's *Categories*, c. 5, 3b10-23.[83]

The Arabian philosophers, v.g., Avicenna (980-1037) and Averroes, do not add any new light to this problem. Furthermore, inasmuch as this study is concerned only with the Latin vocabulary which is used as an adequate translation of those elements found in the Greek text of Aristotle, there would be no reason to quote any sources recorded in Arabic.

Damascene (died about 749) wrote his logic in Greek. The Latin translations of his text contain a traditional vocabulary. For example, he expresses extension by such words as *latius, complectitur,* and *generalius,*[84] and he expresses comprehension by the verb *abundare.*[85]

The philosophical works of Ancius Manlius Severinus Boethius (480-524 or 525) are important inasmuch as they exercised a very great influence on the terminology, method and doctrine of medieval logic. Indeed, the schoolmen, until the beginning of the twelfth century, depended entirely on Boethius for their knowledge of Aristotle's doctrines.

Boethius is responsible for two commentaries on Porphyry's *Isagoge*. His first commentary takes the form of a dialogue and is based on the Latin translation of Victorinus. His second commentary is based on the Latin translation which he himself made of Porphyry's treatise.

In Boethius' *Dialogue on Porphyry,* one finds the word 'collective' which has already been noted in the writings of Cajetan, St. Albert and Daniel Stahl. This particular word is employed by him to indicate the power of the genus to comprehend or collect several species. Such vocabulary is an obvious reference to extension. Thus he says: "For the genus is both a principle to the species and is collective of several species in itself."[86]

This author not only speaks of extension in terms of collecting (*colligere*) but also in terms of unifying (*coadunare*). As already pointed out, the activity of collecting begins with many things and terminates in one, while the activity of unifying begins with one and terminates with many joined in a unified whole.

> For genus, since it is one, is progenitive of several species. For several species are found under one genus. . . . Genus, however, gathers several things, since it is divided again by several species. . . . Therefore, the genus is collective of its species and in a certain manner unitive. But the species is divisive of the genus and in a certain manner multiplicative. Therefore, whatever ascends more to the genera, collects and unites all the multitude of species by the genera.[87]

Boethius employs both the verbs 'to surpass' *(abundare)* and 'to exceed' *(superesse)* when he discusses the extension of the genus to the species. It has already been observed that the verb *abundare* was frequently used by other logicians to signify comprehension.

> Everything that is genus contains several species under it; but everything that is species has several things under it, it has the differences. For the genus, that is animal, in this man, that is species, surpasses and exceeds, because man alone is man. But animal is not only man, but also ox or bird, or others of this sort. But species surpass genera in this, because the species possess these differences in act, the genera do not have them as such. . . . And likewise the species which is man, or other species, as horse, surpass and exceed its genus animal in this, that animal itself per se is neither rational nor irrational.[88]

The word 'collective' is found in Boethius' text as applicable to species as well as to genus, and, in both instances, designates extension.

101

But species and genera are collective, species indeed is collective and unitive of individuals. . . . However, species derives a singular and particular multitude from the unity of singularity, therefore the genus is more unitive than the species.[89]

Besides the use of the word *adunare* in reference to extension, Boethius utilizes still another Latin word to convey the same notion, namely, 'magnitude' *(magnitudo)*.

The name of the genus is proper to the whole species: for the magnitude of the genus is not made equal only to the species, but it even surmounts the species itself. For that reason, every man is an animal, since within the designation of animal are contained both man and other animals. But truly no one would say, Every animal is man; for the name of man does not attain to the whole animal, because since it is less extensive, it is in no way equated with the designation of the genus. And thus those things which are greater are predicated of lesser things, but those things which are lesser, are not converted so that they may be predicated of greater things.[90]

In the following passage, this philosopher once again utilizes the word *abundare*. This time, however, the word is applied to comprehension.

The specific difference is that by which the species surpasses genus, for animal is a genus, man is a species: therefore man has differences in himself, which constitute him rational and mortal. . . .[91]

Finally, Boethius employs the same verb *supervadere* to signify both extension and comprehension.

Genera surpass their species . . . ; but species surpass genera in the plurality of differences. For animal which is a genus surpasses man which is a species, because it not only contains man, but also ox, horse and other species. . . . But species as man surpasses genus as animal in a multitude of differences.[92]

A Greek commentator of the fifth century, Ammonius Hermeae, helps us to understand more clearly how one of the traditional rules of definition is intimately linked to genus and species, and

102

how a transition from genus and species to the rules of definition can be made directly and explicitly through the notion of extension, but indirectly and implicitly through the notion of comprehension. This philosopher, who wrote all of his treatises in Greek, will be cited in this study in a Renaissance Latin translation. In his commentary on Porphyry, Ammonius employs the word ἐπιτείνειν [93] and thereby brings us in closer contact with the vocabulary of Aristotle's *Posterior Analytics.* The Greek verb, meaning literally 'to stretch out' or 'to extend', comes from the same Indo-European root as the Latin verb *extendere.* This translation is important because for the first time in a treatise on the predicables *extenditur* is used to explain the word *latius.* Of course, the original word in the Greek text is more important than the Latin translation.

The more complex things are, the more they are narrowed down; the more abstract [simple] things are, the broader they are and extended over [individuals], for example, those things which are closer to the first and universal principle of all things. And, for that reason, animal considered alone is applied to more things; but if rational is added to it, it is applied to fewer individuals. Now rational animal added to mortal also comprehends still fewer things; if, moreover, you add grammatical, it will contain still fewer things. Wherefore, definitions which are too small make the thing over-large, and definitions which are too large make the thing too small.[94]

If the Latin verbs *continere* and *comprehendere* imply *dilatantur* and *extenduntur,* then this text clearly indicates that extension is presupposed to the logical rule concerning definition formulated in the last sentence of the preceding citation. Furthermore, if this be true, one can see the error of the *Port Royal Logic* which, after treating slightingly the predicables, proceeds to elaborate upon the rules of definition in detail as if there were no connection between the two.

In the following passage which also calls attention to extension, one learns that logic is interested in the power of the first genus which establishes the order of predication.

Species only comprehends individuals in their distinctness, but genus comprehends both species and individuals: indeed, from the inferior, or from individuals ascending to the most general, things are narrowed down as regards their multitude, and yet are increased in their power. Species are fewer than individuals in regard to multitude, but they surpass the individuals in their power and increased size. Genera are related to species in the same way until eventually we arrive at one most general genus. This is rightly thought to happen this way since there is only one cause and origin of all things, for the special reason that those genera which are closer to the first genera are more restricted in multitude, but are increased in power. But those genera which are further away from the first genus are increased in number and diminished in their power.[95]

When Ammonius declares that species surpass the individuals in their power *(potentia)*, the word 'power' means a capacity to contain individuals, whereas the individuals themselves are contained by the species. This so-called 'power' is an active potency in the line of formal causality. And since the species has the power to contain individuals, it is also considered larger (increased) in size. Power *(potentia)* as used here in reference to species and genera is principally in the line of extension and not in the line of comprehension. This power, implying the capacity to contain inferiors, is what establishes the whole order of predication, and consequently, all of logic. Of course, as this power to contain inferiors becomes greater, the number of genera becomes smaller in such a way that the first universal, that is, first predicable, is a unique *genus generalissimum.*

Ammonius should be given due credit because of the explicitness of his reference to extension. For example, he remarks that while the species comprehends individuals, the genus comprehends both species and individuals. In other words, genus is more extensive than the species and individuals contained under it, while species is only more extensive than the individuals it contains.

A similar reference is made to extension by the word *amplius* when he declares that the genus can be said of the species, but not vice versa.

Genus, he says [Porphyry] is always predicated of the species, as animal is predicated of man, and as substance is predicated of animal, but species is not predicated more extensively. . . . Hence, therefore, it is evident that genera are always predicated of the species, while species are never predicated of genera.[96]

Before dismissing Ammonius in this historical survey, it will be profitable to pause momentarily and ask oneself whether his pronouncements in logic have made an important contribution to the doctrine of extension and comprehension. By emphasizing the power of the first genus and its role in predication, Ammonius clearly manifests that extension is more fundamental and more important than comprehension. Although he does not employ such terminology as explicitly as does Cajetan, he leaves no doubt in the reader's mind that the principal role in logic must be assigned to extension by virtue of its explicit connection with genus which is always predicated of its proper species.[97] When one employs Cajetan's vocabulary, namely, *collectivum extensive* and *collectivum intensive,* there is a tendency to commit a serious error because of the peculiar force of the word *intensive,* referring to qualitative perfection as superior to quantitative perfection. One may be inclined to form the opinion that, according to Cajetan, comprehension, and not extension, is more fundamental and important in logic. Perhaps implicit difficulties in the word *intensive* are the reason why many modern logicians maintain that comprehension is more important than, and prior to extension. For example, one nineteenth century logician makes the following statement on the priority of comprehension to extension: "for comprehension, as prior to extension in the order of nature and of knowledge, ought to stand first."[98] This same thought is reiterated by Jacques Maritain when he says,

For just as the comprehension of a concept is a more fundamental property than its extension, so, in affirmation, the logical function of making a Predicate enter into the comprehension of a Subject is more fundamental than the function of making a Subject enter into the extension of a Predicate.[99]

A twentieth century logician offers a more detailed account of

105

this problem of priority in reference to comprehension and extension.

It is of primary importance that we first grasp the comprehension of a concept before its extension. For example, we cannot intelligently use the concept "liberal" until we understand what "liberal" means. We often neglect the priority of comprehension over extension. There is such a deluge of concepts poured out upon us from the press, radio, television and other channels of information with such speed and volume that modern man has become accustomed to witness the application of concepts that he does not adequately understand. One is apt to repeat this application and make it one's own without ever attempting to comprehend the concept employed.

. . . .

Insistence upon the comprehension of concepts is viewed by some contemporary thinkers as Medieval and as outmoded as the cross-bow. This is the position of the nominalists or those who contend that the universal concept is simply an error in grammar; it is really only a common name. In nominalism the concept has no reality other than the individuals which it represents. Its meaning is, therefore, derived from its extension or its particular applicability and so it is the extension that is prior in importance.

It is true sometimes we cannot deduce certain of the intelligible notes of a concept simply by studying the concept itself. We have to determine some concepts by going directly to the facts of the individual that is the starting point of our knowledge and empirically recognizing them. Whereas we can know from the concept "body" that one of its intelligible notes is the property of quantity we cannot know that the bee actually flies by contemplating the concept "bee". For this fact, we look at bees and study their habits. The use of induction is not proof that extension is prior to comprehension. What it proves is that comprehension is more or less dependent upon the data of experience.[100]

On the contrary, Ammonius' text guards us from committing a serious error in this matter of priority relevant to comprehension and extension by setting in bold relief the power of the first genus. Although extension and comprehension are correlatives ascribed to both genus and its species so that one cannot be considered without a consideration of the other, they are related to each other as matter is to form. Comprehension is material with respect to extension, and thus has a material priority. Extension, on the other hand, is formal, and thus its consideration is more basically and necessarily implied in the power of the genus derived from its superiority in the order of predication.

Sir William Hamilton asserts that some later Greek logicians referred to the intensive quantity of concepts by the word *bathos*, and to the extensive quantity of concepts by the word *platos*.[101] Did he mean to refer to Theophrastus or Alexander of Aphrodisias? Evidence points to a negative answer for either possibility. Did he have Porphyry in mind? It seems rather strange that he would refer to Porphyry because the particular work of this Greek author where one expects to find the words *bathos* and *platos*, namely the *Isagoge*, is not a commentary. It is true that Porphyry did write a commentary on the categories. Nevertheless, the two words are not used in either of his works.[102]

Hamilton might have been referring to Ammonius. This Greek logician employs the words *bathos* and *platos* in his commentary on the *Isagoge* when he discusses differences *per se* which do not admit of more or less, in opposition to differences *per accidens* which admit of intention and remission.[103] Since genus does not admit of more or less predication of that of which it is predicated, the words *bathos* and *platos* as used by Ammonius do not signify the intensive and extensive quantities of concepts distinguished by Sir William Hamilton. Hence it would seem that none of the forementioned Greek commentators referred to this twofold distinction by such terminology as *bathos* and *platos*.

Even if the two Greek words already cited cannot be traced to an original source where they comport that signification attributed to them by Hamilton, still research proves to be more fruitful when one attempts to learn the name of one Greek commentator to whom is ascribed the role of announcing the doctrine implied by the distinction between extension and comprehension. In the Introduction to his English translation of the *Port Royal Logic*, Thomas Spencer Baynes admits an indebtedness to Sir William Hamilton for the following information:

107

This distinction, though taken in general terms by Aristotle, and explicitly enounced with scientific precision by one, at least, of his Greek commentators, had escaped the marvellous acuteness of the schoolmen, and remained totally overlooked and forgotten till the publication of the Port-Royal Logic.[104]

It is only when one turns his attention to a paper presented by C. S. Peirce that one learns the identification of this designated Greek commentator.

It is correctly said that the doctrine taught by the Port Royalists is substantially contained in the work of a Greek commentator. That work is no other than Porphyry's Isagoge; and therefore it would be most surprising if the doctrine had been totally overlooked by the schoolmen, for whether their acuteness was as marvellous as Hamilton taught or not, they certainly studied the commentary in question as diligently as they did the Bible. It would seem, indeed, that the tree of Porphyry involves the whole doctrine of extension and comprehension except the names. Nor were the scholastics without names for these quantities. The *partes subjectives* and *partes essentiales* are frequently opposed; and several other synonymes [sic] are mentioned by the Conimbricenses. It is admitted that Porphyry fully enunciates the doctrine; it must also be admitted that the passage in question is fully dealt with and correctly explained by the medieval commentators. The most that can be said, therefore, is that the doctrine of extension and comprehension was not a prominent one in the mediaeval logic.[105]

Hamilton and Peirce seem to be justified in giving credit to a Greek commentator for the development of the doctrine pertaining to extension and comprehension. Though Hamilton's opinion that the Greek words *bathos* and *platos* were employed to designate that distinction cannot be substantiated, Peirce's opinion that the Greek philosopher Porphyry expounded this doctrine in an explicit manner seems to be correct. Since the *Isagoge* is the most explicit source among ancient logical texts for the doctrine of comprehension and extension, every reference to the doctrine by Porphyry will be cited from three widely used translations in English,[106] French,[107] and Latin.[108]

In the first part of his treatise, Porphyry defines three different and distinct realities which have been designated analogically by the word 'genus'. The first use of the word 'genus' applies to a group or a collection which embraces many individuals that have been engendered by a common ancestor. In this instance, the word 'genus' names a relation of many to one *(multa ad unum)*. Notice especially that the reality named by this first use of genus implies the notion of extension[109] because the individuals which belong to the tribe or clan may be greater or lesser, and because there must be at least two individuals. First of all, Porphyry says "for that is called genus which is a collection of certain things subsisting in a certain respect relatively to one thing, and to each other, ..."[110]

In its second usage the word 'genus' signifies a common ancestor or a common place of origin: v.g., Hercules is a genus because he is a common ancestor for the *Heraclidae*, and people are called Athenians because of the generic fact that they are born in Athens. In this case, the word names a relation of one to many *(unum ad multa)*. This second meaning of genus does not name a physical collection or a plurality. It designates a certain person or place which has a power *(potentia)* over such a collection. In other words, according to this second usage, genus is collective but is not a collection.

> Again, after another manner also, the principle of the generation of every one is called genus, whether from the generator or from the place in which a person is generated, ...[111]

Thus father is known as a genus and is collective *(collectivus)* if he has at least two children. In this case, there is the element of plurality or extension from the viewpoint of the children. A man can be called a father if he has only one child. However, a father assumes the name of genus when he has two or more children. Later on the collective power of a father over a plurality of offspring will become a sign leading the logician to recognize that a logical genus must have power over two or more species.

The reality defined in the third usage of the word 'genus' is that sort of genus proper to logic. In its third signification, Porphyry declares:

> Again, in another way that is denominated genus to which the species is subject, called perhaps from the similitude of

these: for such a genus is a certain principle of things under it, and seems also to comprehend all the multitude under itself. As then, genus is predicated triply, the consideration by philosophers is concerning the third, which also they explain by description, when they say that genus is that which is predicated of many things differing in species, in answer to what a thing is, e.g. animal.[112]

In the preceding citation, the word 'extension' is not found explicitly; however, the word 'comprehension' is expressed explicitly in the English translation by the infinitive 'to comprehend'. This same passage not only names a third distinct reality, but it also provides three different manifestations of a logical genus, namely, (1) genus is that to which the species is subject: (2) genus is a certain principle of things under it: and (3) genus is that which is predicated of many things differing in species.

A way to use the word 'extension' is also found in the second and third realities designated by the word 'genus'. However, in these instances, the word 'extension' is not understood in a sense univocal with the first. Extension may be taken passively to refer to the number of individuals included in a collection; or actively, to refer to the unifying collective power dominating the individuals. This needs further explanation.

In spite of differences which characterize these three realities named by genus, a similitude exists among all of them. This similitude can even be traced back to the etymology of genus, namely the activity of generation. A group of offspring is called a genus because generated; a father, because a generator; a certain logical reality, because first in the generation of an essence. By way of contrast, in the first reality where extension is understood in a passive sense, the number of individuals included is related to the second reality as effect is related to cause; yet it is fitting that both effect and cause receive the same name if there is a participation in a common nature. Furthermore, the second reality is collective in nature and hence implies an active extension. Thus, from the viewpoint of such extension, a grandfather can be considered more a father than his son who is also a father, inasmuch as the grandfather can be compared to the *genus generalissimum* which has the greatest extension. In brief, just as the word 'genus' comports an active and passive sense, so too extension can be understood actively and passively. According to the second reality manifested by the word 'genus', extension is understood in the active sense implying a power to embrace or to be collective. In this instance, the collective power of one father is greater than the collective power of another father because the first father has more children.

The third reality named by genus in turn differs from the second reality because the former comprehends things under it and can be predicated of them. On the other hand, a father, who is mentioned in the second reality, cannot be predicated of his children. This third reality is called a genus because the activity of predication engenders distinct knowledge of an essence.

Although the second and third realities already mentioned resemble each other from the aspect of their power to contain, that is, they are collective and not a collection, still they differ from each other. In the second usage of genus, the principle of generation is not found entirely in each one of the individuals engendered by it. On the contrary, the logical genus, expressed by the third reality, is found entirely in each species contained under it. As a concluding note, it may be asserted that according to the second reality, one speaks of a genealogical tree, and, according to the third reality, one speaks of the Porphyrian logical tree.

One finds an explicit reference to extension in the word-forms 'comprehending' and 'comprehended' of the English translation made by Owen:

Also, the most specific has one condition, as to the things prior to it, of which it is the species, yet it has not a different one, as to things posterior to it, but is called the species of individuals, so termed as comprehending them, and again, the species of things prior to it, as comprehended by them, wherefore the most generic genus is thus defined to be that which being genus is not species, and again, above which there cannot be another higher genus.[113]

Notice in the footnote that the French translation employs the verb *contenir* instead of *comprendre*, and the Latin translation makes use of the verb *continere* instead of *comprehendere*.

Both comprehension and extension are indicated by Porphyry

when he talks about species collecting many things in one nature, and genus collecting many more things.

> In descending then, to the most specific, it is necessary to proceed by division through multitude, but in ascending to the most generic, we must collect multitude into one, for species is collective of the many into one nature, and genus yet more so. . . .[114]

Comparing genus to species, Porphyry explains that the former is more extensive than the latter. Note especially the distinct use of the word 'extensive' *(extensif)* in the French translation.

> Genus indeed is always predicated of species, and all superior of inferior, but species is neither predicated of its proximate genus, nor of those superior, since it does not reciprocate. For it is necessary that either equals should be predicated of equals, as neighing of a horse, or that the greater should be predicated of the less, as animal of man, but the less no longer of the greater, for you can no longer say that animal is man, as you can say that man is animal.[115]

The greater extension of genus as compared to the lesser extension of species is based on the fact that genus is predicated of species as well as individuals, whereas species is only predicated of individuals.

> At least, since the superior are always predicated of the inferior, species indeed will always be predicated of the individual, but the genus both of the species and of the individual, but the most generic both of the genus or the genera, (if the media and subaltern be many,) and of the species, and of the individual. For the most generic is predicated of all the genera, species, and individuals under it, but the genus which is prior to the most specific (species), is predicated of all the most specific species and individuals; but what is species alone of all the individuals (of it), but the individual of one particular alone. Now, an individual is called Socrates, this white thing, this man who approaches the son of Sophroniscus, if Socrates alone is his son, and such things are called individuals, because each consists of properties of which the combination can never be the

112

same in any other, for the properties of Socrates can never be the same in any other particular person; . . . .[116]

This same thought as expressed in the preceding passage is reiterated in a passive sense (form) when Porphyry speaks of the individual being comprehended by the species, and of the species being comprehended by the genus.

Wherefore the individual is comprehended in the species, but the species by the genus, for genus is a certain whole, but the individual is a part, and species both a whole and a part; part indeed of something else, but a whole not of another, but in other things, for the whole is in its parts.[117]

In a footnote, the translator Owen misinterprets this passage by erroneously opposing a 'whole in predication' to a 'whole in definition'.[118] Both genus and species are wholes in predication. But genus is a larger whole inasmuch as it is predicated of both species and individuals, whereas species is only predicated of individuals. The *Totum Essentiale*, to which he refers in the footnote, is outside the domain of logic.

Porphyry speaks about comprehension when he explains how the species exceeds the genus. One should observe carefully the French translation and its use of the word 'comprehension' whereby the species exceeds or surpasses the genus.

Difference is that by which species exceeds genus, e.g. man exceeds animal in being rational and mortal, for animal is neither any one of these, (since whence would species have differences?) nor has it all the opposite differences, (since otherwise the same thing would at the same time have opposites,) but (as they allege) it contains all the differences which are under it in capacity, but not one of them in energy. . . .[119]

In this particular passage, the Latin translation is more precise than the English and French translation because it speaks of the genus containing the differences in a determined capacity *(in potestate)* in contrast to an undetermined capacity *(in potentia)*.

In the following quotation, Porphyry points out that, although genus and difference embrace species, genus has a larger extension than difference inasmuch as it contains or comprehends species which are opposed to each other. Difference, on the other hand, comprises a single species since it is determined to one *(ad unum)* by its very nature.

It is common to genus and difference to be comprehensive of species, for difference also comprehends species, though not all such as the genera; for rational, though it does not comprehend irrational, as animal does, yet it comprehends man and divinity, which are species.[120]

Genus is not only more extensive than difference, but also more extensive than the other predicables, namely species, property and accident, because its power of predication is greater.

Now, it is the property of genus to be predicated of more things than difference, species, property, and accident are, for animal (is predicated) of man and horse, bird and snake, but quadruped of animals alone, which have four feet; again, man of individuals alone, and capacity of neighing of horse alone, and of particulars. Likewise, accidents of fewer things . . . .[121]

Contrasting genus with species, Porphyry asserts that the former has a greater extension than the latter. Observe once again the explicit use of the word 'extension' in the French translation.

. . . but they differ, because genus indeed comprehends species, but species are comprehended by, and do not comprehend genera, for genus is predicated of more than species.[122]

In his final reference to extension and comprehension, Porphyry speaks of genus possessing a greater extension and of species possessing a greater comprehension. "Moreover, genera exceed, from comprehending the species which are under them, but species exceed genera by their proper differences; . . . ."[123]

In the Greek text, the Greek word ἐπιτείνειν is not used for the sense of extension; nor is the Latin word *extendere* found in the Latin translation. Porphyry employs the word 'comprehension' in two different senses: one of which is identical with the modern usage of comprehension, and the other of which is identical with extension.

The idea of extension weakly appears in a treatise written by the Roman Quintilianus (30 A.D.–circa 100 A.D.). In the follow-

114

ing passage, he reveals the dependence and subjection of a plurality of species to their genus:

> [An argument based upon genus] has the least value for proving the species, the most value for removing the species. And thus not because some thing is a tree, is it an Oriental plane-tree; rather because it is not a tree, consequently, it is not an Oriental plane-tree: and since something is not virtue, it cannot be justice . . . . Thus a genus will never be taken away because of one species, unless all the species, which are placed under the genus, are removed: in this manner, *because it is neither immortal nor mortal it is not an animal.*[124]

By utilizing the vocabulary *complectatur* and *sub se habeat*, Seneca (4 B.C.–65 A.D.) in one of his letters presents the notion of extension.

> For we are now seeking that first genus on which several species depend, from which every division is born, by which all things are comprehended. It [the genus] will be discovered, however, if we follow in the footsteps of individual things in a manner just the opposite of deduction; in this way we shall be led back to that first genus [which was the starting point]. Man is a species, as Aristotle says: horse is a species; dog is a species; therefore, some common bond must be sought in all these things, which embraces those things, and has them under itself.[125]

Cicero presents the notion of extension when he speaks about something being 'placed under' or 'contained under' the genus. He declares: "For genus is that which embraces several parts as animal: part is that which is placed under the genus, as horse."[126]

Whereas Sir William Hamilton, Thomas Spencer Baynes and C. S. Peirce retrace the doctrine of extension and comprehension explicitly to Porphyry, they retrace this same doctrine implicitly to Aristotle (384 B.C.–322 B.C.), the founder of logic. In this particular section, it will be determined whether or not the modern vocabulary and modern meaning underlying extension and comprehension are to be found either explicitly or implicitly in Aristotle's logical treatises. If so, what are the texts on which this doctrine is based? Do these texts offer sufficient evidence to justify the opinions of Hamilton, Baynes and Peirce that the notion, if not the vocabulary, of extension and comprehension, is contained in the writings of Aristotle? The investigation will center on Aristotle's *Topics* from which Porphyry derived basic material to compose his treatise, namely, the *Isagoge,* then proceed chronologically to the *Categories,* and finally consider the *Posterior Analytics.*

A. *Topics.*

In this treatise, eleven passages worthy of consideration have been found. Aristotle makes an implicit reference to extension by his use of the word 'many' when he says, "Genus, however, is that which is predicated of many things differing in species, in (answer to) what a thing is."[127] Both the Greek text and Latin translations do not contain any kind of vocabulary which would allow one to say that this passage is anything but an implicit reference to extension.[128]

The notion of a diminishing extension is implied in the word 'fewer' when one examines the individual species.

> Another (topic) is, to regard those with which, either all or none, a thing is said to be present, and to consider according to species and not in finites, (individuals) for the investigation (will be) more in the way and in fewer things.[129]

The problem of comprehension is posed by Aristotle when he talks about the species 'partaking' or 'participating' more intensely in a thing than the genus. Once again the Greek text does not provide any distinctive terminology which would herald the kind of vocabulary employed by Aristotle's early commentators, the medievalists or modern logicians when they referred to comprehension.[130]

> The definition of partaking, is to receive the definition of what is participated. Now it is evident that species partake of genera, but not genera of species, since the species accepts the definition of genus, but not genus that of the species.[131]

Aristotle's most explicit reference to extension occurs when he asserts that the 'genus' is wider than the species and also wider than the difference.

The genus is always more widely extended than the species .... Still the element relative to all such is, that the genus is of wider extension than the species and the difference, for difference, also, is predicated of fewer things than the genus.[132]

Another allusion is made simultaneously to extension and comprehension by excluding the difference from the problem. In the following text, it is learned why difference does not directly enter the problem under study because the difference does not partake of the genus.

For everything which partakes of the genus, is either species or individual; but difference is neither species nor individual, wherefore clearly difference, [sic] does not partake of genus. . . .[133]

Once again Aristotle resorts to the Greek words ἐπὶ πλέον[134] when he insists that the genus must be said of more things than the difference: "The genus must necessarily be predicated more extensively than the difference, and must not partake of difference. . . ."[135]

It seems that the doctrine of extension may be negatively inferred when it is said that the genus and species are not predicated of the same number of things: "Again, if genus and species are not predicated with reference to an equal number of things. . . ."[136]

The wholeness that is appropriate to comprehension is implicitly mentioned when Aristotle points out that the entire genus is participated by any particular species.

Further, (notice) whether species partakes of what is said to be genus partially, since genus does not appear to be partially participated, as man is not partially an animal, nor grammar partially a science. . . .[137]

The greater extension of genus is noted in the simple statement that the genus and the species are predicated of the same things. However, inasmuch as the predication of the species applies only to individuals, and that of the genus to species as well as individuals, species has a lesser extension.

Of all then of which genus is predicated, it happens that species is also predicated, since "being", and "the one", are simply

117

predicated of all, when it is necessary that species should be predicated to a less extent.[138]

Comparing genus with difference, Aristotle again employs the Greek words ἐπὶ πλέον (Latin equivalent is *in plus*)[139] to indicate that genus has a wider extension than the difference: Genus is of wider predication than difference. . . ."[140]

Finally, Aristotle declares that neither difference nor species can have as much extension as that of genus. Notice especially in the Greek text that Aristotle uses the superlative form, namely ἐπὶ πλεῖστον[141] to designate that genus has the widest extension of all the predicables.

Moreover, if difference or species be predicated of genus, or something which is the subject of species, there will not be a definition, for nothing of what we have mentioned can possibly be predicated of genus, since genus is the most extensively spoken of all.[142]

B. *Categories.*

In this logical work, Aristotle alludes implicitly to extension and comprehension by an *a posteriori* argument based upon actual predications belonging to the second operation of the intellect. Thus, in order that it be valid to assert 'all men are some animals', 'animals' as a genus must have a greater extension and a lesser comprehension than the species.

For the species is to the genus as subject is to predicate, since the genus is predicated of the species, whereas the species cannot be predicated of the genus.[143]

In still another passage of this treatise, Aristotle employs in collocation with ἐπὶ πλεῖον, the analogical word περιλαμβάνει (Meaning: 'to embrace', 'to grasp', 'to encompass', 'to enclose', 'to comprehend', 'to include', 'to seize').[144] Such vocabulary may refer to the act of grasping a certain number of things (which is meant by the word 'extension'), or to the act of embracing in a certain particular way or with a determinate qualification (which is meant by the word 'comprehension'). And thus one finds confusing this text which discusses both extension and comprehension. In the

118

following translation, this Greek word περιλαμβάνει is taken to refer directly to extension.

> The determinate qualification covers a larger field in the case of the genus than in that of the species: he who uses the word 'animal' is herein using a word of wider extension than he who uses the word 'man'.[145]

The sentence in which the expression 'determinate qualification' occurs means that the determinate qualification (comprehension) of the genus is less determined than the determinate qualification of the species.

It seems that the translators have paraphrased this passage in the *Categories* weakly.[146] For the thought of this entire quotation is determined by the use of the word ἀφορισμόν which means a 'delimitation', 'assignment of boundaries', 'separation', 'distinction', 'determination', 'distinctive character' or 'attainment of definiteness', etc.[147] In this text one finds ἐπὶ πλεῖον first allied with ἀφορισμόν and then with περιλαμβάνει. The translators in question give ἐπὶ πλεῖον an equivocal signification, whereas a univocal interpretation would be preferable. The thought would seem to be that "because the comprehension (determinate qualification) of the genus is broader, the one who uses the genus 'animal' embraces in a broader way". If this interpretation be correct, the direct meaning of the total passage is to comprehension and its indirect meaning is to extension. And thus one finds two explicit Greek words in Aristotle for comprehension. For that reason, it is now clear that ἐπὶ πλεῖον, meaning 'more' is analogical, and can refer to extension or comprehension. Its meaning must be clarified by the context in which it is found.[148]

C. *Posterior Analytics.*

In this work, Aristotle makes a very explicit reference to extension with the appearance of ἐπεκτείνει.

> Now of the attributes which inhere always in each several thing there are some which are wider in extent than it but not wider than its genus (by attributes of wider extent I mean all such as are universal attributes of each several subject, but in their application are not confined to that subject).[149]

119

The Latin Aristotelian translation of this particular citation re-enforces the evidence of the Greek when it is seen that the expression *extenduntur in plus* is used as a synonym for *esse in plus*.

Eorum igitur quae insunt semper unicuique, quaedam extenduntur in plus, non tamen extra genus: dico autem in plus esse quaecunque insunt quidem unicuique universaliter, at vero et alii.¹⁵⁰

Although Aristotle employs the notion of comprehension in his *Posterior Analytics*, I, c. 4, 73a35-73b, when he talks about the species containing the genus and other attributes in its definition, this passage may be passed over here without any detriment to the investigation of this problem.¹⁵¹

D. *Summary.*

Aristotle's *Posterior Analytics*, II, c. 13, 96a24-26, is an explicit and uncontestable reference to extension. In the Greek text one finds the word ἐπεκτείνει (in Latin *extenduntur*) used in direct relation with ἐπὶ πλέον (in Latin *latius* or *in plus*). It should be recalled that Aristotle in his treatise on the *Topics*, composed while he was a comparatively young man, used only εἶναι or ὑπάρχειν ἐπὶ πλέον. Yet the same doctrine presented in that logical work is to be found in this later treatise, namely the *Posterior Analytics*, and it is rendered more clear and manifest by the introduction of a new word ἐπεκτείνειν (to stretch out) to which the Latin words *extendere* and *extensio* are related through a common Indo-European ancestor. On the other hand, the *Categories* gives us an explicit reference to comprehension by the expressions ἐπὶ πλεῖον, ἀφορισμόν and περιλαμβάνει ἐπὶ πλεῖον.

If a student only studied the *Topics*, he would be inclined to agree with the opinions of Hamilton, Baynes and Peirce as regards the implicit existence of 'extension' in Aristotle's logic. But when he also studies the *Posterior Analytics* and discovers therein the usage of ἐπεκτείνει, the opinions of these three logicians seem less valid. Even if the citations pertaining to comprehension are less numerous than those pertaining to extension, yet there is sufficient evidence to judge that the doctrine on comprehension and its vocabulary are explicit and manifested with a certain consistency in the logical writings of Aristotle.

By deliberate intent, only the *Organon* has been submitted to scrutiny. If the doctrine pertaining to extension and comprehension is found in Aristotle's other works, then the research necessary to discover it is outside the scope of this study.

There existed no organized and unified logical doctrine prior to the time of Aristotle. One finds only a logic comprised of examples. Unlike Aristotle and his successors who taught logic, Plato and his predecessors only used logic. In that pre-Aristotelian era, examples were often presented to illustrate and explain some abstract notion, and these examples were couched in a concrete vocabulary. It is interesting to know that Plato (427 B.C.? — 347 B.C.) employed the same two words found in Aristotle, namely ἐπὶ πλέον, when he wished to designate extension.[152] In his dialogue *Euthyphro,* he emphasizes the fact that respect forms a part of fear. Consequently, if there is respect shown to any person, fear is also manifested toward that same person. However, the contrary is not necessarily so because fear is in more (ἐπὶ πλέον)[153] than respect.

It is not within the range of this study to examine other Greek words in Plato's writings to determine whether they contain an explicit or implicit vocabulary of extension and comprehension. It suffices to say that Plato did not refer to extension and comprehension in an explicit manner. Yet he did make an implicit reference to extension when he related how Socrates tries to discover the meaning of piety or holiness by questioning the young Euthyphro who intends to accuse his father of murder. One will notice that the first response offered by Euthyphro is not a true Socratic definition of 'piety'. It is only an example of piety when he says:

> Well then, I say that holiness is doing what I am doing now, prosecuting the wrongdoer who commits murder or steals from the temples or does any such thing, whether he be your father or your mother or anyone else, and not prosecuting him is unholy.[154]

Naturally, Socrates objects to this sort of definition by saying:

At present try to tell me more clearly what I asked you just now. For, my friend, you did not give me sufficient information before, when I asked what holiness was, but you told me that this was holy which you are now doing, prosecuting your father for murder.[155]

Then Socrates commands Euthyphro to give him another definition of 'piety'. The youth replies, "well then, what is dear to the gods is holy, and what is not dear to them is unholy".[156] Although Socrates expresses satisfaction with this definition,[157] he expects the young man to prove the truth of his statement.

After further questioning by Socrates, the lad is compelled to define 'piety' in several different ways as "that which all the gods love is holy and, on the other hand, what they all hate is unholy;"[158] or 'piety' is "that which has to do with attention to the gods;"[159] or 'piety' is "when one knows how to say and do what is gratifying to the gods, in praying and sacrificing;"[160] and, finally, 'piety' is "that which is precious to the gods".[161] None of these definitions are acceptable to Socrates because they fail to provide a common denominator or general idea which makes all pious things to be pious.

Euthyphro has only offered specific examples of 'piety', that is, he has 'extended' the word to certain cases of 'piety'. Similarly, if one asked what are building materials, and then proceeded to define them by giving examples such as brick, wood, glass, steel, stone, etc., these examples would be an extension of the words 'building materials'.

Although Plato never employed the vocabulary of extension and comprehension, his dialogues reveal that he considered some ideas to be more universal than others inasmuch as they can be applied to a greater number of other ideas. This number of inferior ideas may be said to constitute the extension of the more universal idea. Plato also regarded some ideas to be richer in content than others inasmuch as they contain more characteristics. This content of each idea may be regarded as the comprehension of that idea. Hence, without designating this distinction by name, Plato seems to have been aware of the difference which existed between extension and comprehension.

Since most of the *Fragments of Archytas of Tarentum* (430 B.C.

— 360 B.C.) are considered unauthentic,[162] only one brief quotation will be cited from them. The division of genus into its constitutive species, differences and individuals by Archytas implies an allusion to extension.

> However, animal is divided into rational and irrational; rational animal into mortal and immortal; mortal into the subdivisions enclosed under the species, such as man, ox, horse and the rest.[163]

Brevity will also characterize the final name entered in this historical survey because all of the reputed works of Pythagoras are spurious.[164] His name was rarely mentioned by writers who preceded Plato and Aristotle. References were made more frequently to his disciples who became known as the Pythagoreans.

In Chapters I and II, the idea of one thing containing another thing was noted repeatedly. It is natural to wonder when and where such a notion originated. This idea had its source in the mathematical notions of the Pythagoreans who is turn exercised a profound influence on the theories of Aristotle. One reads

> it is thus that he [Aristotle] borrows from the Pythagoreans this great and admirable principle, that the ensemble of beings, the real world of substances, the whole, as the Pythagoreans were saying, is a progression, forms a series linked in which each term contains all the terms which precede it, as, in the system of the Decade, every number contains the numbers placed under it in the natural development of numbers identical to things.[165]

Although genus and species are not mentioned specifically in this particular citation, they are certainly inferred when the Pythagoreans say that "each term contains all the terms which precede it".

The idea of one term containing another is further developed by the following explanation (note especially the presence of the words 'comprehension' and 'extension' used by the translator):

> Much more, these terms are quantitative terms: they express some quantities, and some quantities of the same species, of nature to being measured by a common measure, to being compared one to the other. Fundamentally, it is very precise to say that Aristotle treats them as numbers. It is for that reason that

123

terms can and ought to be considered contained one in the other, as having a quantity suspectible to more or less. Restored to its simplest form, the syllogism is only a proportion: A is in B; B is in C, and consequently, A is necessarily in C. And the relations of capacity and of quantity persist inversely, whether one considers the comprehension or one considers the extension of terms: For comprehension as extension envelops the idea of more and of less, of extent, of quantity. The two extremes in this regard are in the inverse relation; the largest according to extension is the smallest according to comprehension; it is seen that they are contained by turns one in the other: and again the middle ought to be considered in turn as containing each extreme, and as contained in each one of them: either A, B, C. If B is contained in A according to comprehension, A is contained in B according to extension; and again if B contains C according to extension, C contains B according to comprehension. Thus there are in the syllogism, according to Aristotle, only some relations of magnitudes, that is to say, some numerical relations.[166]

General Summary of Chapters I and II.

This chapter will conclude by considering in a general way how the doctrine of extension and comprehension and its vocabulary evolved from the time of Aristotle to the present day. It has already been noted that both the doctrine and words utilized to express this doctrine were found explicitly in the writings of Aristotle and Porphyry. Hence Thomas Spencer Baynes was mistaken when he claimed that the distinction between extension and comprehension was taken only in general terms by Aristotle.[167] Furthermore, Porphyry's *Isagoge* has been regarded as the most explicit source for this ancient distinction. Both Aristotle and Porphyry attached a twofold analogy to words signifying 'comprehension', namely, (1) a usage identical with the modern meaning of comprehension, and (2) another usage identical with extension.

Subsequently, Ammonius Hermeae, by his usage of the word ἐπιτείνειν in his commentary on Porphyry's *Isagoge*, brought us in closer contact with the vocabulary of Aristotle's *Posterior Analytics*. Ammonius helped to explain the use of the Latin word *latius* as a link with the Latin word *extendere* inasmuch as the latter word is related to the Greek word ἐπιτείνειν. By emphasizing the power of the first genus and its role in predication, he also showed that extension is more fundamental and more important than comprehension.

Boethius added a variety of words such as *ambitus, abundare, superesse, magnitudo generis, plurimarum in se specierum collectivum,* and *supervadere* to the vocabulary of extension, as well as *abundare* and *supervadere* to the vocabulary of comprehension.

St. Albert the Great still further enriched the vocabulary of extension and comprehension by speaking of the genus as containing the species *secundum ambitum communitatis,* and by using such expressions as *extenduntur in plus, aptitudo, qualitas differentiae, magis est collectivum et adunativum genus quam species.* Again, in opposition to Baynes' statement, St. Albert showed that the Scholastics did not overlook the distinction between extension and comprehension; instead they presented this doctrine in a language which is not often familiar to modern logicians.

Although St. Thomas Aquinas did not employ the words 'extension' and 'comprehension' as explicitly as the Port Royalists or modern Latinists, still the presence of *extenduntur in plus* and *esse in plus* in his writings served as a foundation for the development of the modern vocabulary frequently employed to designate extension.

Cajetan added a certain preciseness and explicitness to this doctrine when he characterized genus as more collective extensively *(extensive)* and species as more collective intensively *(intensive).*

The traditional Aristotelian and Porphyrian doctrine appeared in England during the sixteenth century (1567) in the logical text of Thomas Wilson. And then twenty years later (1587) the Italian Paulus Barbus Soncinas employed the noun form *comprehensio* to designate extension.

John of St. Thomas (1632) referred to extension in a negative way by saying that the genus is less contracted *(minus contractum)* than the species.

In the early seventeenth century, Daniel Stahl's *Regulae Philosophicae* (1635) contributed to the continuity of the traditional doctrine and vocabulary pertaining to extension and comprehension. He transmitted this doctrine intact whereas the Port Royalists

125

created a new vocabulary. Stahl's explicit reference to Cajetan's words *extensive* and *intensive* served as a forerunner to the modern vocabulary of extension and intension.

It was observed that, prior to the *Port Royal Logic,* the entire tradition of nineteen centuries considered extension and comprehension as properties of the genus and species. But once the Port Royalists originated the modern vocabulary of comprehension and extension of ideas, a radical evolution was noted in reference to the doctrine as well as to the vocabulary itself. Though John Wallis (17th century) and John Regius (18th century) still upheld the Aristotelian and Porphyrian doctrine, V. Cl. Purchotius (1711) translated the Port Royal doctrine into the Latin words *extensio* and *comprehensio* and attached to them the same meaning found in the Port Royal text.

Isaac Watts (1731) clarified the Port Royal definition of extension by applying that word to individuals as well as to species. Somewhat later Richard Kirwan (1807) substituted the word 'denotation' for 'extension'. About the same time Thomas Reid (1806) added confusion to the traditional doctrine by concluding that there are more than five predicables.

Sir William Hamilton (1837-38) tried to show that all concepts ought to be viewed in terms of quantity. Therefore, he distinguished between the extensive and intensive quantity of concepts. In the middle of the nineteenth century, most English writers followed Sir William Hamilton in substituting 'intension' for the word 'comprehension'.

John Stuart Mill (1843) introduced in his writings the words 'denotation' and 'connotation' as substitutes for extension and comprehension, and thus he employed a vocabulary which was in contradiction to medieval usage.

Several modern logicians, v.g., Noah K. Davis (1880) and Henry W. Johnstone, Jr. (1954) confused extension with a class. John Neville Keynes (1906), and subsequently Sylvester J. Hartman (1949), added complexity but not clarity to the traditional distinction by differentiating several kinds of intension or comprehension.

L'Abbé Levesque (1913) restricted comprehension exclusively to difference, property and accident, whereas others associated it with genus and species. Levesque likewise restricted extension to genus and species.

126

C. Willems (1915) considered extension as proper to logic, and comprehension as proper to ontology (science of first intentions and not metaphysics).

James Edwin Creighton and Harold R. Smart employed the words 'extension' and 'comprehension' with a certain fluidity without justifying their usage by a previous tradition. Thus, unlike the majority of logicians who identified extension with breadth and intension or comprehension with depth, these two twentieth century authors considered extension and depth as synonymous, and intension or comprehension and breadth as synonymous. Richard Whately (1848) had already added to this word-confusion by using 'extension' and 'comprehension' as synonymous and convertible.

As a final observation, it would seem quite safe to assert that although the modern logicians have apparently enriched the vocabulary of extension and comprehension by introducing many new words, their additions have not added anything to the clarity of the doctrine. In Part II an attempt will be made to show that their additions could not contribute anything worthwhile to the doctrine because it is erroneous to detach extension and comprehension from the predicables.

The Scholastic or Thomistic manuals seem to suffer from a double heritage. Following the division of logic according to John of St. Thomas into formal and material, the predicables, considered as a part of material logic, are never studied at the beginning. Since the *Port Royal Logic* established a divorce between the predicables and the doctrine of extension and comprehension, the manualists thus arranged to place this distinction immediately at the beginning of their texts.

PART II: A DOCTRINAL SURVEY

CHAPTER III: AN ESSAY IN DOCTRINE

Although the words 'extension' and 'comprehension' have been used in logical textbooks for more than three hundred years without anyone offering a serious appraisal of their validity, the question arises whether this sort of vocabulary is well-grounded, and whether logicians can defend their position concerning this manner of speaking.

In this final chapter of the study, let us examine whether the words 'extension' and 'comprehension' may be employed legitimately within the domain of logic. Let us also examine whether these two words convey adequately the meaning intended by logicians. But before we even consider this vocabulary as a part of logic, the original impositions of meaning given to the words 'extension' and 'comprehension' outside of the realm of logic should command our first attention. A better understanding of their multiple signification will help us to avoid much of the confusion which has been associated with the distinction between these two words.

1. Non-logical meanings of 'extension'.

The word 'extension' is derived from the Latin noun *extensio*, which is based upon the past participle of the verb *extendo, extendere, extendi, extensus*. This verb is composed of two Latin words *ex* out + *tendere* to stretch. The Latin *extensio* translated into English words of Anglo-Saxon origin thus appears to mean a 'stretching out'. Certainly such a translation readily conveys more meaning to us than the words 'expanding', 'dilating' or 'amplifying'.

How *extensio* was used in Latin by classical authors and what different kinds of meaning it acquired in context will be made clear by an ordered series of examples of its usage by noted writers. For clarity, this section will be subdivided into four parts, followed by a summary.

A. The *Thesaurus Linguae Latinae* contains in outline form the various meanings of *extensio*. The primary imposition of meaning given is that of 'stretching out'. As it is clear that the basic notion is that of a certain type of physical activity, it will be of value to study a few examples of the verb itself.

> Funis (se) involvendo circum suculam extenditur et ita sublevant onera (*Vitr.* 10, 2, 2).[1]
> (The rope . . . is stretched taut . . .).

> Deus sanctos suos in modum arcus et sagittarum dicatur extendere (Hier. *Epist.* 34, 4, 2).[2]
> (God may be said to stretch out His saints after the metaphor of a bow and arrows).

This passage gives two meanings: a "stretching out of bow and arrows" which is a literal meaning (primary imposition), and a "stretching out of His saints" which is a secondary imposition (metaphorical usage). The latter meaning is a poetic metaphor.

In a more specialized way, this meaning to 'stretch out' is found in musical art:

> Quemadmodum in psalterio extendamus nervias (Varro *Men.* 366)[3]
> (Just as we pluck [stretch out] the strings on a psalter).

When the *TLL* paraphrases Seneca, it tells us quite frankly that the object being stretched out must possess certain quantitative aspects as boundary, shape, or height.

> Per extensionem mutatur ambitus rei vel animantis, figura, altitudo sim (Cf. *Nat.* 1, 9, 2)[4]
> (The circumference of a thing or a living being, the shape, the height, etc., is changed by its being stretched out).

Tertullian also uses the word in the same univocal sense when he says:

> Cum radius ex sole porrigitur . . . , non separatur a substantia solis, sed extenditur (*Apol.* 21, 12).[5]
> (When a ray is given out from the sun . . . , it is not separated from the substance of the sun but it is a stretching out of the sun).

130

Ovid conveys the notion of 'outstretched' by declaring:

Dum volt succurrere sorori . . . frater et extentas porrigit usque manus (*Fast.* 3, 872).[6]
(When he wishes to bring help to his sister . . . the brother offers his outstretched hands).

Or again one finds this same meaning intended by Jerome:

Videtur . . . mitti ad probationem . . . , extendi autem ad poenas eorum, qui merentur supplicia (*In Ezech.* 16, 27, p. 145 A).[7]
(It seems . . . hands are being put to the test . . . , but they are being stretched out for the punishments of those who merit sufferings).

This idea of stretching out the hands is still retained in the following examples even though it has now become symbolic. In the first instance, the action is linked to a curse, while in the second case, the action is linked to a blessing.

Jesus non avertit manum suam, quam extendit in Gaet. donec anathematizaret omnes (*Itala Jos.* 8, 26).[8]
(Jesus did not turn away his hand, which he extended over the Gaet., until he cursed everyone).

Joseph extendens manum dextram posuit super caput Ephraim . . . benedixitque (*Gen.* 48/14).[9]
(*Joseph* extending his right hand placed it over the head of Ephraim . . . and he blessed him).

The action of stretching out the hands is also associated symbolically with the notion of giving.

Deus cum ad retribuendum his manum extendisset id est auxilium obtulisset (Hil. *In Psalm.* 54, 16 p. 159. 9).[10]
(When God had extended His hand to repay them, that is, He had offered help).

All of the preceding examples contain the first and most obvious meaning of extension, namely, an act of stretching out. From these examples it should be clear that the primary and proper meaning of extension implies two elements: (1) the stretching out of (2) quantitative parts. Extension implies that the parts of quantity have a certain mobility; that they are larger or smaller; that

131

more parts can be compressed into less space and later can be made to occupy a larger space. It also seems to be evident that this word refers to a particular aspect of a whole with regard to the position of its parts, for one material object considered as a whole will occupy the place where its parts are to be found.

B. Now let us focus our attention on certain passages where the meaning of the word is clear, but where the explanations just given cannot be applied so directly. In each example to be cited, the expression 'to stretch out' will be discovered to make sense, yet there will always be a proportional transfer of meaning.

Caesar employs the verb form in a less proper sense. From the notion of "prolonging a trip", he transfers the word to the one who prolongs the trip. Thus he creates a new proportional meaning whereby the Latin verb *extendere* is transferred from the activity of stretching out some other object to the activity whereby the doer of the action performs the action on himself. As a result, *se extendere* comes to mean "to make a journey".

Pompeius . . . cum se magnis itineribus extendere (*Civ.* 3, 77, 3).[11]
(Pompey . . . when he would set out on great journeys).

C. Seneca appeals to the imagination when he speaks of stretching out the ears. In this case, there is no stretching out of the ears in distance, but rather a figure of speech to indicate that the ears are eager to catch the words of the orator. Here again one finds the word used in a less proper sense inasmuch as extension is no longer applied to local motion in space, but to the non-spatial movements of the appetite.

Aeque stillare oratorem . . . nolo quam currere nec extendat aures nec obruat (*Epist.* 40, 3).[12]
(I do not want an orator to speak too slowly anymore than I want him to rush along; neither should he overexcite their curiosity [overstretch their ears]).

This less proper meaning of the word is used again by Seneca to denote a stretching out in the sense of relaxing oneself.

Quidam se domi contrahunt (opp.) dilatant (syn.) foris et extendunt (*Epist.* 20, 3).[13]

(Certain people are puritanical at home and very outgoing and extrovert away from home).

In one classical grammar, the basic notion of quantity is retained when the grammarian speaks of lengthening the vowel.

Syllaba longa fit natura, cum vocalis extenditur (Fortun. *Gramm.* VI, 279, 27).[14]
(*A syllable becomes long by nature* when its vowel is lengthened).

In this example, words are quantitative because the length of vowels can be measured, but they are quantitative in a less strict sense inasmuch as all of the parts do not exist simultaneously. Hence the act of stretching out or lengthening is to be taken in the less proper sense.

D.   Besides referring to passions, emotions and appetites which are common to animals and men, the word 'extension' is also applied to human knowledge and to problems peculiar to man. The *Justinian Code,* for example, speaks of widening the law by enlarging our understanding of the words. This operation is strictly intellectual.

Latius . . . legis interpretationem [extendere] (2, 40, 5, 1).[15]
([To stretch out] more widely the interpretation of the law).

Vergil speaks of propagating or making known (stretching out) courage or glory, a quality which lacks all material ingredients.

Dubitamus . . . virtutem [i.e., *virtutis gloriam*] extendere factis (*Aen.* 6, 806).[16]
(We hesitate . . . to propagate our virtue [i.e., *the glory of virtue*] with deeds).

Livy talks about stretching out hope (another quality of the soul which lacks quantification).

Scipiones in Africam quoque spem extenderunt (24, 48, 1).[17]
(The members of the *Scipio* family also extended hope in Africa).

Summary.

It seems opportune now to summarize the major variations of meaning which pertain to the word 'extension'.

1. *Proper meaning:* the activity of stretching out of a material object. The notion of quantity is linked to this particular meaning. The result, that is, the thing stretched out, is also related to it.

2. *Less proper meaning:* the agent of the action stretching himself out with reference to local motion. This feat is possible because the doer of the action is himself a material, quantitative being.

3. *Still less proper meaning:* human emotions and appetites are said to be stretchable even though they may not be material objects in the same way as in the preceding instances.

4. *Common meaning:* knowledge which is in no way material may also be considered as something stretchable.

Perhaps it would not be amiss to make a few remarks at this juncture concerning the proper and common meanings of words. A proper meaning is one which does not presuppose another definition. For example, if one says that "John is a man", "Peter is a man", the word 'man' is being used in its proper meaning, because the definition of man as 'rational animal' presupposes no other definition. But if one declares "this statue is a man", there is a proportional transfer of meaning. One recognizes here a new meaning having a similitude with a prior meaning. The word 'man' no longer retains a proper meaning; it has now acquired a common meaning because it presupposes another meaning by virtue of the fact that it is predicated of the word 'statue'.

In like manner, the proper meaning of extension (to stretch out) is present whether the word is used in its primary imposition, less proper, still less proper, or common meaning. However, each transition of meaning is somewhat more removed from the original notion. This so-called transition or transference of meaning can likewise be explained in terms of quantity which is always found in some form or other with each variation of meaning. Whenever one refers to extension in the proper sense or less proper sense, the parts or subject extended (stretched out) are always quantitative *per se*. On the other hand, whenever the still less proper meaning is implied, the parts or subject are quantified *per accidens*. The

134

analogical use of extension can be developed further so that the parts are no longer quantitative, but are only spoken of or imagined to be quantitative. This evolvement of meaning has already been designated as the common imposition of the word.

2. Non-logical meanings of 'comprehension'.

Now let us consider the different meanings to be found in the use of the word 'comprehension' which comes from the Latin word *comprehensio*. The latter word is based upon the past participle of the verb *comprehendo, comprehendere, comprehendi, comprehensus*. The verb *comprehendo* is composed of two Latin words *cum* with + *prehendere* to grasp. It seems that the best English translation for the Latin *comprehensio* is 'a grasping completely'. For the sake of brevity and clarity, the analysis of this section will be divided into three parts, followed by a summary.

A. The *TLL* also presents an outline of various meanings for *comprehensio*. The primary meaning given is that of 'grasping' or 'seizing'. Once again let us study examples of the verb itself. First of all, the word seems to refer to the physical motion of grasping something with the hand. According to Cicero,

Quid manibus *opus est,* si nihil comprehendum est *(Nat. Deor.* 1, 92)?[18]
(What *need is there* for hands if there is nothing to be seized)?

The same meaning of a physical grasping with hands is employed by Caesar.

Comprehendunt utrumque et orant *(B. G.,* 31).[19]
(They join them *together* and pray).

The idea of seizing a beast is intended by Cicero in the following passage:

Anguibus domi comprehensis *(Div.* 1, 36).[20]
(Having seized the serpents in the house).

Terence conveys the same meaning when he states:

Aliquem pro moecho comprehendere et constringere *(Eun.* 5, 5, 23).[21]
(To seize and hold someone as an adulterer).

135

Vergil uses the word where the context would allow the translation 'to lay hold of'.

Ignis robora comprehendit *(Georg.* 2, 305).[22]
(Fire lays hold of the trunks).

Other examples can be cited where the word always signifies 'to grasp', and yet its nuances may be best translated by different verbs according to the context.

Cum comprehendit [surculus] (Varr. *R. R.* I, 40 fin).[23]
(When the [graft] *takes root).*

Arbor terram comprehendere dicitur *(Columel).*[24]
(The tree is said to *adhere to* the earth).

From speaking of plants which take root and trees which adhere, one can advance by analogy to speaking of the female of animals as 'conceiving'.

Si mulier non comprehendit *(Cels.* 5, 21. fin).[25]
(If the woman does not conceive).

B.   The second level of meaning is introduced when 'to grasp' may be translated 'to embrace'. Now, however, the word no longer names a local motion, but a human emotional activity either on the part of the sensible appetite or on the part of the rational appetite.

Comprehendere multos amicitia (Cic. *Cael,* 6, 13).[26]
(To embrace many with affection).

The Christian writer, L. Coelius Lactantius Firmianus, talks about embracing virtue with zeal (the words *studio complecti,* 'embraced with zeal', are prefaced to this quotation).

Quid est aliud colere virtutem nisi eam comprehendere animo ac tenere *(Inst.* 1, 20, 21)?[27]
(What else is it to cultivate virtue except to embrace and hold it with desire)?

Cicero also speaks of encircling someone with affection.

Comprehendere adolescentem humanitate tua *(Fam.* 13, 15 fin).[28]
(To embrace the youth with your kindness).

C. The word is still more extended to another level of meaning, that of knowledge, whether sensible or intellectual. When *comprehendere* refers to sense knowledge, it is often translated by 'to perceive' and not 'to grasp'. In the first example, the action of perceiving is performed by such external senses as vision and touch. In the second example, perception is made by the internal sense of memory.

'Quod est' nec visu nec tactu nec ullo sensu comprehenditur: cogitabile est (Sen. *Epist.* 58, 16).[29]
('What is' perceived by neither sight or touch or any other sense: it is thinkable).

Res brevis est, ut facile memoria comprehendatur (Rhet. *Her.* 2, 19, 30).[30]
(The thing is brief in order that it may be perceived by memory).

The notion of perceiving or grasping with the memory is also evidenced in the following example:

. . . has quinque dierum disputationes memoria comprehendamus (Cicero, 5 *Tusc.* 121).[31]
(. . . *let us remember* these arguments of five days).

The word 'comprehension' can likewise be applied to intellectual knowledge. In this case the word names or designates an activity of the intellect which draws the object to itself. Through knowledge, the intellect grasps and possesses the forms of things. In contrast to such activity, the first and second levels of meaning attached to the word 'comprehension' imply a reaching out to the object. Thus in the physical activity of grasping, the hand reaches out toward the thing; and in human emotional activity, the appetite wishes to grasp or reach out to the total entity of a thing.

Here are a few examples where 'comprehension' comports an activity of the intellect:

Omnes scelerum comprehendere formas, omnia poenarum percurrere nomina (Verg. *Aen.* 6, 626).[32]
(To collect all forms of crimes, to mention cursorily all names of punishments).

Neque enim numero comprehendere refert *species ac nomina* (Verg. *Georg.* 2, 104).[33]
(For to gather in number does not refer to *species and names*).

Omnem . . . scientiam comprehendere uno oratoris officio ac nomine (Cic. *De Orat.* 1, 213).[34]
(To embrace all science under one name and one function [namely, that] of a speaker).

This same intellectual activity can sometimes be considered from the viewpoint of the object. For example,

Breviter paucis comprehendere multa *(Lucr.* 6, 1082).[35]
(To describe many things briefly in few words).

Or the same activity can be regarded from the viewpoint of the knower.

Breviter comprehens a sentenia (Cic. *Fin.* 2, 7, 20).[36]
(Expressing briefly by a sentence).

In the following example, although the use of the word *comprehendere* is in the realm of knowledge, yet it refers to the physical activity of containing because 'volumes' contain wars inasmuch as words are contained in books which in turn are signs of wars.

Bella comprehendere viginti voluminibus (Suetonius, *Vit. Plinii*).[37]
(To write of wars in twenty volumes).

Cicero speaks of grasping something by the mind from some sensible sign. This activity implies a kind of argumentation.

Placuit ut Diogenem Habitus emeret . . . , quo facilius aut comprehenderetur res eius indicio aut falsa esse cognosceretur *(Cluent.* 47).[38]
(It was pleasing . . . , in order that the thing would be more easily grasped by its sign or would be known to be false).

Even though, according to one dictionary,[39] the seizure by intelligence is looked upon as an image borrowed from plants, namely that an opinion takes root because it has been implanted in the mind, it would seem more probable to look for a similitude between the hand and the intellect.

Si quam opinionem jam mentibus vestris comprehendistis: si eam ratio convellet, . . . (Cic. *Cluent.* 2, fin).[40]
(If you have seized with your minds any opinion, if reason plucks it, . . .).

In these previous examples belonging to this third part, the Latin verb *comprehendere* is no longer used in its proper or less proper meaning. The word has now acquired a common meaning.

The very citations of Latin classical authors seem to demonstrate clearly that the Latin word *comprehendere* was used on the level of knowledge. It is surprising to observe, therefore, that the famous French etymologists, A. Ernout and A. Meillet, maintaining the word *comprehendere* as used in this manner did not pertain to the classical period. They state that the classical word applied to knowledge was *apprehendere* and not *comprehendere*.[41]

The primary usage of the word *comprehendere* purports a physical grasping of something quantitative by the most universally useful instrument of man, namely, the hand. This activity of grasping can be ascribed to an inanimate element such as fire, or to an animate object such as a plant. This first meaning of part A is always on a material level of physical grasping. It is called the proper meaning of *comprehendere* because all the other usages presuppose this signification of a physical grasping. In other words, all other meanings are measured or weighed according to this physical grasping.

A change occurs in part B. While the object grasped may remain material, one element of meaning is sifted from the word. The activity of reaching out physically with the hand now becomes a grasping of another type. In this next level of meaning, the thing that reaches out to grasp its object employs a different instrument, that is, either the emotions or the will. For example, the sensible appetite can be said to grasp (embrace) someone with affection. This new level of meaning is less proper than the first because it presupposes a similitude, namely, the likeness of things which are different. The likeness is founded on the activity of grasping, while the difference arises from the instrument employed to execute the activity of grasping.

Finally, in part C, there is a further transference or sifting of meaning. Now the intellect, unlike the sensible and rational appetites, brings the object within itself inasmuch as that which is known assumes an intentional existence. Here the knowing subject has no quantitative parts, but it does possess material dispositions whereby that which is known is mentioned as if it were quantitative. In the case of the appetite, the object grasped becomes the measure of the one who grasps. However, in this third state, the level of sensible or intellectual knowledge, the senses or the intellect which grasp also impose their limits on the thing grasped. This third signification of *comprehendere* may be called the common meaning of the word.

Perhaps it may be well to consider a few examples in which the noun *comprehensio* is found before the multiple meanings of the word are presented in a summarized form. On the purely physical level, this noun can purport a corporeal activity.

Non effugies de manu eius, sed comprehensione capieris *(Jer. 34, 3)*.[42]
(Thou shalt not escape out of his hand, but thou shalt be caught in his grasp. . .).

In the following example, *comprehensio* imports a non-corporeal activity or state of affairs:

Sexta comprehensio, qua continetur urbs Roma, amplectitur Caspias gentes (Plin. *Nat.* 6, 217).[43]
(The sixth comprehension, in which the city Rome is enclosed, comprises the Caspian nation).

Or again, the noun-form may be used to designate the activity of grasping with the senses or with the intellect.

Latiore quadam comprehensione per omnes . . . species . . . ire (Quint. *Inst.* 2, 5, 14).[44]
(To go . . . through all . . . species of things with some wider comprehension).

Sin . . . comprehensionem eam dicimus, ut non solum sensu quis et sapientia comprehendat, sed et virtute et potentia cuncta teneat, qui cognovit; non possumus dicere, quod comprehendat filius patrem (Hier. *Epist.* 124, 4, 13).[45]
(But if . . . we call that comprehension, so that anyone who knows may comprehend not only knowledge and wisdom, but also he holds all things in his strength and power; we cannot say that the son comprehends the father).

When he discusses the art of oratory, Cicero employs the noun form of *comprehensio* (Gr. περίοδος) to mean a certain sphere, extension, circle or rounding of a sentence. Commenting on the rhythm of an oration, he declares,

> and in this discussion inquiry has been made, whether it is in the whole of that rounding of a sentence which the Greeks call περίοδος, and which we call *'ambitus'*, or *'circuitus'*, or *'comprehensio'*, or *'continuatio'*, or *'circumscriptio'*, or in the beginning only, or in the end, or in both, that rhythm must be maintained?[46]

Summary.

All of these variations of meaning attached to the word 'comprehension' can be summed up in the following manner:

1. *Proper meaning:* the activity of grasping completely a material object. The notion of quantity is also bound to this primary meaning. And, of course, the object grasped is likewise related to it.
2. *Less proper meaning:* human emotions (non-material) may be said to grasp another person with affection or to grasp something with zeal.
3. *Common meaning:* the external or internal senses are said to grasp, that is, perceive their proper objects with reference to sensible knowledge; or immaterial knowledge is grasped by an immaterial faculty.

The same transference of meaning which evolved with *extensio* is observed to occur with *comprehensio*. In each distinct meaning of the latter word, the notion of quantity is always present. In its proper setting, *comprehensio* implies that the parts or subject grasped are quantitative *per se*. In its less proper meaning, the parts or subject are quantified *per accidens*. Finally, in its common imposition of meaning, the parts are no longer quantitative. They are only said to be quantitative according to virtual quantity.

By way of postscript to this section, it is interesting to note that the sequence of meanings in the English language for the verb 'to comprehend' did not follow the basic order of the Latin significations. Some meanings made an early appearance due to a literal translation from the Latin by Anglo-Saxon expressions: v.g., 'to overtake', 'to come up and seize'.

> If any man do begin to follow after either of them . . . he is not able to comprehend or attain them with a Horse (Topsell, Four-f. *Beasts*, 1673, 561).[47]

But the earliest attested sense of this word was not to 'seize', 'grasp', 'lay hold of', or 'catch'. The primary meaning, based on an English need for such translation from the Latin, was 'to grasp with the mind', 'conceive fully or adequately', 'understand', or 'take in'. The following quotations exemplify such meanings:

> Able to compass and comprehend the greatest matters, and nevertheless to touch and apprehend the least (Bacon, *Adv. Learn.* I, To King, 1605).

> To comprehend is to know a thing as well as that thing can be known (Donne, *Serm. I. Cor.* xiii, 12, 1628).

> Those things which our hands can grasp, our understanding cannot comprehend (Young, *Centaur*, i Wks, IV, 115, 1757).

> Those . . . do not comprehend the real nature of the crisis (Macaulay, *Hist. Eng.* I, 152, 1848).[48]

3. Extension and comprehension with reference to the theory of knowledge.

In the process of examining the various meanings attached to 'extension' and 'comprehension', it was observed that the Latin words were first used to name a certain activity of material things, and were eventually transferred to that special type of activity of certain living beings which is called knowledge. In this section an effort will be made to show that the uses of these two words in such meanings are not only facts of language, but also that these meanings do have bearing in philosophy. It is beyond the domain of this study to pass in review all of the nuances of meaning that these words can convey in the philosophy of nature.[49] This section will treat exclusively that branch of philosophy which is concerned with living mobile beings.

The justification for the above mentioned way of speaking is found when an adequate theory of knowledge is propounded. Consider, for example, the theory of Aristotelian knowledge as explained by St. Thomas.

> Knowing beings are distinguished from non-knowing beings in that the latter possess only their own form; but the knowing being has also the natural capacity to possess the form of another thing, for the species of the thing known is in the knower. Hence it is evident that the nature of a non-knowing being is more contracted and limited; however, the nature of knowing beings has a greater *amplitude* and *extension*.[50]

Because the nature of a non-knowing being is more restricted and limited while the nature of knowing beings has greater amplitude and extension, Aristotle has said that

> the soul [of knowing beings] is in a way all existing things; for existing things are either sensible or thinkable, and knowledge is in a way what is knowable, and sensation is in a way what is sensible.[51]

When the matter is limited by form, the word 'limitation' implies perfection.[52] But when the form is limited by matter, the word 'limitation' implies restriction, contraction and imperfection. Since matter is the root source of inertia, all operations of a material composite flow from the form. It must be remembered that all forms are immaterial since they are non-matter. When, however, composites begin to manifest a greater number of increasingly complex operations, their forms may be said to be immaterial, that is to say, they have emerged from the limiting constraint *(coarctatio)* of matter.

A thing is able to know then by virtue of its immateriality; and the level or degree of knowing depends on the level or degree of immateriality. Thus plants do not know on account of their materiality.[53] But animals are said to be cognitive because they can perform newer and higher operations when they receive the forms of things without all of their individuating conditions. And man is still more cognitive because the operation of his intellect is such an activity carried on a higher level.[54]

In the preceding passage cited from St. Thomas *(Ia,* q. 14, a.1), the Latin word *extensio* is of special interest to us. Although we have used in this English translation the word 'extension', the word

143

extensio could have been adequately translated by the words 'a stretching out' or perhaps 'a stretch'. Words such as 'stretchability' and 'stretchableness', though not found in English dictionaries, could also be substituted and would be clearly understood in the same circumstances. If objection is made to 'a stretching out', it may be found acceptable to say 'a stretching quality'. Thus the text of St. Thomas could read: "the nature of knowing beings has a greater amplitude and stretching quality". In the Latin original the two words *extensio* and *amplitudo* name in a positive way what is meant by the standard Thomistic thesis that immateriality is the root-condition of knowledge. If one wishes to understand what is meant by an immaterial mode of reception proper to knowledge, the explanation must be given in terms of quantity, and yet, strictly speaking, neither knowledge nor its mode of reception is quantity. Even though knowledge is immaterial, it must be spoken of as if it were material. Just as material beings are stretchable, so knowing beings, in a proportionate way, are also said to be stretchable.

It has already been mentioned that the Latin word *comprehensio* is best translated by the English words 'a complete grasp'. This notion of grasping something completely or perfectly by a knowing power in relation to its object is also discussed by St. Thomas. The reader will note that the following passage will be very accurate and still clear if he substitutes mentally the words 'a complete grasp' each time the word 'comprehension' appears in the translation, and likewise if he substitutes the words 'to grasp completely' for the verb 'to comprehend'.

Properly speaking, one thing is said to be comprehended by another if it is included within it; for something is said to comprehend when it can apprehend anything in all its parts simultaneously, that is, to include it in every respect.

Now what is included by another thing does not exceed it, but is less inclusive, or at least equal. However, these things pertain to quantity. Consequently, there are *two modes* of comprehension according to *dimensive* and *virtual* quantity. According to dimensive quantity, as a cask comprehends wine; but according to virtual quantity, as matter is said to comprehend form when no part of the matter is left unperfected by the form.

And in this way any knowing power is said to comprehend its known object, namely, inasmuch as what is known stands perfectly under its activity of knowing. However, when the thing known exceeds the activity of knowledge, then the knowing power fails in comprehension.

But this excess must be considered *differently* in different powers. For in *sensitive* powers, the object is compared to a power not only according to virtual quantity, but also according to dimensive quantity; in this that the sensibles move the sense inasmuch as it exists in space, not only by force of the quality of the proper sensibles, but according to dimensive quantity, as it is manifest from the common sensibles.

Whence comprehension of the sense can be impeded *in a twofold manner: in one way,* from an excess of the sensible object according to virtual quantity: for example, the eye is impeded from comprehension of the sun, because the force of the sun's clarity, which is visible, exceeds the proportion of the visual power which is in the eye. *In another way,* on account of the excess of dimensive quantity: for example, the eye is impeded from comprehending the total area of the earth, but it sees one part and not another, which did not happen in the first impediment; for all parts of the sun are seen by us simultaneously, but not perfectly since the sun is too brilliant.

Now the intelligible object is also compared *to the intellect* indirectly according to dimensive quantity, inasmuch as the intellect receives from the sense. Consequently, our intellect is also impeded from the comprehension of anything unlimited according to dimensive quantity, and this is so because some of it is in the intellect and some of it is outside of the intellect. However, the intelligible object is not related directly to the intellect according to dimensive quantity, since the intellect is a power not using a corporeal organ; but it is related directly to the latter only according to virtual quantity. And, therefore, the comprehension of the intellect is impeded in those things which are understood directly without conjunction to the sense only if there is an excess of virtual quantity: for example, when what is understood has a more perfect mode of being understood than the mode by which the intellect understands. If, e. g., anyone knows the conclusion that a triangle has three angles equal to two right angles because of a probable reason

145

based upon authority, or because it is commonly said, such a person does not comprehend it, not because he is ignorant of one part of it, another part being known, but because that conclusion is knowable by a demonstration, to which the knower has not yet attained; and, therefore, he does not comprehend it, because it does not stand perfectly under his knowledge.[55]

This passage indicates that *comprehensio* has several ways of being used with reference to sensible and intellectual knowledge. Just as 'extension' names the capacity of a knowing being to stretch out toward a certain number of knowable things, so 'comprehension' signifies the complete grasp of knowable things.[56] In this section *(De Ver.*, q. 8, a. 2) it seems that St. Thomas is acting as a psychologist analyzing our activity of knowing. He is explaining the relation between concepts and things, but not the relations between the concepts themselves. It is easy to observe that St. Thomas uses the word *comprehensio* in respect to intellectual knowledge alone with great care. Since intellectual knowledge implies concepts, it would seem consistent with the teaching of St. Thomas to speak of the 'comprehension and extension of concepts'. But, on the other hand, what do many logicians mean when they speak of the comprehension and extension of concepts?[57] Are concepts the proper domain of logic, or are they proper to psychology?

In answer to these questions it would appear that those who speak of the comprehension and extension of concepts needlessly confuse students on the difference between logic and psychology. Logic is not directly interested in the concept but in the multiple and intricate relationships which arise between several concepts when man tries to obtain scientific knowledge about things. This needs further explanation.

In psychology, the concept is sometimes called the intelligible species or the mental word.

The intellect understands something in a *twofold way: in one manner formally,* and thus it understands by means of the intelligible species by which it is put into act; *in another manner* as an instrument which it uses in order to understand anything, and in this way the intellect understands by means of a con-

146

cept, because it forms the concept for this purpose that it understands the thing.[58]

A concept, an intelligible species, or a mental word, is said to be an instrument by which the intellect knows a thing. As such it is a quality of the intellect, a personal possession. One does not say that the concept is the thing known because a concept and its object are not physically identical. This distinction between a concept and its object is implied when one refers to the 'object' of knowledge which signifies something that is different from knowledge. Whereas the concept itself as an instrument or means of knowing is a real being, the object of knowledge may be either a being or a non-being. For example, although Cinderella may not exist, a concept of her is nonetheless real.

Inasmuch as they exist in the mind for the purpose of bringing the knower in contact with things, concepts are called intentions. If these concepts are directed toward objects real or not, they are called 'first intentions'. But when these concepts of things are considered in relation to each other, relations between the concepts arise because of the things known. These relationships are called 'second intentions'.

Those things which are first understood are the things outside the soul toward whose understanding the intellect is first borne. But the intentions following upon our mode of knowing are said to be the second things understood: for by this second activity the intellect understands inasmuch as it is bent back on itself, understanding (1) that it understands and (2) the mode by which it understands.[59]

Logic is not immediately concerned with the existence of a thing. "For the logician considers the mode of predication and not the existence of a thing."[60] It is only directly concerned with relationships between concepts which are beings of reason. "And a being of this kind, namely, a being of reason, is properly the subject of logic."[61]

Further, it is worthwhile noting that unlike psychology which considers concepts independently of any relationship with words, logic is interested in concepts insomuch as they are bound to words.

147

Therefore, these are the three speculative sciences, and there are no more, as we remember that we said in our *III Book On The Soul*, because the logical sciences do not consider a being or any part of a being, but rather the second intentions about things implied by language, through which are had ways of moving from the known to the unknown according to an inductive or deductive syllogism.[62]

That part of philosophy, which is often called psychology, studies concepts as one of the many properties of the soul. Logic, on the other hand, studies the relations (second intentions) between concepts. Hence it is possible for psychology to be interested in only one concept, that is, any concept insomuch as it is a quality of the soul. On the contrary, logic presupposes the existence of at least two concepts about things because it is not interested in concepts as qualities of the soul, but rather in concepts as related to each other with reference to things. In fact logic demands a multiplicity of concepts because one must be able to say something of inferiors before science can prove any conclusions.

The ambiguity of the expression 'extension and comprehension of concepts' should now be obvious. Taken literally, the expression belongs properly to psychology. If the words 'extension' and 'comprehension' are to have any non-psychological meaning in logic, it would be because somewhere among the many second intentions studied by the logician, some new and more restricted usage must be found. Or again, since the subject of logic is not concepts but the relations between concepts, then extension and comprehension should never be employed to designate concepts but rather to indicate the relationships existing between concepts, or they should not be employed at all. Confusion on this point in a logical text can be taken as a sign of defective knowledge on the part of its author. L'Abbé Levesque, for example, confuses the two viewpoints when he discusses extension and comprehension in his treatise on psychology.[63] In that text he considers the relations between ideas, a topic which is exclusively proper to logic.

The Port Royalists and their admirers, in speaking of the extension and comprehension of ideas or concepts, displayed a weakened knowledge of logic. Although the Port Royalists were aware that logic studies relations between concepts, yet they attached insufficient importance to such relationships. They treated certain foundations of logic, that is, the concepts, as more important than these relations. As shall be seen more clearly, their lack of respect for the predicables seems to be mirrored in their statement, "This is more than sufficient touching the five universals, which are treated at such length in the schools".[64] Even if the Port Royalists had assigned a proper role to the predicables in logic, still their use of such vocabulary as the 'extension and comprehension of ideas' would continue to be a constant source of confusion to the neophyte in logic. Basing himself on such an expression, a beginner in logic cannot be expected to discern the fine nuances which separate psychology from logic. For a similar vocabulary that confuses beginners on this point, consult Appendix II.

4. Extension and comprehension in logic.

Now that the distinction between psychology and logic has been set forth, a proper way to use 'extension' and 'comprehension' in a strictly logical setting can be discussed in which these two words will have meaning with reference to second intentions. The best way to proceed would be by looking at the purpose and divisions of logic, and then the three operations of the intellect in reverse order.

A. Extension and comprehension with reference to the purpose and divisions of logic.

At this point it should not be forgotten that certain logicians have attempted to divide logic into a logic of extension and a logic of comprehension (intension).[65] Whether logic is so divided on the basis of these particular aspects (v.g., extension and comprehension) will not be manifest until we consider the purpose of logic itself.

Since it may be said that logic is utilized by the philosopher of nature, the mathematician, and the metaphysician, the total ulterior end of logic is science. This total ultimate end embraces the attainmen of both the incomplex and the complex unknown. The philosopher of nature needs the instrument of attaining the incomplex and complex unknown objects in order to grasp reality in nature; the mathematician also relies on logic for clarity in his grasping of the formal properties of quantity; and the metaphysician needs logic to understand the properties of all beings.

149

The unity of logic, a speculative and liberal art, is derived from its end. As an art, the whole of logic may be divided into two parts according as the unknown object of research is incomplex or complex. The perfect attainment of the end of logic presupposes a threefold operation on the part of man's reason, and it is this threefold operation which establishes the division of the subject matter of the science of logic. Since Aristotle actually uses the distinction of the incomplex and complex in his treatise *On The Soul* by dividing the activity of the intellect into two radically distinct operations, the divisions of logic according to the operations of reason need only be discussed here.[66] Furthermore, it should not be forgotten that St. Thomas makes explicit the thought of Aristotle when he points out that this second operation embraces what in modern Thomistic manuals are called the second and third operations.[67]

The objects which form the basis for the division of logic as an art, namely the incomplex and complex unknown, are outside the realm of logic. And similarly the objects which form the basis for the division of logic as a science, namely the three operations of the intellect, are also outside the domain of logic. Therefore if logic should be divided according to extension and comprehension, then these two words ought to name things outside of logic. Since Father Clark's division of logic into one of extension and one of comprehension does not name things outside of logic, it is faulty.

B. Extension and comprehension with reference to the third operation.

At this point the discussion can be restricted to an adverse argument. In an objection posited by St. Thomas, the word 'comprehension' is employed both with reference to definitions and to syllogisms. This is strange because it would mean that comprehension is proper to the logic of the third operation as well as to the logic of the first operation. Since the third operation is more directly ordained to the total ulterior end of logic, the meaning of the word 'comprehension' in reference to syllogisms should be discussed first. But before such discussion is undertaken, it may be well to explain briefly the third operation.

The third act of our intellect consists in a process of moving from a first element to a third element by means of a middle element because "to reason is to advance from one thing understood to another in order to know an intelligible truth".[68] In this process of reasoning, one moves in thought from knowledge already possessed to something new, or from something previously known in an imperfect way to a possession of it in a more perfect way. Is comprehension intimately and properly linked to this process of reasoning? Or does it belong equally to the third operation and the first operation? While reading an objection in which St. Thomas applies the word 'comprehension' to demonstration, a process of reasoning which belongs to the third operation of the intellect, the reader should again substitute in his own mind the words 'to grasp completely' every time the verb form 'to comprehend' appears in the translation.

> Besides, just as the most perfect way of knowing complex things is to know them by demonstration, so the most perfect way of knowing incomplex things is to know what they are. But every complex thing that is known by demonstration is comprehended. Therefore, everything concerning which the essence is known is comprehended. But those who see God through His essence have a quidditative knowledge about Him, since to know what a thing is, is nothing other than to know the essence of the thing. Therefore, angels comprehend the divine essence.[69]

In this passage, the verb form 'to comprehend' is used properly in two ways: there is a direct use and a derivative use of the word. The direct usage is found in the first operation of the intellect. The derivative usage, which presupposes a prior use in the first operation, is found in the third operation. St. Thomas responds to the objection by declaring that before anything can be comprehended, its definition (matter which comprises part of the first operation) must itself be comprehended.

> A thing is comprehended whose definition is known if only the definition itself is comprehended. But just as it is possible to know a thing without comprehension, so it is possible to know the thing itself without comprehension; and so the thing itself remains uncomprehended. But the angel, although he may see in some manner what is God, nevertheless he does not comprehend this.[70]

151

Aristotle offers another example of extension in the third operation when he discusses the variables of syllogistic reasoning. These terms are also derived basically from genus and species in the first operation.

The truth is that cause, effect, and subject are reciprocally predicable in the following way. If the species are taken severally, the effect is wider than the subject (e. g. the possession of external angles equal to four right angles is an attribute wider than triangle or square), but it is coextensive with the species taken collectively (in this instance with all figures whose external angles are equal to four right angles). And the middle likewise reciprocates, for the middle is a definition of the major; which is incidentally the reason why all the sciences are built up through definition.

We may illustrate as follows. Deciduous is a universal attribute of vine, and is at the same time of wider extent than vine; and of fig, and is of wider extent than fig: but it is not wider than but coextensive with the totality of the species. Then if you take the middle which is proximate, it is a definition of deciduous. I say that, because you will first reach a middle next the subject, and a premiss asserting it of the whole subject, and after that a middle — the coagulation of sap or something of the sort — proving the connexion of the first middle with the major: but it is the coagulation of sap at the junction of leaf-stalk and stem which defines deciduous.

If an explanation in formal terms of the interrelation of cause and effect is demanded, we shall offer the following. Let A be an attribute of all B, and B of every species of D, but so that both A and B are wider than their respective subjects. Then B will be a universal attribute of each species of D (since I call such an attribute universal even if it is not commensurate, and I call an attribute primary universal if it is commensurate, not with each species severally but with their totality), and it extends beyond each of them taken separately. Thus, B is the cause of A's inherence in the species of D: consequently A must be of wider extent than B; otherwise why should B be the cause of A's inherence in D any more than A the cause of B's inherence in D?[71]

In this passage the verb *extendere* occurs only once. But the Latin text of Aristotle contains several other words which are synonymous with the verb *extendere*: v.g., *esse in plus* (to be wider), *excellere* (to surpass—again with reference to extension), and *excedere* (to exceed, that is, to be wider or to have a greater extension). One should note especially that the words *'in plus'* are used four different times in this citation.

In the original Greek text, this same passage contains the verb παρεκτείνειν [72] which is translated by the Latin verb *extendere*. The Greek word means 'to stretch out' or 'to extend'. It is translated into Latin as *"logice, eundem habere ambitum"*[73] (logically, to have the same extension). Aristotle also employs the words ἐπὶ πλέον with the verb παρεκτείνειν. This expression is translated by the Latin words *"latiorem ambitum habere"*[74] (to have a wider extension). ἐπὶ πλέον is also translated by the Latin words *'in plus'* which mean 'to be in more' or 'to be wider'.

In lines 99, 33-34, Aristotle uses the verb ὑπερέχειν which is translated by the Latin word *excedere*. In the logical sense, the word signifies *"maiorem ambitum habere"*[75] (to have a greater extension). In line 99, 42, the verb ὑπάρχειν means *"esse in eius ambitu"*[76] (to be in its extension).

Aristotle reduces this problem of relating the cause, effect and subject to the genus which he considers to be the first universal. Hence the problem of extension is not one of the third operation, but is rooted fundamentally in the genus and the first operation of the intellect.

In his *Commentary* on this particular Aristotelian text, St. Thomas utilizes the expression *in plus* five times and the verb *excedere* thrice to convey the meaning of Aristotle with reference to extension.[77] In still another lesson, St. Thomas employs *in plus* nine times[78] and *excedere* twice.[79]

If 'comprehension' can be used in the third operation of the intellect, but only by presupposing a prior use in the first operation, perhaps if the same is true for 'extension', we shall have proved that the two words are correlatives—wherever one is found, so will be found the other. Here is an example of extension in the *Posterior Analytics* which presupposes a prior use with reference to genus in the first operation.

Therefore, of those things which are always present in any one thing, certain ones are extended in more: not, however,

153

outside the genus: but I say in more to be whatever are present indeed in any one thing universally, and truly in others.[80]

Because Aristotle confines 'extension' to the genus (a relation of the first operation), the word is employed here in its direct and not derivative usage.

Since extension and comprehension are found in the third operation of the mind only derivatively, are modern logicians correct when they speak about the 'extension and comprehension of terms'?[81] According to Aristotle, the word 'term' signifies the resolution of the premises in a syllogism (part of the third operation): "I call that a term into which the premiss is resolved, i.e. both the predicate and that of which it is predicated, 'being' being added and 'not being' removed, or vice versa."[82] Even the testimony of the medieval *Grammatica Speculativa* is completely in accord with Aristotle's assertion that the word 'term' is applied to the third operation.

But the *term* bespeaks the reason of terminating the resolutions of a syllogism, because the dialectician resolves the syllogism into propositions, and propositions into subject and predicate; which are called *terms* according to the logician.[83]

Therefore, even if modern logicians intend to name an activity of the first operation when they refer to the 'extension and comprehension of terms', still their terminology is ambiguous and reveals a similar carelessness of thought and lack of precision exhibited by logicians who confuse psychology with logic by speaking about the 'extension and comprehension of concepts'. However, this mistake is less serious because to speak of the 'extension and comprehension of terms' is a problem of anticipation. Such logicians intend to speak about the first operation of the intellect.[84]

C. Extension and comprehension with reference to the second operation.

Since extension and comprehension belong to the third operation only derivatively, may it be said that they are derived from the second act of understanding whereby two concepts are identified or separated from each other? It would seem so because the propositions entering in a syllogism are composed of subjects and predicates. In the historical part of this study, several authors were found to confuse the problem of subject and predicate with that of comprehension and extension.[85] According to these authors, the problem of comprehension is identified with the predicate being contained in the subject, and the problem of extension is confused with the subject being contained in the predicate. Subject and predicate pertain to the second operation of reason.

There are, however, *three* acts of reason. . . . But the *second* operation of the intellect is composition or division of the intellect in which there is now the true or false.[86]

This act of affirming or denying by stating that a thing is or is not denotes more than a mere conception of essences; it concerns the very existence of a thing. Hence one may speak of a concept such as 'a stick with one end', but one may not make a valid statement that 'a stick with one end is possible'. Although logic treats of true and false enunciations,[87] it does not treat of true or false concepts because the product of the first operation, namely, the concept, does not say anything about the existence of a thing. It is only in the product of the second operation, namely the enunciation, composed of subject and predicate, that one finds truth or falsity following upon the declaration in the intellect that something exists in reality. One must remember that what is being considered in an enunciation is not two concepts, but either two realities, or one reality under two aspects, which are either composed or divided. St. Thomas explains this second operation of the mind in the following manner:

But the second operation concerns the very existence of a thing, which results from the union of the principles of a thing in composites, or, as in simple substances, it accompanies its simple nature. And because the truth of the intellect is from the fact that it conforms to a thing, it is evident that according to this second operation, the intellect cannot truly abstract what has been joined in reality, because in abstracting a separation would be signified according to the very existence of the thing, just as if I abstract man from whiteness by saying: 'man is not white', I signify that there is a separation in reality. Consequently, if according to reality man and whiteness are not separated, the intellect will be false. By this

155

operation, therefore, the intellect can truly abstract only those things which are separated according to reality. . . .[88]

Some modern logicians speak of a judgment of extension whereby the subject is in the predicate because the predicate includes more objects than the subject, and a judgment of comprehension or intension whereby the predicate is in the subject because the subject embraces more attributes than the predicate.[89] Though logicians are naming certain results or effects whose cause is in the first operation, they do not seem to make it clear that in every enunciation and in every subject and predicate there is a problem of extension and comprehension. Extension and comprehension can be applied to this second act of understanding only in a derivative sense, because only in an enunciation can the total possible extension and comprehension be *de facto* limited to a particular context. Therefore, if extension and comprehension are used with reference to second intentions as explained before, the proper *locus* for determining their role is within the first operation of the mind. In other words, the supposition of an enunciation presupposes its meaning.

By way of anticipation, it may be said that simple apprehension expresses its intelligible content in the form of a concept or idea because "one act of the intellect is the understanding of indivisible or incomplex things according to which one conceives what a thing is".[90] For example, one may have a concept of a 'river', 'mountain', or 'valley'. This act of simple apprehension does not involve any judgment or enunciation. Something is conceived without affirming or denying anything about it.[91] It is an act of the intellect knowing something. This act of the mind tells us only what a thing is rather than that it exists:

the first operation is indeed concerned with the very nature of the thing according to which any understood thing holds some grade among beings, whether it be a complete thing, as any whole, or whether it be an incomplete thing, as a part or accident.[92]

Nor does this operation entail any error because " . . . simple objects are neither true nor false, and because the intellect is not deceived in that which a thing is. . . ."[93]

If 'extension' and 'comprehension' are found properly in the logic of the first operation, and found conjointly in every enunciation, further evidence is seen why it would be ridiculous to have a logic of extension and a logic of comprehension. This would mean that every enunciation requires two logics: one of extension and one of comprehension. Such a position seems to destroy the *per se* unity of an enunciation. Needless to say, such a division has nothing to do with the expression 'extension and comprehension' which is derived from the *Port Royal Logic*.

D. Extension and comprehension with reference to the first operation.

In the course of studying the first operation of the mind, the second intentions which should be given principal consideration are the predicaments and the predicables because they are necessary tools for the formulation of definitions and the execution of divisions. The predicaments are related to the predicables as matter is related to form. In nature, matter is ordained to form, but as the less dignified to the more dignified. But in the case of certain liberal arts, form is ordained to matter, as the less dignified to the more dignified; and in this part of logic, the predicables as form are ordained to the predicaments as matter as to something more dignified. The predicaments will be considered first because they are more dignified and closer to the end of logic than the predicables.

i)   The predicaments.

Some logicians classify the predicaments as first intentions instead of second intentions. Their error is caused by the fact that they neglect to distinguish between modes of being and modes of predicating *(modi praedicandi)*.

It must be known that being is not divided univocally into ten predicaments, as genus into species, but according to the diverse mode of being. But the modes of being are proportionate to the modes of predicating. For by predicating anything of any other, we say that this is that: whence the ten genera of being are said to be the ten predicaments.[94]

Although the modes of being are proportionate to the modes of predicating, the former are first intentions belonging to metaphysics,

157

while the latter are second intentions belonging to logic. Hence if one speaks of a first intention as a predicament, he is in fact naming a mode of being, even though the reason for the name is found in the intellect. Here our interest is confined to a predicament as a mode of predication, that is, as a second intention in logic.

In order that anything be predicated of another, it must be, first of all, universal. At this point a clear understanding of the use of the word 'universal' is necessary.[95] The word 'universal' can be considered in two different ways: and consequent upon the first way, it will be used with reference to both the predicaments and the predicables. In the first way, the word 'universal' can be used to name a common nature when it underlies an intention of universality, that is, a substitute mode of existence provided by the mind. For example, something can be ascribed to this common nature accidentally by reason of the thing in which it exists. Thus when we say that a man is 'white', white may be considered substantial because it exists in substance and yet it is only accidentally substantial.

In still another way, the word 'universal' can be used with reference to the common nature itself without any consideration being given to a mode of existence. Nothing is true of it except what belongs to it as such. Thus it pertains to man to be 'rational', 'animal', 'sentient', 'living', and whatever else the definition of man includes, whereas the accidents 'tall', 'young', 'American', etc., which are not included in the concept of man, do not belong to man as man.

This common nature has a twofold existence: materially in individuals, and immaterially in the intellect. In both modes of existence, the common nature which is called a universal is found to exist according to the peculiar properties of that which gives it existence. When this common nature is considered as existing in particular things, that is, with the intention of universality proper to the mind left aside, the universal is said to exist in the particular. Otherwise, one could not say that the nature of man exists in the individual. The intention of universality is not found in the particular because it is opposed to the individuating power of prime matter. When the common nature assumes a mode of existence in and provided by the intellect, it takes on an intention of universality because of the abstractive power of the intellect. In this case it may be said that the universal nature exists in the universal.[96]

Perhaps the thought of St. Thomas in the paraphrase will be clearer if summarized in an outline.

(1) A common nature considered with reference to a universal mode of existence may be called a universal.[97]
(2) The word 'universal' can also be considered with reference to the common nature without any regard to the mode of existence either particular or universal.

The universal mode of existence which is implied by the intention of universality can in turn be considered in two ways: (1) from the viewpoint of the intellect which actually makes the existence, or (2) from the viewpoint of the common nature which receives the existence. The necessity for such a distinction is seen to be implied when the citation from the treatise *On The Physics* is contrasted with that *On the Soul*. However, to make the implication clear, certain grammatical observations are necessary.

The Latin expression *modus praedicandi* (mode of predicating) is proportionally equivocal because it can signify either the activity of predicating or the passivity of being predicated. The gerund form[98] *praedicandi* may be interpreted as the genitive case of either the active infinitive *praedicare* (the activity of predicating) or the passive infinitive *praedicari* (the passivity of being predicated). Hence *modus praedicandi* is analogical because according to the context it may have an active or a passive signification.

It may be well to consider, for example, other Latin verbs such as *amo* and *tango*: both verbs have an active infinitive form (*amare*: to love; *tangere*: to touch) and a passive infinitive form (*amari*: to be loved; *tangeri*: to be touched). The infinitive forms of these two verbs do not create a problem, but as soon as the active infinitives *amare* and *tangere* are used as nouns, their genitive forms *amandi* and *tangendi* give rise to confusion. *Amandi* as the genitive of *amare* means 'of loving actively', and as the genitive of *amari* means 'of being loved'. Likewise, *tangendi* as the genitive of *tangere* means 'of touching actively', and as the genitive of *tangeri* means 'of being touched'. So while there is precision in the Latin infinitive

159

forms, there is ambiguity in the gerund forms since the latter purport two meanings: one active and one passive.

In English, clarity of expression is also lacking. The English infinitive is neither active nor passive. The infinitive is generic inasmuch as it has indifferently an active or a passive meaning. If one considers the infinitive forms of the verbs 'to read' and 'to do' outside of a sentence structure, their meaning is ambiguous since they can denote either activity or passivity. Of course, this ambiguity could be eliminated if a compound tense were introduced: v.g., 'to be read' or 'to be done'. But we are only interested here in the simple tenses as we compare the Latin and English infinitive and gerund forms. In context the infinitives 'to read' and 'to do' may possess two meanings. If one declares, 'I am going to read a book', the infinitive is active. But if one states, 'I have a book to read', the infinitive is passive because the sentence really means 'I have a book to be read'. The infinitive 'to do' also has an active sense in the sentence 'I am going to do some chores', and a passive nuance in the sentence 'I have some chores to do', that is, 'some chores to be done'.

English present participles are likewise equivocal. 'Cooking' and 'selling' may be either active or passive in meaning depending upon their context. In the sentences 'his wife is cooking dinner' and 'he is selling books', the participial forms 'cooking' and 'selling' are active; but in the sentences 'the food is cooking slowly' and 'the book is selling well', the present participles are passive in meaning.

The same ambiguity exists in the English gerunds. If one refers to the 'process of ageing', the gerund may denote either an active meaning, namely, "the process of ageing wine', or a passive sense, namely, 'the process of becoming older'. The same equivocation can be found in the expression 'the act of graying'. The gerund 'graying' may signify either the active meaning of coloring an object gray, or the passive sense of becoming gray, that is, when it refers to a person's hair.

Similarly, the terminology 'mode of predicating' *(modus praedicandi)* is equivocal because it can be interpreted actively or passively. If one interprets the 'mode of predicating' in an active sense, he names a 'predicable'; but, if he construes the 'mode of

160

predicating' in a passive sense (the more accurate expression would be the 'mode of being predicated'), he names a 'predicament'. That is the reason why St. Albert used the adjective 'predicable' *(praedicabilis)*[99] with a passive meaning to designate a predicament, because predicable means 'that which can be predicated'. At the same time he employed the words *universalis* and *ordinatio praedicabilium* when he referred to the predicables, in order to emphasize the intellectual activity of producing the universal intentions.[100] When the word 'universal' is being used in the intellect from the viewpoint of actually making existence, it is a mode of predicating called the 'predicable'. But when the word 'universal' is being used from the aspect of the common nature receiving existence, it is a mode of predicating called the 'predicament'.

Now that we have examined the two modes of active and passive predication, we shall consider whether or not extension and comprehension are proper to the passive mode of predicating, namely, the predicaments. Such an investigation, whether it yields positive or negative information, will deepen our understanding of extension and comprehension as we proceed to find the basic source of these two properties. Aristotle enumerates ten different ways in which things can be predicated (note the passive form 'can be predicated'). These ways are called by logicians today either the ten categories, predicaments, predicates, or supreme genera.

> Expressions which are in no way composite signify substance, quantity, quality, relation, place, time, position, state, action, or affection. To sketch my meaning roughly, examples of substance are 'man' or 'the horse', of quantity, such terms as 'two cubits long' or 'three cubits long', ...[101]

Due to lack of space, only the predicaments of quantity and substance will be considered here: first of all, quantity, because some logicians have recognized 'extension' and 'comprehension' as quantities.[102] They identified extension as an external quantity with the dimension of breadth, and comprehension as an internal quantity with the dimension of depth. These men were inclined to call concepts quantities containing 'under' themselves (extension) and 'in' themselves (comprehension) certain attributes. In view of their way of speaking, it would seem at first glance that the words 'extension' and 'comprehension' belong to the predicament or category of quantity. According to Aristotle, quantity is either continuous or discrete.[103] After citing examples of these two species of quantity, he remarks that "strictly speaking, only the things which I have mentioned belong to the category of quantity: everything else that is called quantitative is a quantity in a secondary sense".[104] In other words, if extension and comprehension are used within the limitations of the predicament 'quantity', their meaning is restricted to their first univocal usage. But such a restriction is not adequate to the total usage of these two words in logic because no allowance would be made for their analogical usage with reference to virtual quantity. Consequently, if and when extension and comprehension are employed in these analogical senses, they cannot belong properly to the predicament of quantity.

For this to be clear, it should be remembered that the first meaning of extension is synonymous with that of quantity. But when one declares that the genus of quantity has a greater extension than a species of quantity (v.g., a triangle), then the word 'extension' has a non quantitative sense.

When the English logician, Sir William Hamilton, said that "a concept is, therefore, necessarily a quantity",[105] he made a very important observation on the methodology proper to logic. If this passage is understood to mean that concepts are to be univocally placed under the predicament of 'quantity', the meaning is misconstrued. But if the statement is interpreted to mean that concepts are virtual quantities and that their properties, second intentions, are to be named and analyzed as properties of virtual quantities, such an interpretation is in accord with the manner in which man is obliged to analyze immaterial realities.

Thus the usage of extension and comprehension, which is the subject of this study, is not proper to the predicament of 'quantity'. If the accidental category of quantity cannot, it would seem likely that no other predicamental accident could found the proper logical usage of extension and comprehension. Therefore, no further analysis of the other eight categories of accident will be given here.

The category of 'substance' should now be treated. Because substance may be extended to, or may contain under it, such beings as body, living body, animal, man and individuals, it may be inquired whether the predicament of 'substance' is the source or cause of extension and comprehension.

> Substance indeed, is itself genus, under this is body, under body animated body, under which is animal, under animal rational animal, under which is man, under man Socrates, Plato, and men particularly.[106]

Substance cannot be regarded as quantity in the univocal sense of the word because the first substance is neither material nor immaterial. When, however, the genus of 'substance' is extended to two species, the same situation prevails as when the genus 'quantity' is extended to two species. This extension of substance, which is generic, to the species is not due to its nature as a predicament, but rather to the predicables which organize it. Therefore, the predicament 'substance' cannot be the cause of extension and comprehension.

Extension and comprehension are not, first of all, concerned with the relationships involved in the passivity of that which is predicated, but with the relationship involved in the activity of predicating. Consequently, extension and comprehension cannot be immediate properties of the predicaments which are modes of being predicated; instead, they must belong to the predicables which are modes of organizing the activity of predicating.

ii)   The predicables.

When something is attributed to another thing, that something is said to be predicated about that thing. That thing about which something may be said is called the subject, while that something which may be said about the subject is known as the predicate. The different ways in which a predicate can be related to a subject are called 'predicables'. All predicables are universals because 'being said of several things' implies a certain universality or repeatability. "And thus a universal is that which is apt to be in many and to be predicated of many."[107] St. Albert makes clear why the predicables are five in number, and only five. The word 'universal'[107a] can be used with reference to either the essence of a subject of which it is predicated, or something which is not the essence. If it signifies the essence, it may express the whole formal essence (spe-

163

cies, v.g., man), an essential part in inchoation (genus, v.g., animal), or an essential part in act (difference, v.g., rational). If it designates something which is not the essence, it may express something which is necessarily connected to the essence of the subject (property, v.g., risibility), or something which is only contingently connected to that essence (accident, v.g., tall).

But the universal thus taken as it is a predicable that is in many and of many, either it is present essentially or accidentally: whether as an essence or as an accident. If it is present as an essence: either it is present as a whole essence or as an essential part. If it is present as a total formal essence, it is evident that it is a species, because species is the whole formal being of individuals concerning which it is predicated: because whatever comes after the species comes from matter or from individuating elements. If, however, as an essential part: then it is present either after the manner of a potency in which there is some inchoate sort of being, or it is present after the manner of an act in which there is some completely actuated being. And in the first way it is a genus, but in the latter way it is a difference. But if it is present as an accident: either it is present as an accident of nature which is caused and flows from the aptitude of its nature, or as a common accident which is an accident of the individual. And in the first way it is the property, but in the second way it is called the accident.[108]

In the first sentence of this paragraph, St. Albert presents one word, namely, the word 'universal' and gives it two meanings by considering it from two different aspects: (1) as a predicament, when he says "it is a predicable that is in many and of many", and (2) as a predicable when he adds the phrase, "either it is present essentially or accidentally". The reader is cautioned to remember that St. Albert employs the words *ordinatio praedicabilium (universale id quo)* to denote the predicables and the word *praedicabilia (universale id quod)* to signify the predicaments.

The five predicables are defined by Porphyry in his *Isagoge*. According to the order of knowledge, Porphyry defines them in the following sequence: genus, species, difference, property and accident. If, however, one follows the order of things in nature, difference should precede the species because the former is constitutive of the latter. Here the definitions of Porphyry will be considered in reverse order beginning with the common accident in order to ascertain in which predicable or predicables 'extension' and 'comprehension' are rooted. Porphyry offers three definitions for accident.

(1) Accident is that which is present and absent without the destruction of its subject.[109]

(2) Accident is that which may be present and not present to the same thing.[110]

(3) Also that which is neither genus, nor difference, nor species, nor property, yet is always inherent in a subject.[111]

In his *Topics*, Aristotle offers a negative and affirmative definition of the predicate 'accident' in the same sentence.

Accident, again, is that which is not any of these, neither definition, nor property, nor genus; yet it is present with a thing, and is that which may possibly be present with some one and the same thing and may not be present, ...[112]

Here the predicate 'accident' presupposes a knowledge of the predicable 'accident'; therefore, if extension and comprehension are related to 'accident', it should be rather to the predicable than to the predicate.

Although several logicians have considered extension or comprehension in reference to the predicable 'accident',[113] these words could be ascribed to 'accident' only in a derivative and not a direct sense; for the law of inverse ratio (namely, the greater the comprehension, the lesser the extension, and vice versa) does not hold sway, in fact it becomes utterly ridiculous. Suppose, for example, one considers the modern medical notion of 'syndrome' in which a group of signs and symptoms occur together and characterize a certain disease. Occasionally such diseases do appear and they are not characterized by all of the signs and symptoms. Hence the law of inverse ratio does not apply to the predicable 'accident'. If one still wishes to speak of extension and comprehension of 'accident', it must be only in a derived sense inasmuch as these words are

165

employed in a more direct sense with reference to one or to several of the other predicables.

Four definitions are given by Porphyry for the predicable 'property'.

(1) For it is that which happens to some one species alone, though not to every (individual of that species), as to a man to heal, or to geometrize;

(2) that also which happens to a whole species, though not to that alone, as to man to be a biped;

(3) that again, which happens to a species alone, and to every (individual of it), and at a certain time, as to every man to become grey in old age;

(4) in the fourth place, it is that in which it concurs (to happen) to one species alone, and to every (individual of it), and always, as risibility to man; for though he does not always laugh, yet he is said to be risible, not from his always laughing, but from being naturally adapted to laugh, and this is always inherent in him, in the same way as neighing in a horse.[114]

Aristotle defines the predicate 'property' in a similar way.

Property, indeed, is that which does not show what a thing is, but is present to it alone, and reciprocates with the thing.[115]

It should be noticed that Porphyry and Aristotle do not distinguish property from accident as flowing necessarily from the essence, but rather as coextensive and convertible with its subject. By the word 'subject' is meant 'species' because when Porphyry compares property to species, he declares that "it is common then to species and property, to be reciprocally predicated of each other, ..."[116] Although property and species have an equal extension, they do not have an equal comprehension. When one speaks of the species 'man', he does not speak of 'risibility'. Yet the property 'risibility' is implied because all men have a natural capacity to laugh. In this case, the property 'risibility' belongs to man in potency. But when one says that 'man is risible', the property becomes actual. Hence the property has a greater comprehension than the species because the more actual and less potential a being, the more determined and knowable it is.

Porphyry proposes five definitions for the predicable 'difference'.

(1) Difference is that by which species exceeds genus, ...[117]

(2) Difference is that which is predicated of many things differing in species in answer to the question, of what kind a thing is, ...[118]

(3) Difference is what is naturally adapted to separate things which are under the same genus, ...[119]

(4) Difference is that by which each singular thing differs, ...[120]

(5) They however who more nicely discuss what pertains to difference, say that it is not any casual thing dividing those under the same genus, but such as contributes to the essence, and to the definition of the essence of a thing, and which is part of the thing.[121]

According to Aristotle, the difference is the determining part of the species: "every specific difference united with genus produces species; . . .".[122] Although the difference, like the property, possesses a certain extension and comprehension, the ultimate specific difference is coextensive with the species. Since the species embraces explicitly the genus and difference, it contains more comprehension than the difference inasmuch as the latter is not explicitly referred to the genus.

As a final remark on these three predicables, it is curious to observe that 'accident', 'property' and 'difference', which do not directly imply extension and comprehension, are expressed for the most part by those grammatical forms which today are called adjectives, and which the ancients referred to as adjective nouns. The time has now arrived to focus attention on those two predicables (species and genus) which are expressed by substantive nouns.[123] Porphyry points out that the word 'species' is employed in three different ways. However, only the second and third meanings are proper to logic.

(1) Species indeed is predicated of every form. . . .

(2) Still that is called species also, which is under the genus stated, ...

(3) Species is what is arranged under genus, and of which genus is predicated in reply to what a thing is: moreover, thus species is what is predicated of many things differing in number, in reply to what a things is.[124]

Before considering whether extension and comprehension belong properly to species or to genus, or whether they belong to both predicables, it may be well to present, first of all, the definitions offered by Porphyry and Aristotle concerning the genus. It was noted in Chapter II that the reality defined in the third usage of the word 'genus' in the *Isagoge* is that sort of genus proper to logic. In its third signification, Porphyry has already been seen to declare:

> Again, in another way that is denominated genus to which the species is subject, called perhaps from the similitude of these; for such a genus is a certain principle of things under it, and seems also to comprehend all the multitude under itself. As then, genus is predicated triply, the consideration by philosophers is concerning the third, which also they explain by description, when they say that genus is that which is predicated of many things differing in species, in answer to what a thing is, e. g. animal.[125]

Genus is also defined as "that which is predicated of many things differing in species, in (answer to) what a thing is; . . .".[126]

From the interpretation of these definitions, three important facts can be discerned: (1) extension belongs to genus; (2) extension belongs also to species; and (3) the extension of the genus is greater than the extension of the species.

The extension of the genus is attested by Aristotle when he asserts that genus is predicated of 'many things' which differ in species.[127] The very notion of extension implies a relation of one to many, or a 'stretching out' (extension) of one to embrace many. The preceding statement may be paraphrased by declaring that the extension of genus is a relation of genus to its proper species, or a 'stretching out' of genus to those species, and consequently to individuals.

This logical relation of one to many is prepared for by way of similitude when Porphyry defines the first non-logical use of genus as "a collection of certain things subsisting in a certain respect relatively to one thing, and to each other, . . .".[128] In this example, genus designates a relation of many to one (*multa ad unum*) inasmuch as many individuals form one group related to one head or ancestor. The notion of extension is attached to genus in this similitude because the individuals of a tribe or clan may be greater or lesser in number, and because such collection implies at least two individuals.

The extension of the genus is further exemplified by Porphyry in his second non-logical usage of the word 'genus'.

> Again, after another manner also, the principle of the generation of every one is called genus, whether from the generator or from the place in which a person is generated, ...[129]

According to this similitude, the father is recognized as a genus and is collective if he has at least two children. From the viewpoint of the children, there is the element of plurality or extension. This collective power of the father can be employed as a transition to realize that a logical genus must also have power over two or more species.

Extension is also attributed to species when Aristotle mentions that "of all then of which genus is predicated, it happens that species is also predicated, . . ."[130] In other words, inasmuch as predication implies a relation of one to many, species is 'stretched out' to the same individuals to which genus is extended.

The extension of the species is explicitly and actively asserted by Porphyry when he says, "species indeed will always be predicated of the individual, . . .",[131] and passively when he states, "the individual is comprehended in the species, . . .".[132] In the active sense, it may be said that species is 'stretched out' (extended) to one or more individuals — it is a relation of one to many. Passively, the individual or individuals are contained under the species — it is a relation of many to one.

In his *Metaphysics*, Aristotle offers additional evidence for the logical use of extension when he treats the word 'genus' under the formality of a whole;[133] because the relation of whole to parts is basically a problem of extension. As the human intellect relies on

169

the principle that the 'whole is greater than its parts', so too everything in logic is to be reduced to the principle of quantity and considered as if it were quantitative in nature.

Further, Aristotle accepts and utilizes the greater extension of the genus as a fundamental principle in the *Topics* when he says,

> The genus is always more widely extended than the species. . . . Still the element relative to all such is, that the genus is of wider extension than the species and the difference, for difference, also, is predicated of fewer things than the genus.[134]

In other citations, he reiterates the greater extension of the genus when he says, "it is necessary that species should be predicated to a less extent [than genus]";[135] "genus is the most extensively spoken of all";[136] "the genus is predicated of the species, whereas the species cannot be predicated of the genus".[137]

Porphyry likewise affirms that genus has a greater extension than the species.

> Genus indeed is always predicated of species, and all superior of inferior, but species is neither predicated of its proximate genus, nor of those superior, since it does not reciprocate.[138]

The greater extension of the genus is based on the fact that one genus is predicated of two species as well as of individuals under both species, whereas one species is only predicated of the individuals under itself.

> At least, since the superior are always predicated of the inferior, species indeed will always be predicated of the individual, but the genus both of the species and of the individual, ...[139]

The greater extension of the genus is emphasized by contrasting it with all of the other predicables.

> Now, it is the property of genus to be predicated of more things than difference, species, property, and accident are, ...[140]

Again, in an explicit manner, the greater extension of the genus is manifested by differentiating genus from species.

... but they differ, because genus indeed comprehends species, but species are comprehended by, and do not comprehend genera, for genus is predicated of more than species.[141]

Finally, Porphyry speaks of genus possessing a greater extension because "genera exceed, from comprehending the species which are under them, . . .".[142]

Ammonius emphasizes the greater power of the genus when he insists that while the species comprehends or contains individuals, the genus comprehends both species and individuals.[143] Consequently, genus is more extensive than the species and individuals embraced by it, whereas species is only more extensive than the individuals it contains.

It may be concluded that while extension is ascribed to both species and genus, it belongs in the very first instance to the predicable 'genus' which possesses the greater power to comprehend or to contain more things under it, and it then belongs to the predicable 'species' inasmuch as the species participates in the unifying power of the genus.

Although the references to comprehension are found less frequently in the logical texts of Porphyry and Aristotle, still the few that are found suffice to show that comprehension belongs to species and genus. Porphyry speaks about comprehension when he explains how the species exceeds or surpasses the genus: "Difference is that by which species exceeds genus. . . ."[144] In order to associate the word 'exceeds' in the preceding quotation with the notion of comprehension, one must remember that the word 'comprehension' is basically analogical: it can mean 'what is grasped' or 'how many are grasped'. In modern manuals on logic, the word 'comprehension' has been limited to one signification, and that one meaning becomes clear by the use of the word 'exceed'.

The action of grasping or seizing by the mind as an instrument is further clarified when Porphyry speaks of the collective power of the genus (in the sense of how many species are grasped, or seized, or comprehended) and the collective power of the species (in the sense of what is grasped, or seized, or comprehended): "for species is collective of the many into one nature, and genus yet more so. . . ."[145]

Aristotle links comprehension to both genus and species when

171

he talks about the species 'partaking' or 'participating' more intensely in a thing than the genus.

> The definition of partaking, is to receive the definition of what is participated. Now it is evident that species partake of genera, but not genera of species, since the species accepts the definition of genus, but not genus that of the species.[146]

In this case, the species comprehends or grasps more of the whatness or nature of a thing inasmuch as it contains not only the more remote differences (which qualify the nature of a thing) which the genus contains, but the species also contains the specific difference which constitutes its very nature. For example, the genus 'animal' and the species 'man' contain the difference 'sentient', 'living', and 'material', but only the species 'man' contains the specific difference 'rational'. Hence, as it has been said before, the species participates more intensely in a thing than the genus, that is, it has a greater comprehension than the genus because it grasps or seizes more of the whatness or nature of a thing.

Comprehension is also ascribed to genus and species by the use of the expression 'determinate qualification' (ἀφορισμόν).

> The determinate qualification covers a larger field in the case of the genus than in that of the species: he who uses the word 'animal' is herein using a word of wider extension than he who uses the word 'man'.[147]

Thus it seems doctrinally sound to say in English that both genus and species have comprehension as well as extension. And it also seems safe to declare that genus has greater extension while species possesses greater comprehension. Extension and comprehension are intrinsic to the definitions of genus and species. They can only be manifested and are not properties to be proved by a *propter quid* demonstration.

5. General Summary of Chapter III.

It would have been difficult to arrive at any decisive conclusions concerning the problem of extension and comprehension in the realm of logic if one neglected to explore the various significations of these two words in other domains. An examination of the word 'extension' in a non-logical setting reveals four major variations of meaning whereby a transition is made from the activity of the stretching out of a material object or the object stretched out, to the agent of the action stretching himself out with reference to local motion, to the stretching out of human emotions and appetites, and ultimately to the capacity of a knowing being to stretch out toward a certain number of knowable things. A threefold transition occurs with the word 'comprehension' when it is shown how the word can vary in meaning from the physical activity of grasping a material object, to the activity of the emotions grasping objects, to the activity of the knowing powers, whether sensible or intellectual, grasping knowable objects.

There is certainly a valid usage for these two words in psychology because all knowledge can be spoken of in terms of extension and comprehension. In the theory of knowledge, knowing beings differ from non-knowing beings by virtue of a certain amplitude or extension. Every sense power (v.g., sight, hearing, imagination, memory, etc.) is by its operation extended to an object and comprehends an object. Nevertheless, in psychology, extension and comprehension pertain to acts of knowledge and do not name second intentions or relations which are proper to logic. For that reason, one is obliged to reject as dangerous the expression 'extension and comprehension of concepts' frequently found in modern logic textbooks.

To ascertain precisely where the distinction between extension and comprehension can be localized in logic, one must be familiar with the purpose and divisions of logic. The end of logic is science which embraces both the incomplex and complex unknown. Perfect attainment of such end presupposes a threefold operation of man's reason. Although extension and comprehension are found in the third operation of reason, they are used there only derivatively. Hence certain modern logicians deserve to be chided when they speak of the 'extension and comprehension of terms' inasmuch as the word 'term' signifies a part of the third operation.

Extension and comprehension also belong to the second operation of reason in a derivative sense. When some modern logicians speak of a judgment of extension whereby the subject is in the predicate, and a judgment of comprehension whereby the predicate is in the subject, they are naming certain results or effects whose cause is in the first operation of the mind. Further, such a position renders absurd the division of logic into one of extension and one of comprehension, a division which would necessitate two logics for every enunciation. This dichotomy would also destroy the demonstrative syllogism which contains extension as well as comprehension.

In the first operation of the mind, one finds two modes of predicating: a passive mode designated by the word 'predicament' and an active mode known by the word 'predicable'. Although some logicians refer to extension as an external quantity and comprehension as an internal 'quantity' still these two words cannot be ascribed to the predicament 'quantity' because such usage would restrict their meaning to the univocal meaning of dimensive quantity and would make no allowance for their analogical usage with reference to virtual quantity. Furthermore, extension and comprehension cannot belong to the predicament 'substance' because the extension of substance to two or more species is not due to its nature as a predicament, but rather to the predicables which organize it. Therefore, extension and comprehension are not immediate properties of the predicaments or passive modes of predication; instead, they are properties of the predicables or active modes of predicating.

Some logicians have considered extension and comprehension in reference to the predicable 'accident'. They belong to that predicable solely in a derivative and not direct sense because the law of inverse ratio (namely, the greater the comprehension, the lesser the extension) does not always hold true in such cases. Nor do extension and comprehension belong properly to the predicable 'property' because property and species are equal in extension but unequal in comprehension. Finally, extension and comprehension do not belong directly to the predicable 'difference' since the difference has less comprehension than the species.

Ample evidence is found in the texts of Aristotle and Porphyry to indicate that extension belongs, first of all, to the predicable 'genus' which possesses the greater power to contain more things under it, and, secondly, to the species inasmuch as the species participates in the unifying power of the genus. Those same texts also

174

reveal that while both genus and species possess comprehension as well as extension, species has the greater comprehension and genus the greater extension.

A better understanding of this problem of extension and comprehension will be achieved if the student of logic is cognizant of two important facts: (1) Extension and comprehension imply a plurality. When anything is extended (stretched out), it is extended to several or many things. And when anything comprehends (grasps completely), it can likewise comprehend several or many things. (2) The words 'extension' and 'comprehension' are analogical in meaning. Oftentimes the same word designates different aspects of the same reality. For example, comprehension may sometimes be used to signify the modern notion of extension, namely, the number of things grasped, or it may simply signify what kind of things are grasped. Such usage permits us to conclude that comprehension is more analogical in meaning than extension.

When extension and comprehension are applied to genus, it may be said that genus offers a clear (comprehensive) and more extended (extension) knowledge; when those same words are applied to species, it may be asserted that species offers a clearer (more comprehensive) and less extended (extension) knowledge. In other words, genus has the greater extension and species the greater comprehension.

EPILOGUE

If a student will take the time to examine many of the modern textbooks on logic, he will discover that a prominent place, and occasionally an entire chapter, is given to the distinction between extension and comprehension. Frequently this doctrine is introduced in the manuals before the predicables are ever considered, and it is presented in such a manner that the reader would never suspect that extension and comprehension belong to the predicables of genus and species.[1]

Because the discussion of extension and comprehension is badly placed in logical treatises, there is a tendency to magnify the importance of this distinction out of proportion to its real value. Thus Jevons claims, "to anyone desirous of acquiring a thorough command of logical science, nothing is so important as a careful study of the intensive or comprehensive meaning of terms, propositions, and syllogisms".[2] Jolivet also considers the distinction of capital importance for formal logic.[3] And Bachhuber believes that comprehension and extension pervade the whole of logic to such an extent that a thorough and correct understanding of them is imperative if one wishes to establish a solid foundation for logic.[4]

It may be conceded that extension and comprehension are significant, but it must be emphasized that extension and comprehension are important only inasmuch as implied in the very definitions of the predicables. Any logical treatise which includes in its contents a section on extension and comprehension, and yet at the same time excludes the predicables, is badly oriented because extension and comprehension present only two ways in which a predicate may be said of a subject, whereas the predicables present five different modes of predication.

Modern logicians also seem to overlook other important facts: the rules of definition are derived from an understanding of the

177

genus and species. The definition of the genus, for example. is the first proper principle of logic. It is of the utmost necessity to manifest this first principle adequately and properly. But such a task cannot be accomplished unless a study of the predicables is made at the beginning of logic. Many of the errors in logic textbooks could be avoided if this procedure were followed. The old adage certainly rings true in this instance: *"parvum quantitate, magnum virtute"*. Applied here, the expression means that if a small error is made in the beginning, it will grow to huge proportions in the end. Such a phenomenon was amply manifested in the historical part of this study where it was seen how the moderns rejected the fixity of meaning imposed on extension and comprehension by the ancients, and introduced not only new words but also new meanings for the old words.

Therefore, the most fitting way to teach logic seems to imply beginnings with a study of the predicables. Once those active modes of predication have been mastered, the student will be better prepared to understand correctly the doctrine of extension and comprehension in logic. Furthermore, when logic is taught it must not be forgotten that these two words, namely, 'extension' and 'comprehension', should be understood analogically with reference to quantity. In fact all relations of reason are named analogically from quantity.

APPENDIX I

GRAMMATICAL SOURCES

Steele differentiates between the distinct and confused signification of a name. He designates the latter meaning by the word 'connotation'.

> But the Reason, that renders a Name uncapable of subsist-
> ing by itself, is when, besides its distinct Signification, it has
> another more confused, which we call the CONNOTATION
> of a Thing, to which that agrees, which is meant by the distinct
> Signification. Thus the distinct Signification of *Red*, is *Redness*,
> but it signifies the Subject of that Redness, confus'dly, which
> makes it not capable of Subsisting by itself in Discourse, be-
> cause we must express, or understand the word which signifies
> the Subject. As, therefore, that *Connotation* makes the *Ad-
> jective*, or *Quality*, so when that is taken away from Words,
> which signify Accidents, they become *Substantives* or *Names*.
> As from *Colour'd, Colour;* from *Red, Redness;* . . . .[1]

It will be observed that James Mill also designates as connotation
what the term or name signifies indirectly.

The distinction of extension and comprehension as found in the
Port Royal Logic did not only appear in most of the subsequent
works on logic, but it was also included in some grammar books.
When the French grammarian Sicard discusses the parts of speech,
he declares that articles determine extension while adjectives affect
comprehension.

> The *extension* of a word is the place that it occupies for
> the mind which considers it; the *comprehension* is the totality
> of partial ideas which constitute it. Thus, the words which are
> called articles, and of which I will treat in the following chapter,
> determine *extension;* and the adjectives, of which it is a ques-

179

tion here, affect the *comprehension;* and they affect it by adding to the name one or several secondary ideas which form part of the total nature of the object stated by the name.[2]

It is quite easy to understand why articles are associated with extension, while adjectives are related to comprehension. For example, the word 'house' signifies a quantity of complex characteristics. This quantity designates a class of objects each of which is a house. In this instance, the word 'house' has unlimited and indefinite extension. But as soon as one adds the article 'the' to the word 'house', the application or extension of 'house' is now limited. Likewise, if one adds adjectives such as 'colonial', 'two-story', and 'brick' to the word 'house', the comprehension of the word is affected as already mentioned by R. A. Sicard.

MacKaye has recourse to the words 'connotation' and 'denotation' when he discusses the internal and external quantities of a species and a genus.

A species always has a larger connotation than its genus; that is, the qualities which are signified by its name are more numerous, because they include all those of the genus plus those of the difference. Fish have all the characteristics of vertebrates in general plus the characteristic of breathing by means of gills. The denotation of the species, however, is smaller than that of the genus, since the number of specimens include only part of the number included in the genus. There are fewer fish than vertebrates in general.[3]

It is worth noting how a modern French grammarian speaks of comprehension and extension. Grevisse says that "the 'comprehension' of the idea expressed by the name is the number of notes more or less great which comprise this idea. Its 'extension', or the 'extent' of the signification of the name, is the number of beings more or less great to which the idea can be applied."[4] He observes that an increase in the comprehension of an idea leads to a diminution of its extension, and vice versa.

Harris and Jarrett employ the words 'denotation', 'connotation' and 'comprehension' when they consider the applications of words and their meanings.

180

(1) The word "eraser" means or refers to any member of the class of erasers; (2) The word "eraser" means an instrument for obliterating marks. (1) is denotation. (2) is connotation. A word *denotes* an object or a set of objects. "Jane" denotes that girl. . . . A word *connotes* a complex of properties or qualities. "Vertebrate" connotes animal-with-a-backbone. . . . The entire set of properties which is possessed in common by the whole denotation of a term has been called the *comprehension* of that term.[5]

APPENDIX II

Different Terminology and Meanings studied in this Treatise

PART I: CHAPTER I

Authors:	*Terminology*:	*Meaning*:
1. Port Royalists:	Extension of an idea:	All subjects to which the idea applies (it is not mentioned whether the subjects are fictional as well as real).
	Comprehension of an idea:	All essential and proper attributes.
2. John Ozell:	Extent:	Cf. Port Royalists.
	Comprehension:	Cf. Port Royalists.
3. Pierre Nicole:	Cf. Port Royalists.	Cf. Port Royalists.
4. Richard Crakanthorpe:	Genus and Species:	Implicit references to extension are contained in his definitions of genus and species.
5. John Wallis:	*Amplior, latior, minimae amplitudinis, omnium amplissimum*:	Genus is wider than species.
6. John Bapt. Du Hamel:	*Species subjicibilis* and *species praedicabilis*:	Extension of genus to species and of species to individuals.
7. John Norris:	Inlargement, extensive, contains under it, contains in it:	Extension of thought; inferior actually contains more; the superior represents more.

8. Johannes Regius:	Genus and Species:	Genus is in the species; genus is wider than the species.
9. Joshua Oldfield:	Extension: Comprehension:	Kinds, sorts and individuals. Attributes, marks or characteristics.
10. V. Cl. Edmundus Purchotius:	Extension: Comprehension:	Subjects to which an idea can be proper. Attributes without which the idea of a thing cannot stand.
11. Jean Pierre de Crousaz:	Genus: Species:	Genus contains under it the species. Species contains in it attributes.
12. Isaac Watts:	Extension of an idea: Comprehension of an idea:	Application of an idea to real species and individuals. Essential modes and properties of an idea.
13. William Brattle:	Genus and Species:	Genus is predicated of several things specifically different; species is predicated of several things numerically different.
14. Peter Van Musschembroek:	Species:	Formation of a universal idea from common attributes.
15. Gottfried Wilhelm Leibniz:	Extension: Comprehend and Intension:	Refers to individuals. Refers to ideas or forms.
16. Francis Hutcheson:	Logical whole or Extension: Metaphysical whole or Comprehension:	Enumeration of several things contained in a common idea or name. Simple ideas joined in an ensemble.
17. Dominicus Angeloni:	Extension Comprehension:	Aggregate of all individual subjects to which the idea belongs. Aggregate of all attributes contained in an idea.

18. Alexander G. Baumgarten:	*Umfang*: *Inhalt*:	Extension of concepts. Comprehension of concepts.
19. Unknown author of the 18th century:	Including, agreeing, comprehending:	Extension of genus to species and of species to individuals.
20. Antonio Genovesi:	Species comprehends: Genera comprehend:	Embraces common things in individuals. Embrace common things in species.
21. William Best:	Extension of a term: Comprehension of a term:	Aggregate of all individuals which belong to a name. Aggregate of all simple ideas which constitute a complex idea.
22. Immanuel Kant:	Extent of cognition or extensive quantity: Intent of cognition or intensive quantity:	Number and variety of the contents of a cognition; embraces individual representations. Cognition is treated as a principle instead of a quantity.
23. John Andrews:	Extension: Comprehension:	Application of the universal idea to genera, species and individuals. Several parts of the compound idea.
24. William Duncan:	Extension: Comprehension:	Application of a universal idea to individuals. Number of parts and properties of an idea.
25. Richard Kirwan:	Denotation: Comprehension:	Refers to things. Refers to the obvious, less obvious and relative properties of a word.
26. Thomas Reid:	Predicables:	His explanation is contrary to tradition.

27. Georg W. F. Hegel:	Quantity:	Applies to spiritual facts (concepts).
28. Levi Hedge:	Extension of a term: Comprehension of a term:	Number of individual subjects to which a term is applied. Aggregate of all known properties of a thing or class of things.
29. Sir William Hamilton:	Extensive quantity, (breadth, *platos*, extension, circuit, *ambitus*, domain, sphere): Intensive quantity (depth, *bathos*, comprehension, *complexus*):	Number of classified concepts or realities contained under a concept. Number of constituent characters contained in a concept.
30. Le Baron de Reiffenberg:	Extension (*omnis*): Comprehension (*totus*):	Number of individuals to which an idea is proper. Sum total of all the particular ideas which compose an idea.
31. S. E. Parker:	Extension of a term: Comprehension of a term:	Number of species into which a genus, or number of individuals into which a species is divided. Aggregate of all known properties of a genus, species, or class.
32. Thomas Solly:	Sphere of a conception: Matter of a conception:	Things which are contained under a conception. Various representations contained in a conception.
33. J. S. Mills:	Denotation: Connotation:	Subjects of which a term can be predicated. Character or attribute possessed by a subject.
34. M. Rattier:	Extension of the idea: Comprehension of the idea:	Refers to classes formed from a group of species or a group of individuals. Ensemble of parts of a complex.

35. William Thomson:	Extension:	Capacity of a conception; vague and general conception.
	Intension:	Narrower and more definite conception.
36. *Marino De Boylesne:	Extensive:	Idea which represents simultaneously all things to which any property belongs.
	Comprehensive:	Idea which considers all the properties of a thing.
37. William Barron:	Genus:	Contains fewer properties.
	Species:	Contains its own properties as well as those of the genus.
38. Augustus De Morgan:	Scope:	Extension of classes.
	Force:	Comprehension of real external attributes.
39. Henry Longueville Mansel:	Generalization:	Concept contains subordinate notions.
	Specification:	Concept contains a plurality of attributes.
40. John Leechman:	Extension of a term:	Number of individuals of which a term is predicated.
	Comprehension of a term:	Union of simple ideas which constitute what the term denotes.
41. Thomas Shedden:	Extension (Denotation):	Number of individuals or real external objects to which the comprehension of a general name applies.
	Comprehension (Connotation):	Sum of real external attributes possessed by a general name.
42. *Salvator Tongiorgi:	Extension of an idea:	Width or amplitude of the idea in representing individuals.
	Comprehension of an idea:	Combination of notes which constitute the idea.

*Indicates an author consulted but not cited in this study.

187

43. Francis Bowen:	Quantity of Extension:	Number of objects (reduced in thought to a class or species) which possess all marks in common.
	Quantity of Intension:	Number of marks inhering in one object or thing.
44. S. H. Emmens:	Extension of a term:	Number of objects predicated of the term of intension.
	Intension of a term:	Marks contained by the subject.
45. Henry N. Day:	External quantity or extension:	Objects contained under a concept.
	Internal quantity or comprehension:	Attributes contained in a concept.
46. W. Stanley Jevons:	Extent of meaning of a term:	Number of objects denoted.
	Intent of meaning:	Embraces the whole infinite series of qualities and circumstances which a thing possesses.
47. *James M. Willcox:	Genus is broader than species and has a greater extension of numbers:	Extension is said of numbers of individuals.
	Species is narrower than genus and more complex in comprehension:	Comprehension is said of numbers of attributes.
48. P. Venceslao Pieralisi:	Extension, width, or sphere of an idea:	Denotes the number of individuals represented by an idea.
	Comprehension of an idea:	Indicates the number of simple notes which concur to constitute its being.
49. Joseph Prisco:	Extension of a concept:	Totality of subjects which a concept contains under itself.
	Comprehension of a concept:	Totality of elements which a concept contains in itself.

*Indicates an author consulted but not cited in this study.

188

50. Cajetano Sanseverino:	Extension, circuit, sphere of a notion: Comprehension of a notion:	Applies to species and individuals. Embraces the *differentia*.
51. J. H. Gilmore:	Species is in the genus: Genus is in the species:	Conceptual existence. Actual existence.
52. R. P. Ludovicus Jouin:	Extension: Comprehension:	Multitude of objects or individuals of which the idea can be predicated. Collection of properties embraced by the universal idea.
53. Alexander Bain:	Extension or Denotation: Comprehension or Connotation:	Individuals to which the term applies. Community of attributes or points of agreement making up the definition of a term.
54. Noah K. Davis:	Extension: Intension:	Class. Mark.
55. F. Thomas Maria Zigliara:	Extension: Comprehension:	More powerful in a universal idea. More powerful in the inferiors of a universal idea.
56. F. H. Bradley:	Extension: Intension:	Objects to which the meaning is applicable. Idea in its content.
57. *P. F. A. Jaffre:	Extension of an idea: Comprehension of an idea:	Number of individuals which the idea includes. Number of essential properties which the idea represents.
58. Bernard Bosanquet:	Extension or Denotation of a concept: Intension or Connotation of a concept:	Designates individual things. Designates relations.

*Indicates an author consulted but not cited in this study.

189

59. John Neville Keynes:	Extension (or Application) of a name:	Objects of which a name can be predicated.
	Intension (or Implication) of a name:	Properties which can be predicated of a name.
	A. Conventional Intension or Connotation:	Embraces all qualities essential to a name.
	B. Subjective Intension:	May include some nonessential qualities of a name.
	C. Objective Intension or Comprehension:	Includes all the qualities of conventional and subjective intension and often many others.
	D. Denotation or Objective Extension:	Excludes all fictitious or conceptual beings.
60. Jno. J. Tigert:	Extension:	Number of individuals possessing marks.
	Intension:	Sum total of marks or properties which an object must possess for admission to a given class.
61. *P. Joseph Mendive:	Extension of a concept:	Number of individuals.
	Comprehension of a concept:	Number of notes contained in a concept.
62. John Veitch:	*Umfang* (Extension, Compass, or Breadth):	Objects or classes denoted by a concept.
	Inhalt (Comprehension, Meaning, or Content):	Attributes of a concept.
63. Charles Coppens:	Extension:	Total number of individuals to which an idea applies.
	Comprehension:	Total signification or all the notes contained in an idea.

*Indicates an author consulted but not cited in this study.

64. Herman Lotze:	Extension (*Ambitus*):	Species contained under the genus.
	Content (*Materia*):	Marks essential to the genus contained in the species.
65. *A. Dupeyrat:	*Ambitus*:	Collection of subjects to which a notion is extended.
	Complexus:	Sum total of attributes required to constitute the thing by a notion.
66. Richard F. Clarke:	Whole of Extension:	Class containing a number of smaller classes.
	Whole of Comprehension:	Idea comprising a number of simpler ideas.
67. P. Joannes Josephus Urraburu:	Extension of an idea:	Multitude of subjects of which any idea can be enunciated.
	Comprehension of an idea:	Combination of distinguishing marks.
68. James H. Hyslop:	Extension:	Quantitative power of terms. It may refer to individuals or class-wholes, whether substantive or attributive, real or conceptual.
	Intension:	Qualitative power of terms. It may refer to a single quality or group of qualities in an individual-whole, whether substantive or attributive, real or conceptual.
69. Alfred Sidgwick:	Denotation of a name:	Things or cases to which a name is intended to be applied.
	Connotation of a name:	Conditions under which a name is intended to be applicable.
70. *J. B. Jaccoud:	Extension:	Individual objects.
	Comprehension:	Complexus of notes which the idea contains.
71. William Minto:	Denotation, Extension, or Scope of a name:	Individuals or groups of individuals.

*Indicates an author consulted but not cited in this study.

191

	Connotation, Intension, Comprehension, or Ground of a name:	Attributes or groups of attributes.
72. *George L. Fonsegrive:	Extension of a concept:	Individual beings to be attributed or to which a concept can be ascribed.
	Comprehension of a concept:	Interior determinations of a concept.
73. Brother Louis of Poissy:	Extension of a universal term:	Number of beings to which a term applies.
	Comprehension of a universal term:	Sum of the elements which a term contains.
74. Élie Blanc:	Extension:	Genus is extended to more individuals than the species.
	Comprehension:	Genus comprehends less notes than the species.
75. *L'Abbé L. Du Roussaux:	Extension, Quantity, or Scope of a concept:	Subjects to which a concept can belong.
	Comprehension, Quality, or Meaning of a concept:	Notes which an object expresses.
76. Thomas Fowler:	Denotation:	A term designates individuals or groups of individuals.
	Connotation:	A term refers to attributes in a secondary manner.
77. Dr. Christoph Sigwart:	Extension of a concept:	Sum total of lower concepts which are subordinated to it.
	Comprehension:	Includes all necessary and accidental attributes of a name.
78. *Vincentius Remer:	Extension of a term:	Number of subjects to which a term is extended.
	Comprehension:	Complexus of notes with which the notion itself is composed.

*Indicates an author consulted but not cited in this study.

79. *E. Gille:	Extension of an idea:	Number of beings or objects to which the idea is applied.
	Comprehension of an idea:	Elements which compose an idea.
80. *R. P. Chabin:	Extension of a term:	Number of individuals to which it is applied.
	Comprehension of a term:	Ensemble of properties which it expresses.
81. George H. Smith:	Meaning of a term:	Embraces both denotation (extension) and connotation.
	Connotation:	Synonymous with intension.
82. John Rickaby:	Extension:	Predicate is represented as containing the subject.
	Intension:	Subject is viewed as containing the predicate.
83. D. Mercier:	Extension of a concept:	Applied to the logical whole.
	Intension of a concept:	Applied to the metaphysical whole.
84. Élie Rabier:	Extension of an idea:	Circumscription or sphere of application of a concept.
	Comprehension of an idea:	Proper matter of the concept; sum total of characters which the idea includes.
85. Herbert Austin Aikins:	Connotative terms:	Point out an object of thought and describe it.
	Non-Connotative terms:	Do not point out an object of thought or describe it.
	Denotation:	Identified with extension.
	Connotation:	Identified with intension.
86. John G. Hibben:	Extension and Intension:	Applied to concepts.
	Denotation and Connotation:	Applied to terms.

*Indicates an author consulted but not cited in this study.

193

87. *A. Farges and   Extension: Sum total of individuals to
    D. Barbedette: which the idea is applied.
                  Comprehension: Designates the sum total of notes
                      by which the idea exists.

88. John Venn: Denotation: Exists in reality and is perceived
                      directly.
                  Connotation: Exists in the mind and is per-
                      ceived indirectly.

89. W. R. Boyce   Intension: Equal to connotation plus de-
    Gibson: notation.
                  Denotation: Differentiation of meaning to be
                      interpreted disjunctively.
                  Extension: Application of meaning to in-
                      dividual objects to be interpreted
                      conjunctively.

90. John Dewey: Extension: Groups of particulars identified
                      and distinguished.
                  Intension: Meaning as a principle of
                      identifying particulars.

91. *G. H. Luquet: Extension of a   Number of individual objects to
                  term: which a term can be attributed.
                  Comprehension   Total characters which consti-
                  of an idea: tute its essence.

92. Nicolaus   Extension: Number of things or subjects to
    Monaco: which a term can be applied.
                  Comprehension: Sum total of perfections or notes
                      to which the term refers.

93. William   Extension: Term is viewed in a horizontal
    Turner: position and applied to individ-
                      uals.
                  Comprehension: Term is viewed vertically to
                      include attributes or qualities.

94. Robert   Denotation and   According to him, this distinc-
    Adamson: Connotation: tion is a grammatical and not a
                      logical problem.

*Indicates an author consulted but not cited in this study.

95. L'Abbé Levesque:	Extension:	Associated with genus and species.
	Comprehension:	Associated with the difference, property and accident.
96. *Michaele de Maria:	Extension of a term:	Number of subjects to which a term can be predicated.
	Comprehension:	Concept signified by the term.
97. *Dr. Seb. Reinstadler:	Extension of an idea:	Sum total of beings which any idea can manifest.
	Comprehension of an idea:	Sum total of notes by which an idea exists.
98. L'Abbé Arthur Robert:	Extension of an idea:	Embraces all present, past and future objects designated by the idea.
	Comprehension of an idea:	Ensemble of elements which comprises an idea.
99. Tilmanus Pesch:	Circuit or Extension of a concept:	Number of subjects to which some concept can be applied.
	Ensemble or Comprehension of a concept:	Collection of notes which the concept of a thing contains.
100. C. Willems:	Extension:	Identified with the material object of cognition and proper to logic.
	Comprehension:	Identified with the formal object of cognition and proper to ontology.
101. H. W. B. Joseph:	Extension:	Variety of kinds over which the predication of a term may extend; or a variety of species in which a common character is exhibited.
	Intension of a term:	What we intend or mean by a term when predicating it of any subject; or a common character exhibited in this variety.

*Indicates an author consulted but not cited in this study.

		Denotation:	Applied to individuals (unlike extension which is applied to species).
102.	R. W. Sellars:	Meaning of a term:	Includes both its denotation and its connotation.
103.	Attilius Munzi:	Extension:	All that which can perform the function of subject or predicate in any proposition.
		Comprehension of a term:	Intelligibility contained in that in which a proposition is resolved.
104.	Edmond Goblot:	Extension or Denotation of a term:	Number of individuals contained in the genus.
		Comprehension or Connotation of a term:	Number of qualities common to the individuals of a genus; embraces all the concepts contained in a particular generic or specific concept.
105.	*Professors of Louvain University:	Extension of an idea:	Sphere of applicability.
		Comprehension of an idea:	Content of characters or notes which analysis can discover.
106.	R. P. Seb. Uccello:	Extension of an idea:	As extrinsic to the idea, it is the sum total of beings which can be manifested by the idea.
		Comprehension of an idea:	As intrinsic to the idea, it is the ensemble of notes of which any idea is composed.
107	*P. F. Zachariam Van De Woestyne:	Extension of an idea:	Combination of inferiors in regard to what an idea is constituted.
		Comprehension of an idea:	Combination of notes which an idea embraces.
108.	*Stanislaus A. Lortie:	Extension of an idea:	Collection of individuals to which the idea belongs.
		Comprehension of an idea:	Collection of notes of an idea.

*Indicates an author consulted but not cited in this study.

196

109. *Josephus Donat:	Extension:	*Complexio* of things to which the sum total of notes belongs.
	Comprehension:	Sum total of notes which the idea manifests.
110. W. E. Johnson:	Extension:	Stands for a set of substantives (more general than denotation).
	Intension:	Stands for a set of adjectives (more general than connotation).
111. Charles Kay Ogden and I. A. Richards:	Denotation:	Some reference which a word symbolizes.
	Connotation:	Selection of properties or adjectives.
112. George Hayward Joyce:	Extension of a term:	Individuals to which a term is applicable.
	Comprehension or Intension:	Characteristics or attributes which are expressed by a common concept.
	Denotation:	Refers to real objects expressed by concepts.
	Connotation:	Concerns a thing as known and not in its objective reality.
113. H. E. Cunningham:	Denotation or Extension:	Reference to things.
	Connotation or Intension:	Reference to attributes or qualities.
114. John J. Toohey:	Extension of an idea:	Sum total of individuals of which the idea can be predicated.
	Comprehension of an idea:	Sum total of notes which the idea explicitly represents in the object.
	Implicit Comprehension:	Sum total of notes determined by an analysis of the formal object of the idea.
115. Pio De Mandato:	Extension or *Amplitudo* of a term:	The width of a term in relation to those things concerning which it can be predicated.

*Indicates an author consulted but not cited in this study.

197

	Comprehension of a term:	Sum total of notes to which the term refers concerning the thing signified.
116. Carolus Frick:	Extension, *Ambitus,* or *Amplitudo:*	Capacity of an idea representing several or fewer objects.
	Comprehension:	Sum total of notes which are expressed by the subjective idea and constitute the objective idea.
117. Matthew Thompson McClure:	Extension:	'Meaning' inasmuch as it has an extrinsic reference.
118. Thomas Crumley:	Application of a term:	The things that possess common qualities.
	Implication of a term:	Common qualities that form an essence.
119. James Edwin Creighton and Harold R. Smart:	Refer:	Names or identifies things.
	Describe:	Represents qualities or attributes belonging to things.
120. Mortimer J. Adler:	Denotative meanings of words:	Names which refer to objects.
	Connotative meanings of words:	Notational entities.
121. *R. P. Dubois:	Extension of a concept:	Number of things which the concept can represent.
	Comprehension of a concept:	Complex of notes which the concept represents intentionally concerning any thing.
122. Robert Latta and Alexander Macbeath:	Denotation:	Reference of term to one or more systems of qualities each considered as a unity.

*Indicates an author consulted but not cited in this study.

198

	Connotation:	Reference of a term to a system of qualities related to one another so as to form a unity.
123. *Joseph Stanghetti:	Extension:	Complexus of subjects to which the term can be applied.
	Comprehension:	Complexus of notes which are signified by any term.
124. Joseph Gredt:	Extension:	Sum total of all objects whose image is the concept.
	Comprehension:	Sum total of notes which constitute a concept.
125. W. H. Forbes and Dennis Hird:	Extension or Denotation:	Refers to genus and species considered as classes.
	Intension or Connotation:	Refers to genus and species considered as attributes of classes.
126. Federigo Enriques:	Comprehension or Connotation:	Contains the real meaning of a concept.
127. Émile Meyerson:	One term should be included in another as in a whole:	Extension.
	The other term should be predicated of all of the first:	Intension.
128. Gottlob Frege:	Indication or Denotation:	Opposed to meaning as something outside the mind is opposed to something inside the mind; it is a term designating an object existing independently of thought.
	Connotation:	Imagery or interpretation which each person brings to a word.
129. Ralph M. Eaton:	Extension or Denotation:	Instances of a universal in the actual world.
	Intension or Connotation:	Universal taken in abstraction from its instances.

*Indicates an author consulted but not cited in this study.

130. Charles Gray Shaw:	Extension of a concept:	Assortment of nouns.
	Intension of a concept:	Variety of adjectives.
	Denotative term:	Exemplification of an idea in individual things.
	Connotative term:	Expresses the essence of an idea.
131. Jacques Maritain:	Extension of a concept:	Breadth of a concept in relation to the individuals and objective concepts in which it is realized.
	Comprehension of a concept:	Breadth of a concept in relation to its characteristic notes (includes essential notes and also properties).
132. Henricus Grenier, Regis Jolivet, and J. B. Bouvier:	Extension of a concept:	Collection of individuals and objects in general to which a universal concept belongs.
	Comprehension of a concept:	Collection of notes which constitute the concept.
133. F. Gonseth:	Cf. Port Royalists:	Cf. Port Royalists.
134. D. Luther Evans and Walter S. Gamertsfelder:	Denotation or Extension:	Refers to the thingness or individuality which everything that can be named must have.
	Connotation or Intension:	Refers to the descriptive features and constituent elements of a thing, idea, or a person.
135. *Émile Filion:	Extension:	Collection of objects to which a concept can be applied.
	Comprehension:	Collection of more simple concepts or notes.
136. Peter Coffey:	Comprehension:	Includes more than connotation: it includes all the attributes which are common to all members of a class.

*Indicates an author consulted but not cited in this study.

200

	Connotation:	Comprises only those qualities essential to a name.
137. Henry Bradford Smith:	Extension, Extent, Breadth, or Denotation:	Individual things to which a term applies.
	Intension, Intent, Depth, or Connotation:	Qualities that serve to define the term.
138. Albert M. Frye and Albert W. Levi:	Psychological Connotation:	Signifies what we think of upon hearing any word.
	Logical Connotation:	Signifies the idea or quality represented by the name.
139. Celestine N. Bittle:	Extension of an idea:	Sum total of all individuals and groups (actual and imaginary) to which an idea can be applied.
	Comprehension of an idea:	Sum total of all the attributes or thought-elements which constitute the idea.
140. L. Susan Stebbing:	Extension:	Refers to classes and not individuals.
	Denotation:	Membership of the classes, not the classes.
	Connotation of a term or Conventional Intension:	Characteristics which anything must have if the term can be correctly applied to it.
141. Alburey Castell:	Extension:	Applies to things.
	Intension:	Applies to properties possessed by those things.
142. Max Black:	Denotation:	Includes all the individuals which exist or have existed.
	Connotation:	Includes all those properties which an individual must possess in order to be what it is.
143. Morris R. Cohen and Ernest Nagel:	Denotation or Extension of the term:	Class of objects.

	Connotation or Intension of the term:	Set of attributes which determine the objects.
144. Raymond J. McCall:	Extension of an idea:	Sum of real (actual and possible) things to which an essence can be applied.
	Comprehension of an idea:	Sum total of notes which constitute the essence.
145. Sylvester J. Hartman:	Essential Comprehension of a universal concept:	Includes all the essential notes of the corresponding class of objects.
	Distinctive Comprehension of a universal concept:	Includes the logically proximate genus and the properties of the pertinent class of objects.
	Complete Comprehension of a universal concept:	Includes the proximate genus, the specific difference, and the properties of the class of objects represented.
	Comprehension of a singular concept:	Includes all the notes of one identified object.
	Extension of a universal concept:	Class of objects which it represents.
146. Thomas Gilby:	Extension, Area Range, Span, or Sweep of an idea:	Number of objects contained.
	Comprehension, Intensity, Force, Depth, Fullness, or Penetration of an idea:	Depends on the ability of an idea to express special characteristics as well as general features.
147. Paul Henle et al.:	Extension:	Meaning applied to the actual world.
	Intension:	Meaning independent of the extensional property of the truth or falsity of any proposition.

148. Francis H. Parker and Henry B. Veatch:	Extension of a concept: Comprehension of a concept:	Includes only possibilities and not actualities. A certain 'what' or essence.
149. Henry W. Johnstone, Jr.:	Extension: Intension:	Embraces all class-objects. Comprises meaningful qualities.
150. Kenneth F. Dougherty:	Extension or Denotation of a concept: Comprehension of a concept:	Individuals to which a concept applies. Sum of the intelligible notes.
151. Herbert L. Searles:	Denotation of a term: Connotation of a term:	Actual things to which the term applies. Set of characteristics common to the members of a class.
152. Maylon H. Hepp:	Application of a name: Signification of a name:	Applies to cases or instances. Signifies a set of characteristics.
153. Edith W. Schipper and Edward Schuh:	Personal Intension: Social Intension:	Connotation of a term used by a given individual. Meaning of a term common to a group of people.
154. Vincent Edward Smith:	Extension of a concept: Comprehension or Intension of a concept:	Number of inferiors to which the concept applies. Number of characteristics or qualifications which determine the content of a concept.
155. Andrew H. Bachhuber:	Absolute Extension: Functional Extension: Comprehension of a term:	All those subjects which exist or can exist. Those subjects which exist. Sum total of the intelligible elements of the quiddity signified by the term.
156. John W. Blyth:	Denotation:	Relation between a word and the objects named by that word.

	Signification:	Relation between a word and the properties of objects called by that word.
	Connotation:	Relation between a word and other words.
157. Monroe C. Beardsley:	Comprehension, Extension, Application, or Denotation of a term:	Class of things over which the term extends.
	Signification, Intension, Implication, Designation, or Connotation of a term:	Consists of those characteristics which the term implies.
158. Louis Couturat:	Extension:	Subject is contained in the predicate.
	Comprehension:	Subject contains the predicate.
159. I. M. Bochenski:	Extension and Comprehension:	Allied with simple and personal supposition.
160. Romane Clark and Paul Welsh:	Denotation of a word:	Objects to which the word applies.
	Connotation of a word:	Properties or traits of an object.
161. John A. Mourant:	Extension:	Embraces individual instances or subjects.
	Comprehension:	Comprises essential characteristics.
162. Daniel J. Sullivan:	Extension:	Applicability of a concept.
	Comprehension:	Essential content of a concept.
163. Samuel S. S. Browne:	Denotation of a term:	Refers to a thing.
	Intension of a term:	Attributes that a thing must possess to be denoted by a term.

204

164. Wilhelm Traugott Krug:	Sphere of a concept:	Multiplicity of representations found under a concept.
	Content of a concept:	Interior quantity.
165. Gottlob E. Schulze:	Matter or *Stoff:*	That which is conceived; applies to species in the mind and to individuals outside the mind.
	Form:	The attribute by which is conceived only what is common to several things.
166. Jakob Friedrich Fries:	Sphere, *Umfang,* or Extension of a concept:	Totality of a concept's projections; actual representations.
	Content or Comprehension of a concept:	Partial projections of a concept.
167. Ernst Reinhold:	Extension *(Umfang),* Sphere, Extensive quantity of a concept, or Content of the category *(fach):*	Individual ideas belonging to one category.
	Content or *Inhalt* of a concept:	Differentiation from the grammatical designation.
168. Wilhelm Esser:	Quantity of Extension, *Umfang, Quantitas Externa, Extensiva, Ambitus:*	Consists in the number of actual or possible objects or things to which the concept can be applied.
	Quantity of Content, *Quantitas Interna, Intensiva, Complexus:*	Differentiating characteristics which are connected to a whole by the concept.
169. Karl Fischer:	Extension *(Umfang)* of a concept:	Sequence of specific concepts proceeding from the superior to the inferior.

	Contents (Inhalt) of a concept:	Inner development of the general concept.
170. Dr. Heinrich Ritter:	Extension (Umfang), Sphere, Area (Gebeit), or Amplitude (Weite) of a concept:	Application to different phenomena; embraces variable marks (actual or possible).
	Content (Inhalt) of a concept:	Meaning of many phenomena united in one individual concept.
171. Moritz Wilhelm Drobisch:	Extension (Umfang), Ambitus, or Sphere of a concept:	Ordered totality of all the species of the content of a concept.
	Content (Inhalt) or Complexus of a concept:	Totality of characteristics of an object-concept.
172. Dr. Friedrich Ueberweg:	Extent, Ambitus, Sphaera, or Extensio of a conception:	Totality of those conceptions whose similar elements of content make up its content.
	Content or Complexus of a conception:	Sum total of the part-conceptions.
173. *Trendelenburg[1]:	Comprehension:	Elements of intuition.
174. *Friedrich Fischer[2]:	Extension:	Limited to real species and single beings.
175. *Bachmann[3]:	Extension:	Refers to real, actual, external, individual objects and not to species.
176. *Strumpell[4]:	Extension:	Psychical concepts.
177. *Herbart[5]:	Extension:	Actual and not merely possible concepts.

*Indicates an author consulted but not cited in this study.

178. *Gerlach: Extension: Applies to merely possible things.[6]

Comprehension: Includes all necessary or accidental marks which are universally predicable of the object of the concept.[7]

*Indicates an author consulted but not cited in this study.

1. Cf C. S. Peirce, "Upon Logical Comprehension and Extension", *Proceedings Of The American Academy Of Arts and Sciences* (Boston and Cambridge: Welch, Bigelow, And Company, November 13, 1867), p. 421.
2. *Ibid.*, p. 422.
3. *Ibid.*
4. *Ibid.*
5. *Ibid.*, p. 423.
6. *Ibid.*
7. *Ibid.*, p. 421.

APPENDIX II (CONTINUED)

PART I: CHAPTER II

Authors:	*Terminology:*	*Meaning:*
179. Petrus Gassendus:	What belongs to the Genus, belongs to the Species:	Comprehension.
	What belongs to the Species, belongs to the Genus:	Extension.
180. F. P. Burgersdijck:	Genus is wider than Species, and Species is wider than the individuals:	Extension.
	Species includes its genus and essential difference:	Comprehension.
181. Lorenzo Valla:	Genus is predicated of its Species; Species is predicated of its individuals:	Extension.
182. R. P. Roderico De Arriaga:	*Species subjicibilis:*	Extension of genus to species.
	Species praedicabilis:	Extension of species to the individuals.
183. Daniel Stahl:	Universal whole:	Extension of genus to species and individuals, and extension of species to individuals.
	Subjective parts:	Species under genus, and individuals under species.

	Genus is wider than species:	Extension.
	Species is collective of many things in one nature:	Comprehension.
	Genus is still more collective:	Extension.
184. John of St. Thomas:	Genus is predicated of several specifically different things:	Extension.
	Genus is less contracted *(minus contractum):*	Extension.
	Genus is predicated immediately of species and mediately of individuals:	Extension.
	Genus is a part of the thing conceived and signified:	Comprehension.
	Species is gathered under the assigned genus:	Extension.
185. Pierre Du Moulin:	Species is a nature comprehended under the genus:	Extension.
	Where the Species is, there the Genus needs be also:	Comprehension.
186. Cosmus (Mediolanensis) Alamannius:	*Genus est in plus:* Species exceeds the genus by means of the difference *(Species abundare a genere . . . .):*	Extension. Comprehension.

209

187. P. Raphaele Aversa A. Sanseverino:	Species is predicated essentially of many things different in number:	Extension.
	Species is composed of Genus and Difference:	Comprehension.
188. Petrus Molinaeus:	Genus contains all Species in potency:	Extension.
	Species contains the Genus in act:	Comprehension.
189. *Thomas Blundeville:	Genus and Species comprehend more or less, or extend further:	Extension.
190. Petrus Fonseca:	Among universals, certain ones are less universal; others, more universal:	Extension.
	Specific difference is that by which the Species exceeds the Genus; individual difference is that by which the individual exceeds the lowest Species.	Comprehension.
191. *Edward Brerewood:	Genus exceeds Species in the power of its nature:	Extension.
	Species exceeds Genus in act and in perfection of nature:	Comprehension.
192. Paulus Barbus Soncinas:	Generic concept comprehends *(comprehendere)* several Species indifferently; *comprehensio:*	Extension.

*Indicates an author consulted but not cited in this study.

193. Dudley Fenner:	Part comprehended under the whole kinde or generall forme:	Designates the extension of the whole to its specific parts.
194. D. Franciscus Toletus:	Genus is more universal *(universalius);* Genus comprehends under it many Species; the more universal is more collective extensively; Genus is predicated of more things than the Species:	Extension.
	The less universal is more collective intensively:	Comprehension.
195. Francis Titelmannus:	Species exceeds *(abundare)* its Genus:	Comprehension.
196. Thomas Wilson:	Largenesse and narrownesse; Species are comprehended under a worde more universall:	Extension.
197. *Alonso de la Veracruz:	Species is placed under the Genus; Genus contains the Species; Species are contained; *Ambitus:*	Extension.
198. Rudolf Agricola:	*Sub se comprehensam; Genus complectitur partes:*	Extension.

*Indicates an author consulted but not cited in this study.

211

199. *Joachim Sterck von Ringelbergh:	Genus is common to several Species; Species is common to individuals:	Extension.
200. Philipp Melanchthon:	Species is in many individuals:	Extension.
201. Thomas de Vio Cardinalis Cajetanus:	Genus collects more extensively *(extensive):* Species collects more intensively (intensive): *Species abundat a genere:*	Extension. Comprehension. Comprehension.
202. Aloysius Antonius Verneus:	Individual embraces more than the Species:	Comprehension.
203. Pseudo-Thomas:	*Latitudo Generis: Abundare* and *Excedere:*	Extension. Comprehension.
204. Joannis Duns Scotus:	Genus is a greater universal than the Species: Genus has less actual and essential intelligibility:	Extension. Comprehension.
205. St. Thomas Aquinas:	*Extenduntur in plus; Esse in plus; Excedere;* Genus contains more members in potency: Species contains more members in act:	Extension. Comprehension.

*Indicates an author consulted but not cited in this study.

212

206. St. Albert the Great:	*Secundum ambitum communitatis; Extenduntur in plus; Aptitudo:*	Extension.
	Qualitas Differentiae:	Extension and comprehension.
	Magis est collectivum et adunativum Genus quam Species:	Extension.
	Species uniat plura in se:	Comprehension.
207. Nicephorus Blemmida:	*Species superat Genus:*	Comprehension.
208. John of Salisbury:	*Nominare:*	A process of naming which refers to individuals.
	Significare:	A process of signifying whereby the individual is brought under a community of meaning.
209. Avicenna:	Genus is predicated of specifically different things; Species is predicated of numerically different things:	Extension.
210. St. John Damascene:	*Latius, Complectitur,* and *Generalius:*	Extension.
	Abundare:	Comprehension.
211. An. Manlius Severinus Boetius:	*Collectivum:*	Extension: genus is collective of several species.
	Adumare, Ambitus, Abundare, Superesse, Magnitudo Generis, Supervadere and *Maius:*	Extension.
	Abundare and *Supervadere:*	Comprehension.

213

212. Ammonius Hermeae:	ἐπιτείνειν Genus comprehends both Species and individuals; Species comprehends individuals; *Amplius*:	Extension 'to stretch out'. Extension.
213. Porphyry:	*Continere*: *Collectivum*: Genus is predicated of Species and individuals; Species is predicated of individuals: *Abundare*: Genus is predicated of more things than Difference, Species, Property, or Accident:	Extension. Extension and comprehension. Extension. Extension and comprehension. Extension.
214. Marcus Fabius Quintilianus:	Subjection of Species to Genus:	Extension.
215. Lucius Annaeus Seneca:	*Complectatur* and *sub se habeat*:	Extension.
216. Cicero:	*Genus plures partes amplectitur; pars subest Generi*:	Extension.
217. Aristotle:	ἐπὶ πλέον, περιλαμβάνει, ἐπεκτείνειν : ἐπὶ πλεῖον, ἀφορισμόν, περιλαμβάνει ἐπὶ πεῖον : πλεῖον	Extension. Comprehension.
218. Plato:	ἐπὶ πλέον :	Extension.
219. Archytas:	Consult p. 123.	
220. Pythagoras:	Consult p. 123.	

214

BIBLIOGRAPHY

A. ANCIENT SOURCES

Ammonius Hermeae. *In Aristotelis Categorias Commentarius.* Ed. Adolfus Busse, Berolini: Typis et impensis Georgii Reimeri, 1895, Vol. IV, Pars IV.

————. *In Porphyrii Isagogen Sive V Voces.* Ed. Adolfus Busse. Berolini: Typis et impensis Georgii Reimeri, 1891, Vol. IV, Pars III.

————. *In Quinque Porphyrii Voces Commentarium.* Ed. Joannes Baptista Rasarius A. Vallevzia A. Graeco in Latinum vertebat. Venetiis: Apud Hieronymum Scotum, 1542.

Archytas. "Les Fragments D'Archytas de Tarente," *Pythagore et la Philosophie Pythagoricienne.* Paris: Didier et Cie, 1873, Vols. I, II. Trans. Anthelme Edouard Chaignet.

Aristotelis. *Opera Omnia Graece Et Latine.* Parisiis: Editoribus Firmin — Didot Et Sociis, 1927, Vol. I.

————. *The Basic Works of Aristotle.* Ed. R. McKeon. New York: Random House, 1941.

————. *The Works Of Aristotle.* Ed. and trans. W. D. Ross. First edition. London: Oxford University Press, 1950, Vol. I.

————. *Organon.* London: Henry G. Bohn, 1853. 2 vols. Trans. Octavius Freire Owen.

————. *The Organon Or Logical Treatises Of Aristotle.* London: G. Bell And Sons, Limited, 1910. 2 vols. Trans. Octavius Freire Owen.

————. "Categories", *Organon.* Paris: Libraire Philosophique J. Vrin, 1959. Trans. J. Tricot.

————. "Les Topiques", *Organon.* Paris: Libraire Philosophique J. Vrin, 1938. 2 vols. Trans. J. Tricot.

————. *Aristotle's Prior and Posterior Analytics.* Ed. W. D. Ross. Reprinted from the first edition. Oxford: At The Clarendon Press,1957.

Augustinus, Aurelius. *Confessiones.* Introduction and notes by Josephus Capello. Taurini: Marietti, 1948.

Boetius, Manlius Severinus. Opera Omnia. Cf. Migne, J. P. *Patrologiae Cursus Completus, Series Latina.* Parisiis: Bibliothecae Cleri Universale, 1891, Vol. LXIV.

Chaignet, Anthelme Edouard. *Pythagore et la Philosophie Pythagoricienne.* Paris: Didier et Cie, 1873. 2 vols. This treatise contains fragments of Philolaus (lived at the end of the fifth century B.C.) and Archytas (430 B.C. - 360 B.C.) which have been translated into French for the first time by A. E. Chaignet.

Cicero, Marcus Tullius. *Opera.* Ed. Aldus Pius Mannuccivus. Venetiis: Carolum Emmanuelem, 1583. Vol. I, Topica, ad C. Trebatium, cum commentario Anicii Manilii Severini Boetii et Petri Velleii Guevarae, pp. 133-235.

————. *Opera.* Ed. C. F. A. Nobbe. Lipsiae: Ex Officina Car. Tauchnitii, 1828. 10 vols.

————. *Academicorum Priorum".* Opera. Ed. C. F. A. Nobbe. Lipsiae: Ex Officina Car. Tauchnitti, 1828, Vol. VIII.

————. "The Orator", *Orations.* London: Henry G. Bohn, 1852, Vol. IV. Trans. C. D. Yonge.

David. *In Porphyrii Isagogen.* Cf. *Commentaria In Aristotelem Graeca.* Ed. Adolfus Busse. Berolini: Typis et impensis Georgii Reimeri, 1904, Vol. XVIII.

Plato. *Euthyphro.* Cf. *Plato.* London: William Heinemann Ltd., 1943, Vol. I. Trans. Harold North Fowler.

————. "Euthyphron", *Oeuvres Complètes.* Deuxième édition. Paris: Societé D'Édition, 1925.

————. *Statesman.* Cf. *The Dialogues of Plato.* Third Printing. New York: Random House, 1937. 2 vols. Trans. B. Jowett.

————. *Theaetetus.* Cf. *Plato.* London: William Heinemann Ltd., 1942. Trans. Harold North Fowler.

Plotinus. *Enneades.* Basileae: Ad Perneam Lecythum, 1580.

Porphyry. *Isagoge.* Paris: Librairie Philosophique J. Vrin, 1947. Trans. J. Tricot.

————. *Porphyrii Isagoge Et In Aristotelis Categorias Commentarium.* Ed. Adolfus Busse. Berolini: Typis et impensis Georgii Reimeri, 1887, Vol. IV, Pars I.

————. "Porphyrii Introductio." Cf. Maurus, Sylvester. *Aristotelis Opera Omnia.* Ed. Franciscus Ehrle, S. J. Parisiis: P. Lethielleux, 1886, Vol. I, pp. 6-26. Trans. Julius Pacius.

————. "The Introduction Of Porphyry", *The Organon, Or Logical Treatises Of Aristotle.* London: Henry G. Bohn, 1853, Vol. II, pp. 609-33. Trans. Octavius Freire Owen.

Quintilianus, Marcus Fabius. *De Institutione Oratoria.* Lipsiae: Sumptibus et typis Caroli Tauchnitii, 1829. 2 vols. in 1.

Seneca, Lucius Annaeus. *Opera Omnia.* Lipsiae: Sumptibus et typis Car. Tauchnitii, 1832. 3 vols.

B. MEDIEVAL SOURCES

Abaelardus, Petrus. *Dialectica.* First complete edition of the Parisian Manuscript by L. M. De Rijk. Assen: Van Gorcum & Company, 1956.

Agricola, Rudolf. *De Inventione Dialectica*. Coloniae: Martinus Gymnicus, 1548.

Alamannius, Cosmus (Mediolanensis). *Summa Totius Philosophiae S. Thomae*. Ticini: Excudebat Jo. Baptista Rubeus, 1624, Pars Prima.

Albertus Magnus, St. "Metaphysica", *Opera Omnia*. Ed. Bernhardus Geyer. Germania: Monasterium Westfalorum In Aedibus Aschendorff, 1960, Liber I.

——. *Commentaria In Perihermenias Aristotelis*. Parisiis: Ludovicus Vivès, 1890.

——. "Physicorum lib. VIII", *Opera Omnia*. Ed. Augustus Borgnet. Parisiis: Apud Ludovicum Vivès, 1890, Liber III.

——. *Commentaria In Posteriora Analytica Aristotelis*. Parisiis: Ludovicus Vivès, 1890. Mimeographed by Michel Doyon, 1215, Chemin Ste — Foy, Quebec, Canada, 1956.

——. *Commentaria In De Praedicabilibus*. Parisiis: Ludovicus Vivès, 1890. Mimeographed by Michel Doyon.

——. *Commentaria In Praedicamenta Aristotelis*. Parisiis: Ludovicus Vivès, 1890. Mimeographed by Michel Doyon.

——. *Commentaria In Libris Topicorum*. Parisiis: Ludovicus Vivès, 1890. Mimeographed by Michel Doyon.

Alexander of Hales. *Summa Theologica*. Florentia: Ex Typographia Collegii S. Bonaventura, 1924. 3 vols.

Alonso de la Veracruz. *Dialectica Resolutio*. Mexici: Excudebat Joannes Paulus Brissensis, 1554.

——. *Recognitio Summularum*. Mexici: Excudebat Joannes Paulus Brissensis, 1554.

Alsted, Johann. *Clavis Artis Lullianae Et Verae Logicae*. Argentorati: Lazari Zetzneri, 1609.

Anselm, St. *Opera Omnia*. Edinburgh: Apud Thomam Nelson Et Filios, 1946. 6 vols.

Aquinas, St. Thomas. *Opera Omnia*. Parmae: Tipis Petri Fiaccadori, 1852. 25 vols.

——. *In Aristotelis Librum De Anima*. Editio Quarta. Ed. P. F. Angeli M. Pirotta, O. P. Taurini: Marietti, 1959.

——. *In XII Libros Metaphysicorum Aristotelis*. Ed. Cathala-Spiazzi. Taurini: Marietti, 1950.

——. *In Libros Peri Hermeneias*. Ed. P. Fr. Raymundi M. Spiazzi, O. P. Taurini: Marietti, 1955.

——. *In VIII Libros Physicorum Aristotelis*. Ed. Maggiolo. Taurini: Marietti, 1955.

——. *In Libros Posteriorum Analyticorum*. Ed. Spiazzi. Taurini: Marietti, 1955.

——. "De Potentia" in *Quaestiones Disputatae*. Ed. P. Bazzi et al. Taurini: Marietti, 1953, Vol. II.

217

————. *Quaestiones Quodlibetales.* Ed. P. Fr. Raymundi Spiazzi, O. P. Taurini: Marietti, 1956.

————. *In Scriptum Super Sententiis Magistri Petri Lombardi.* Ed. R. P.M.F. Moos. Parisiis: Lethielleux, 1956. 4 vols.

————. *Summa Theologiae.* Edidit Commissio Piana. Ottawa: College Dominicain, 1953. 5 vols.

————. *Expositio Super Librum Boethii De Trinitate.* Editio Altera. Ed. Bruno Decker. Leiden: E. J. Brill, 1959.

————. "De Veritate" in *Quaestiones Disputatae.* Ed. Spiazzi. Taurini: Marietti, 1953, Vol. I.

Arriaga, R. P. Roderico De. *Cursus Philosophicus.* Parisiis: Apud Jacobum Quesmel, 1639.

Aurivillius, Petrus. *Elementa Logicae.* Upsaliae: H. Curio, 1672. This book was published earlier in 1630.

Avicenne. *Livre des Définitions.* Caire: Publications de l'Institut Français d'Archéologie Orientale, 1963. Trans. A. M. Goichon.

————. *Livre des Directives et Remarques.* Paris: Librairie Philosophique J. Vrin, 1951. Trans. A. M. Goichon.

Blemmida, Nicephorus. *Epitomes Logicae Prooemium.* Cf. MG, Vol. CXLII.

Blundeville, Thomas. *The Arte Of Logick.* London: William Stansby, 1617.

Bonaventura, S. *Opera Omnia.* Ed. A. C. Peltier. Parisiis: Ludovicus Vivès, 1867. 15 vols.

————. Cf. Marc, Antonius de Carpenedulo, O.M.C. *Summa Totius Dialecticae Ad Mentem S. Bonaventurae.* Romae: Apud Andream Phraeum, 1634.

Brerewood, Edward. *Elementa Logicae.* Londini: Apud Joannem Billium, 1615.

————. *Tractatus Quidam Logici De Praedicabilibus Et Praedicamentis.* Oxoniae: Excudebat Guilielmus Turner, 1631. This treatise presents a detailed explanation of how the predicables (according to Porphyry) agree and disagree among themselves.

Bumannus, Carolus. *Hypomnemata Logica.* Francofurti: Apud Andreae Wecheli heredes, 1597.

Burgersdijck, F. P. *Institutionum Logicarum.* London: Ex officina Rogeri Danielis, 1651.

Burleigh, Walter. *De Puritate Artis Logicae Tractatus Longior.* Ed. Philotheus Boehner. St. Bonaventure, N.Y.: The Franciscan Institute, 1955.

Caesarius, Johannes. *Dialectica.* Lugduni: Apud Antonium Vincentium, 1545.

Cajetanus, Thomas de Vio Cardinalis. *Commentaria In Porphyrii Isagogen Ad Praedicamenta Aristotelis.* Ed. P. Isnardus M. Marega. Romae: Apud Institutum Angelicum, 1934.

218

Crucius, Jacobus. *Medulla Logicae Contracta*. Lugduni Batavorum: Ex Officina Joannis Maire, 1640.

Damascene, St. John. *Dialectica*. Cf. *MG*, Vol. XCIV.

Du Moulin, Pierre. *The Elements Of Logick*. London: Printed by I. Dawson for Nicholas Bourne, 1624. Trans. Nathanael De-Lavvne.

Duns Scotus, Joannis. "In Universam Logicam Quaestione", *Opera Omnia*. Editio nova. Parisiis: Apud Ludovicum Vivès, 1891, Vol. I.

Fenner, Dudley. *The Artes Of Logike And Rhetorike*. Middelburg?: R. Schilders?, 1584.

Fonseca, Petrus, S. J. *Institutionum Dialecticarum*. Coloniae: Apud Petrum Cholinum, 1616.

————. *Isagoge Philosophica*. Coloniae: Apud Petrum Cholinum, 1616.

Freigius, Joannes Thoma. *Quaestiones seu Logicae Et Ethicae*. Basileae: Per Sebastianum Henricpetri, 1584.

Frisner, Erasmus. *Exertitium* [sic] *totius noue logicae Analyticorum: Priorum, Posteriorum, Thopicorum, et Sophisticorum*. Colophon: Impressum Liptzk per Jacobum Thaner, 1511.

Gassendus, Petrus. *Opera Omnia*. Lugduni: Sumptibus Laurentii Anisson, & Joan. Bapt. Devenet, 1658, Vol. I.

Javelli, Chrysostomus, O.P. *Compendium Logicae*. Venetiis: Apud Haeredes Joannis Mariae Bonelli, 1572.

Joannis Saresberiensis Episcopi Carnotensis. *Metalogicon*. Ed. Clemens C. I. Webb. Oxonii: E. Typographeo Clarendoniano, 1929, Libri IIII.

John of St. Thomas O.P. *Cursus Philosophicus Thomisticus*. Nova editio a P. Beato Reiser, O.S.B. Taurini: Marietti, 1948. 3 vols. The second part of the *Ars Logica, in Isagogen Porphyrii*, was first published in 1632.

John XXI (Petrus Hispanus). *Dialectica*. Milan: Leonardus, Pachel and Ulrich Scinzenzeler, 1487.

————. *Summulae Logicales*. Ed. I. M. Bochenski, O. P. Romae: Domus Editorialis Marietti, 1947.

————. *Summulae Logicales*. South Bend: University of Notre Dame, 1945. Trans. Joseph P. Mullally. This treatise was written prior to 1261.

Maimonides, Moses (1135-1204). *Treatise On Logic*. Proceedings Of The American Academy For Jewish Research. Philadelphia: Press of the Jewish Publication Society, 1937-38, Vol. VIII. Trans. Israel Efros.

Marc, Antonius de Carpenedulo, O.M.C. *Summa Totius Dialecticae Ad Mentem S. Bonaventurae*. Romae: Apud Andream Phraeum, 1634.

Melanchthon, Philipp. *Compendiaria Dialectices Ratio*. ?: Apud Inclytam Basileam, 1521.

Molinaeus, Petrus. *Elementa Logica*. Bremae: Apud Thoman Villerianum, 1619.

Ockham, William. *Summa Logicae*. Ed. Philotheus Boehner, O.F.M. St. Bonaventure, N.Y.: The Franciscan Institute, 1951. 3 vols. in 2.

Pisani, Francesco. *De Universae Philosophiae Ornamentis Oratio.* Venetiis: Joannes Antonius et fratres, 151?.

Prideaux, John. *Tabulae Ad Grammatica Graeca Introductoriae.* Editio Tertia. Oxoniae: Impensis Eliae P. T. Allam, 1639.

Pseudo-Thomas. *De Totius Logicae Aristotelis Summa.* Cf. Aquinas, St. Thomas. *Opera Omnia.* Parmae: Petri Fiaccadori, 1864, Vol. XVII, Opusculum XLIV, pp. 54-117.

Ringelbergh, Joachim Sterck von. *Dialectica et Rhetorica.* Parisiis: ?, 1534?

Sanderson, Robert. *Logicae Artis Compendium.* Editio quarta. Oxoniae: Impensis Wm. Davis. 1640.

Sanseverino, P. Raphaele Aversa A. *Logica.* Romae: Apud Jacobum Muscardum, 1623.

Smaglecki, Marcin, S. J. *Logica.* Oxonii: Excudebat H. Crypps, et al., 1634.

Smith, Samuel. *Aditus Ad Logicam.* Editio quinta. Oxoniae: Excudebat Guil. Turner, 1639.

Soncinas, Paulus Barbus de. *Quaestiones Metaphysicales Acutissimae.* Venetiis: Apud Haeredem Hieronymi Scoti, 1587.

Stahl, Daniel. *Expositionis Regularum Philosophicarum.* Oxoniae: J. Webb, 1663. This book was published earlier in 1635.

Stierius, Joannes. *Praecepta Doctrinae Logicae, Ethicae, Physicae, Etc.* Editio quarta. Londini: Ex officina Rogeri Danielis, 1652.

Tataretus, Petrus. *In Summulas Petri Hispani Exactae Explicationes.* Venetiis: R. P. F. Salvatorem Bartol, 1581.

Thomas of Erfort. *Grammatica Speculativa.* Parisiis: Ludovicus Vivès, 1890. Mimeographed by Michel Doyon.

Titelmannus, Francis. *De Consideratione Dialectica.* Venetiis: Apud Franciscum, Gasparem Bindonum, & Fratres, 1571.

Toletus, D. Franciscus, S. J. *Commentaria In Universam Aristotelis Logicam.* Venetiis: Apud Iuntas, 1576.

Turre, Dionysius de. O.F.M. *Dialecticae Libri XII.* Romae: Apud Paulum Profilium, 1614.

Valla, Loreno. *Dialectice.* Parisiis: In edibus Ascensianis, 1509.

Verneus, Alovsius Antonius. *De Re Logica.* Romae: In officina viduae Josephi De Orga, 1369.

Wilson, Thomas. *The Rule Of Reason.* London: Ihon Kingston, 1567.

Zazarelia, Jacobus. *Opera Logica.* Venetiis: Apud Paulum Meietum Bibliopol. Patavinum, 1586.

C. MODERN SOURCES

Abbott, T. K. *The Elements Of Logic.* Fourth Edition. London: Thomas Nelson And Sons Ltd., 1951.

Adams, E. M. *The Fundamentals Of General Logic.* New York: Longmans, Green And Co., 1954.

Adamson, Robert. *A Short History Of Logic.* Ed. W. R. Sorley. Edinburgh: William Blackwood And Sons, 1911.

Adler, Mortimer J. *Dialectic.* New York: Harcourt, Brace & Company, Inc., 1927.

Aikins, Herbert Austin. *Principles Of Logic.* 2nd. Edition. New York: H. Holt & Co., 1904.

Aldrich, Henry. *Artis Logicae Rudimenta.* Fourth edition. London: W. Barter, 1829.

————. *Artis Logicae Rudimenta.* Third edition Ed. Rev. Henry L. Mansel. Oxford: W. Graham, 1856.

Altieri, A. F. Laurentius. *Elementa Philosophiae.* Venetiis: Apud Franciscum Andreola, 1829, Vol. I.

Andrews, John. *A Compend Of Logick.* Philadelphia: Budd And Bartram, 1801.

Angeloni, Dominicus. *Institutiones Logicae.* Neapoli: Ex Typographia Raymundiana, 1772.

Argyropulus, Joannes. *Dialectica Ad Petrum De Medicis.* Montis Casini: D. M. Muller, 1943.

Arnauld, Antoine and Lancelot. *Grammaire Générale et Raisonnée de Port-Royal.* Seconde édition. Paris. Chez Bossange et Masson, 1810.

Arnauld, Antoine et Nicole, M. *Logique de Port-Royal.* Nouvelle Édition. Paris: Librairie De 1. Machette Et Cie, 1869.

————. *The Port Royal Logic.* Sixth Edition. Edinburgh: Oliver and Boyd, 1865. Trans. Thomas Spencer Baynes.

Atkinson, William Walker. *The Art Of Logical Thinking or The Laws Of Reasoning.* Chicago: The Progress Company, 1909.

Atwater, Lyman H. *Manual Of Elementary Logic.* Revised edition. Philadelphia: J. B. Lippincott Company, 1867.

Author Unknown. *Logic, Ontology And The Art Of Poetry.* Being The Fourth And Fifth Volumes Of The Circle Of The Sciences. London: Printed for T. Carnan, and F. Newberry, at Number 65, in St. Paul's Church Yard, 1776.

Author Unknown. *The Oxford Elements Of Logic.* London: W. Green, 1816.

Avey, Albert E. *The Function And Forms Of Thought.* New York: Henry Holt And Company, 1927.

Bachhuber, Andrew H. *Introduction To Logic.* New York: Appleton-Century-Crofts, Inc., 1957.

Bain, Alexander. *Logic.* London: Longmans, Green, & Co., 1879. 2 vols.

Balmes, Rev. J. *Elements Of Logic.* New York: P. O'Shea, 1878. Trans. from the Spanish by James M. Spelissey.

Barker, Stephen F. *The Elements of Logic.* New York: McGraw-Hill Book Company, 1965.

Barnes, Winston H. F. "The Doctrine Of Connotation And Denotation." *Mind,* July, 1945, Vol. 54, pp. 254-63.

Barrett, Solomon. *The Principles Of Grammar.* Revised edition. Boston: Geo. C. Rand And Avery, 1862.

Barron, William. *Elements Of Logic.* Edited and compiled by Rev. James R. Boyd. New York: A. S. Barnes & Co., 1856.

Baumgarten, Alexander Gottlieb. *Acroasis Logica.* Halae Magdeburgae: C. H. Hemmerde, 1773.

Bayer, Raymond. *Épistémologie et Logique depuis Kant jusqu'a nos jours.* Paris: Presses Universitaires de France, 1954.

Baynes, Thomas Spencer. *New Analytic Of Logical Forms.* Edinburgh: Sutherland And Knox, 1850.

Beardsley, Monroe C. *Practical Logic.* New York: Prentice-Hall, Inc., 1950.

————. *Thinking Straight.* Second Edition. Englewood Cliffs, N.J.: Prentice-Hall, Inc., 1958.

Bennett, Albert A. and Baylis, Charles A. *Formal Logic.* New York: Prentice-Hall, Inc., 1939.

Bensa, L'Abbé M. *Manuel de Logique.* Paris: J. Leroux Et Jouby, 1855.

Bentham, Edward. *An Introduction To Logick, Scholastick And Rational.* Oxford: W. Jackson, And J. Lister, 1773.

————. *Reflexions upon Logick.* Second edition. Oxford: Printed at the Theatre for James Fletcher in the Turl, 1755.

Bergomus, Petrus de. *Tabula Aurea.* Romae: Editiones Paulinae, 1960.

Best, William. *A Concise System of Logics.* New York: Printed by Samuel Campbell, 1796.

Bierman, A. K. *Logic: A Dialogue.* San Francisco: Holden-Day, Inc., 1964.

Binder, Frank. *Dialectic.* London: Eric Partridge Ltd. At The Scholartis Press, 1932.

Bishop, R. H. *A Manual of Logic.* Oxford, Ohio: Printed at the Societies' Press, 1830.

Bittle, Celestine N. *The Science of Correct Thinking.* Fifth printing. Milwaukee: The Bruce Publishing Company, 1941.

Black, Max. *Critical Thinking.* New York: Prentice-Hall, Inc., 1946.

Blakey, Robert. *Historical Sketch Of Logic.* London: H. Bailliere, 1851. This book contains a comprehensive list of classical works on logic.

Blanc, Élie. *Traité de Philosophie Scolastique.* Nouvelle édition. Lyon: Emmanuel Vitte, 1893, Vol. I.

Blyth, John W. *A Modern Introduction To Logic.* Boston: Houghton Mifflin Company, 1957.

Boas, George. *Our New Ways Of Thinking.* New York: Harper & Brothers, 1930.

Bochenski, I. M. *Ancient Formal Logic.* Amsterdam: North-Holland Publishing Company, 1951.

————. *Elementa Logicae Graecae*. Romae: Anonima Libraria Cattolica Italiana, 1937.

————. *A History Of Formal Logic*. Ed. and trans. Ivo Thomas. South Bend: University of Notre Dame, 1961.

————. *La logique de Théophraste*. Fribourg en Suisse: Librairie de l'université, 1947.

Bode, Boyd Henry. *An Outline of Logic*. New York: Henry Holt And Company, 1910.

Bodkin, Richard. *Logic For All*. Chicago: Henry Regnery Company, 1955.

Boehner, Philotheus. *Medieval Logic*. Manchester: The University Press, 1952.

Boll, Marcel et Reinhart, Jacques. *Les Étapes de la Logique*. Paris: Presses Universitaires de France, 1946.

Bonitz, H. *Index Aristotelis*. Secunda editio. Graz: Akademische Druck U. Verlagsanstalt, 1955.

Bonnot, Lucien. *Essai sur les Fondements de la Logique et sur la Méthodologie causale*. Paris: Presses Universitaires de France, 1943.

Bosanquet, Bernard. *Knowledge And Reality*. London: Kegan Paul, Trench & Co., 1885.

————. "Logic As The Science Of Knowledge", *Essays in Philosophical Criticism*, ed. Andrew Seth and R. B. Haldane. London: Longmans, Green, And Co., 1883. Pp. 67-101.

————. *Logic or the Morphology of Knowledge*. Second Edition. London: Oxford University Press, 1911. 2 vols.

Bourke, Vernon J. *Thomistic Bibliography* (1920-40). St. Louis: McMullen Printing Co., 1945.

Bouvier, J. B. *Institutiones Philosophicae*. Duodecima editio. Parisiis: Apud Méquignon Juniorem, 1858.

Bowen, Francis. *A Treatise On Logic, Or, The Laws Of Pure Thought*. Cambridge: Sever And Francis, 1865.

Boylesne, Marino de, S. J. *Cursus Philosophiae*. Lutetiae Parisorum: Sumptibus Julien, Lanier Et Sociorum, 1855.

Bradley, F. H. *The Principles of Logic*. Second edition. London: Oxford University Press, 1928. 2 vols.

Brattle, William. *Compendium Logicae*. Boston: ? not recorded, 1735.

Brenan, Justin. *Old And New Logic*. London: Thomas Tegg, 1839.

Brough, J. *The Study Of Mental Science*. London: Longmans, Green, And Co., 1903.

Brown, Paul L. and Stuermann, Walter E. *Elementary Modern Logic*. New York: The Ronald Press Company, 1965.

Browne, Samuel S. *Fundamentals of Deductive Logic*. Dubuque, Iowa: Wm. C. Brown Company, 1964.

Burtt, Edwin Arthur. *Principles And Problems Of Right Thinking*. New York: Harper & Brothers, 1928.

223

Bushby, Rev. Edward. *The Elements Of Logic.* Cambridge: Printed by John Smith, 1826.

Butani, H. L. *Elements Of Logic.* Bombay: Kitab Mahal Publishers, 1962.

Carnap, Rudolf. *Introduction to Semantics.* Cambridge, Mass.: Harvard University Press, 1942.

————. *Philosophy and Logical Syntax.* London: Kegan Paul, et al, 1935.

Casey, Fred. *Thinking.* Chicago: Charles H. Kerr & Company, 1926.

Castell, Alburey. *A College Logic.* Eight Edition. New York: The Macmillan Company, 1944

Chabin, R. P. *Cours de Philosophie.* Quatrième Édition. Paris: Berche Et Tralin, 1896.

Chapman, Frank M. and Henle, Paul. *The Fundamentals Of Logic.* New York: Charles Scribner's Sons, 1933.

Charles, M. Em. *Éléments de Philosophie.* Paris: V. Eugène Belin Et Fils, 1885, Vol. II.

Charma, M. A. *Leçons de Logique.* Paris: Librairie Classique et Élémentaire de L. Hachette, 1840.

Chase, Stuart. *Guides To Straight Thinking.* New York: Harper & Brothers Publishers, 1956.

Churchman, C. West. *Elements Of Logic and Formal Science.* Chicago: J. B. Lippincott Company, 1940.

Clark, Joseph T. *Conventional Logic And Modern Logic.* Woodstock, Md.: Woodstock College Press, 1952.

Clark, Romane and Welsh, Paul. *Introduction to Logic.* Princeton, N.J.: D. Van Nostrand Company, Inc., 1962.

Clarke, Richard F. *Logic.* New York: Benziger Brothers, 1889.

Clericus, Joannes. *Logica: Sive, Ars Rationandi.* Londini: Impensis Awnsham & Johan. Churchill, 1692.

Coffey, Peter. *The Science Of Logic.* Second Edition. New York: Peter Smith, 1938. 2 vols.

Cohen, Morris R. *A Preface to Logic.* Fourth Printing. New York: Henry Holt And Company, 1946.

Cohen, Morris R. and Nagel, Ernest. *An Introduction To Logic and Scientific Method.* Third Edition. London: Routledge & Kegan Paul Ltd., 1951.

Coleridge, Samuel Taylor. *A Dissertation on the Science of Method.* Sixth edition. London: Richard Griffin And Company, 1854.

Comenius, J. A. *Sapientiae Primae Usus Tertium Catholicum.* Lugduni Batavorum Apud Haeredes Jacobi Heeneman, 1681.

"Commune". *Classics In Logic.* Ed. Dagobert D. Runes. New York: Philosophical Library, 1962.

"Commune". *Encyclopaedia Britannica.* 1960 edition. Chicago: London: Toronto: Encyclopaedia Britannica, Inc. William Benton, Publisher, 1960. Vols. 6, 7, 8, 15, and 16.

"Commune". *Essays in Logic.* Ed. Ronald Jager. Englewood Cliffs, N.J.: Prentice-Hall, Inc., 1963.

"Commune". *An Introduction To Reflective Thinking.* Boston: Houghton Mifflin Company, 1923.

"Commune". *Logico-Philosophical Studies.* Ed. Albert Menne. Dordecht-Holland: D. Reidel Publishing Company, 1962.

"Commune". *The Oxford English Dictionary.* Oxford: At The Clarendon Press, 1961, Vol. II.

"Commune". *Readings in Logic.* Ed. Roland Houde. Dubuque, Iowa: William C. Brown Company, 1958.

"Commune". *Thesaurus Linguae Latinae.* Ed. Academiae Germanicae Berolinensis Gottingensis Lipsiensis Monacensis Vindobonensis. Lipsiae: In Aedibus B. G. Tenubneri, 1906, Vols, III, V.

"Commune". *Traité Élémentaire de Philosophie.* Cinquième Édition. Louvain: Institut Supérieur de Philosophie, 1920, Vol. II.

Condillac, Étienne Bonnot de. *La Logique, ou Les Premiers Dévellopements De l'Art De Penser.* Paris: De L'Imprimerie D'Auguste Delalain, 1831.

Conway, Pierre. *Grammar * Logic * Rhetoric.* Columbus: College of St. Mary of the Springs, 1961.

Cooley, J. C. *An Outline Of Formal Logic.* Cambridge, Mass.: Harvard Cooperative Society, 1939. 4 vols.

Copi, Irving M. *Introduction to Logic.* Second Edition. New York: The Macmillan Company, 1961.

Coppée, Henry. *Elements Of Logic.* Philadelphia: E. H. Butler & Co., 1858.

Coppens, Charles. *Logic and Mental Philosophy.* New York: Schwartz, Kirwin & Fauss, 1891.

Corriol, L'Abbé. *Compendium de la Philosophie Chrétienne.* Avignon: Adolphe Coriolana, 1880, Vol. I.

Cotter, A. C. *Logic and Epistemology.* Boston: The Stratford Company, 1930.

Couturat, Louis. *La Logique de Leibniz.* Hildesheim: Georg Olms Verlagsbuchhandlung, 1961.

Crakanthorpe, Richard. *Logicae Libri Quinque.* Oxoniae: L. Lichfield & H. Hall, 1677.

Creighton, James Edwin. *An Introductory Logic.* Fourth Edition. New York: The Macmillan Company, 1926.

Creighton, James Edwin and Smart, Harold R. *An Introductory Logic.* Twenty-Fourth Printing. New York: The MacMillan Company, 1958.

Croce, Benedetto. *Logic As The Science Of The Pure Concept.* Third Edition. London: Macmillan And Co., Limited, 1917. Trans. from the Italian by Douglas Ainslie.

Crousaz, Jean Pierre de. *Examen du Pyrrhonisme.* A la Haye: Chez Pierre de Hondt, 1733.

————. *A New Treatise Of the Art Of Thinking.* London: Printed for

Tho. Woodward at the Half-Moon over-against St. Dunstan's Church in Fleet-Street, 1724. 2 vols.

Crumley, Thomas. *Logic: Deductive And Inductive.* New York: The Macmillan Company, 1926.

Cunningham, H. E. *Textbook Of Logic.* New York: The Macmillan Company, 1924.

Damiron, M. Ph. *Cours de Philosophie.* Paris: Chez L. Hachette, 1836, Vol. III.

Das, Adhar Chandra. *An Introduction To Logic.* Calcutta: Kamala Book Depot, 1949, 2 vols.

Davies, Arthur Ernest. *A Text-Book Of Logic.* Columbus, Ohio: R. G. Adams And Company, 1915.

Davis, Noak K. *The Theory Of Thought, A Treatise On Deductive Logic.* New York: Harper & Brothers, 1880.

Day, Henry N. *Elements of Logic.* New York: Charles Scribner And Company, 1867.

————. *The Logic Of Sir William Hamilton.* Cincinnati: Moore, Wilstach & Baldwin, 1865.

Deferrari, Roy J. and Barry, Sister M. Inviolata. *A Lexicon of St. Thomas Aquinas.* Baltimore: The John D. Lucas Printing Co., 1949.

De Mandato, Pio. *Institutiones Philosophicae.* Editio Quarta. Romae: Pontificia Universitas Gregoriana, 1925, Vol. I.

De Morgan, Augustus. *First Notions Of Logic.* Second Edition. London: Printed for Taylor and Walton, 1840.

————. *Syllabus Of A Proposed System Of Logic.* London: Walton And Maberly, 1860.

De Rijk, L. M. *Logica Modernorum.* Assen: Van Gorcum & Company, 1962.

Descartes, René. *Les Principes de la Philosophie.* Paris: Victor Cousin, 1824.

Dewey, John. *How We Think.* Boston: D. C. Heath & Co., Publishers, 1910.

————. *Logic, The Theory Of Inquiry.* New York: Henry Holt And Company, 1938.

————. *Studies In Logical Theory.* Chicago: The University Of Chicago Press, 1903.

Dictionnaire Étymologique de la Langue Latine. Quatrième édition. Paris: Librairie C. Klincksieck, 1959.

Dinwiddie, William. *Essentials of Logic.* New York: The Neale Publishing Company, 1914.

Donat, Josephus, S. J. *Logica.* Editio 4 et 5. Innsbruck: Typis Et Sumptibus Feliciani Rauch, 1922, Vol. I.

Dopp, M. Joseph. *Formal Logic.* New York: Joseph F. Wagner, Inc., 1960. Trans. J. Roland, E. Ramirez and Robert D. Sweeney.

226

Dougherty, Kenneth F. *Logic*. 2nd. Edition. Peekskill, New York: Graymoor Press, 1956.

Drobisch, Moritz Wilhelm. *Neue Darstellung Der Logik*. Leipzig: Leopold Voss, 1863.

Dubois, R. P., S. J. *Compendium Philosophiae*. Montreal: Auditorum Collegii Sanctae Mariae, 1927.

Du Hamel, Joh. Bapt. *Philosophia*. Editio quinta. Amstaelodami: G. Gallet, 1700, Vol. I.

Duncan, William. *The Elements Of Logic*. New York: L. Nichols & Co., 1802. The first edition was published in 1792.

Dupeyrat, A. *Manuductio Ad Scholasticam, In Primis Vero Thomisticam Philosophiam*. Editio Altera. Parisiis: Apud Victorem Lecoffre, Bibliopolam, 1887, Vol. I.

Du Roussaux, L'Abbé L. *Éléments de Logique*. Bruxelles: Société Belge De Libraire, 1894.

Du Trieu, A. R. P. Philippus. *Manuductio Ad Logicam*. London: B. M'Millan, 1826. This text is based on the Oxford edition of 1662.

Duval-Jouve, J. *Traité de Logique*. Paris: Librairie Philosophique de Ladrange, 1844.

Du Verger, Jean de la Barbe. *La Logique ou L'Art De Penser*. Nouvelle edition. Paris: Chez Humblot, 1763.

Eaton, Ralph M. *General Logic*. New York: Charles Scribner's Sons, 1931.

Egger, D. Franciscus. *Propaedeutica Philosophica-Theologica*. Editio Quinta. Brinxinae: Typis Et Sumptibus Wegerianis, 1898.

Emmens, S. H. Esq. *A Treatise On Logic*. London: Virtue Brothers & Co., 1865.

Emmet, E. R. *Thinking Clearly*. London: Longmans, Green And Co. Ltd., 1960.

————. *The Use of Reason*. London: Longmans, Green And Co. Ltd., 1960.

Enriques, Federigo. *The Historic Development Of Logic*. New York: Henry Holt And Company, 1929. Trans. from the Italian by Jerome Rosenthal.

Erdmann, Johann Eduard. *Outlines Of Logic And Metaphysics*. London: Swan Sonnenschein & Co., Limited, 1896. Trans. from the 4th. (revised) edition by B. C. Burt.

Ernout, A. et Meillet, A. *Dictionnaire Étymologique de la Langue Latine*. Quatrième édition. Paris: Librairie C. Koincksieck, 1959.

Esser, Gerard. *Logica*. Techny, Illinois: Typis Domus Missionum ad St. Mariam, 1942.

Esser, Wilhelm. *System der Logick*. Munster: Buchhandlung, 1830.

Evans, D. Luther and Gamertsfelder, Walter S. *Logic: Theoretical And Applied*. New York: Doubleday, Doran & Company, Inc., 1937.

Everett, Charles Carroll. *The Science Of Thought*. Boston: William V. Spencer, 1869.

Farges, A. et Barbedette, D. *Philosophia Scholastica*. Editio Decima. Parisiis: Apud Berche Et Trailin, Editores, 1906, Vol. I.

Filion, Émile. *Elementa Philosophiae Thomisticae*. Montreal: Librairie Beauchemin Limitée, 1937.

Fischer, Karl. *Grundzüge der Systems der Philosophie*. Erlangen: Berlag von Gender & Zimmer, 1848.

Fonsegrive, George L. *Éléments de Philosophie*. Troisième Édition. Paris: Alcide Picard Et Kaan, Editeurs, ?, Vol. II.

Forbes, W. H. and Hird, Dennis, *Palaestra Logica*. Fifth Edition. Oxford: J. Thornton & So., 1929.

Fortescue, G. K. *Subject Index Of The Modern Works Added To The Library Of The British Museum In The Years 1881-1900*. London: William Clowes And Sons, Limited, 1903. Vol. II, pp. 764-67.

Fowler, Thomas. *Logic Deductive And Inductive*. Tenth Edition. Oxford: At The Clarendon Press, 1895.

Franck, Ad. *Esquisse d'une Histoire de la Logique*. Paris: Librairie Classique De L. Hachette, 1838.

Freund, Guill. et Theil, N. *Grand Dictionnaire de la Langue Latine*. Paris: Librairie de Firmin Didot Frères, Fils et Cie, 1866, Vol. I.

Frick, Carolus. *Cursus Philosophicus*. Editio Sexta Emendata. Friburgi Brisgoviae: Herder & Co., 1925, Pars I: Logica.

Fries, Jakob Friedrich. *Grundris der Logik*. 3rd. edition. Heidelberg: Winter, 1827.

Frye, Albert Myrton and Levi, Albert William. *Rational Belief*. New York: Harcourt, Brace & World, Inc., 1941.

Galen, *Institutio Logica*. Baltimore: John Hopkins Press, 1964. Trans. John Spangler Kieffer.

Gardeil, H. D., O. P. *Initiation à la Philosophie de S. Thomas d'Aquin*. 2nd. édition. Paris. Les Éditions Du Cerf, 1953.

Garnett, A. Campbell. *The Perceptual Process*. Madison: The University Of Wisconsin, 1965.

Geach, Peter Thomas. *Mental Acts*. London: Routledge & Kegan Paul, 1956.

―――――. *Reference and Generality*. Ithaca, N.Y.: Cornell University Press, 1962.

Genovesi, Antonio. *Elementorum Artis Logico-Criticae*. Editio novissima. Venetiis: Apud Remondini, 1794. 2 books in 1.

Gianelli, A. P. *Meaningful Logic*. Milwaukee: The Bruce Publishing Company, 1962.

Gibson, W. R. Boyce. *The Problem Of Logic*. London: Adam And Charles Black, 1908.

Gilbart, James William. *Logic For The Million*. London: Bell & Daldy, 1865.

Gilby, Thomas. *Barbara Celarent*. London: Longmans Green And Co., 1949.

Gill, William I. *Analytical Processes; or The Primary Principle Of Philosophy*. New York: The Authors' Publishing Company, 1876.

Gille, E. *Cours de Philosophie*. Sixième Édition. Paris: Victor Lecoffre, 1896.

Gilmore, J. H. *Outlines Of Logic*. New York: D. Appleton And Company, 1879.

Glenn, Paul J. *Dialectics*. St. Louis: B. Herder Book Co., 1929.

Goblot, Edmond. *Traité De Logique*. Deuxième Édition. Paris: Librairie Armand Colin, 1920.

Gonseth, F. *Qu'Est-Ce Que La Logique?* Paris: Herman & Cie, Éditeurs, 1937.

Gratry, A. *Logic*. La Salle, Illinois: The Open Court Publishing Company, 1944. Trans. Helen and Milton Singer.

Gredt, Joseph. *Elementa Philosophiae Aristotelico-Thomisticae*. Editio secunda. Friburgi Brisgoviae: Sumptibus Herder, 1909, Vol. I.

Gregory, D. S. *Practical Logic*. Philadelphia: Eldridge & Brother, 1881.

Grenier, Rev. Henri. *Thomistic Philosophy*. Editio tertia. Charlottetown, Canada: St. Dunstan's University, 1950, Vol. I. Logic. Trans. Rev. J. P. E. O'Hanley.

——————. *Cursus Philosophiae*. Quebec: L'Actio Sociale Ltée, 1937, Vol. I.

Grevisse, Maurice. *Le Bon Usage, Cours de Grammaire Française et de Langage Français*. Cinquième édition; Paris: Librairie Orientaliste Paul Guethner, 1953.

Grundy, Rev. William. *Aristotelianism, The Logical Treatises, The Metaphysics, The Psychology, The Politics*. Third Edition. New York: E. & J. B. Young & Co., 1889.

Hahan, Hans. *Logique, Mathématiques et Connaissance de la Realité*. Trans. Ernest Vouillemin. Paris: Herman & Cie, Éditeurs, 1935.

Hamilton, Edward John. *The Modalist*. Boston: Ginn & Co., 1891.

Hamilton, Sir William. *Lectures on Logic*. Third Edition, Revised. Ed. Rev. H. L. Mansel and John Veitch. Edinburgh And London: William Blackwood and Sons, 1874, Vols. I and II.

Harris, Robert T. and Jarrett, James L. *Language and Informal Logic*. New York: Longmans, Green And Co., 1956.

Hartman, Sylvester J. *Fundamentals of Logic*. St. Louis: B. Herder Book Co., 1949.

Harvey, Nathan A. *The Thinking Process*. Ypsilanti, Michigan: State Normal College, 1910.

Hedge, Levi. *Elements Of Logick*. Fourth Edition. Boston: Cummings, Hilliard & Co., 1824.

Hegel, Georg Wilhelm Friedrich. *The Logic Of Hegel*. Second Edition. London: Oxford University Press, 1950. Trans. from *The Encyclopaedia Of The Philosophical Sciences* by William Wallace.

229

Henle, P., Kallen, H. and Langer, S. *Structure, Method And Meaning.* New York: The Liberal Arts Press, 1951.

Hepp, Maylon H. *Thinking Things Through.* New York: Charles Scribner's Sons, 1956.

Hibben, John Grier. *Logic Deductive And Inductive.* New York: Charles Scribner's Sons, 1905.

Holmes, Roger W. *The Rhyme Of Reason.* New York: D. Appleton-Century Company, 1939.

Holyoake, George Jacob. *A Logic of Facts.* London: J. Watson, 1866.

Hope, Richard. *How Man Thinks.* Pittsburgh: University of Pittsburgh Press, 1949.

Houde, Roland and Fischer, Jerome. *Handbook Of Logic.* Second Printing. Dubuque: Wm. C. Brown Company, 1954.

Howell, Wilbur Samuel. *Logic and Rhetoric in England, 1500-1700.* Princeton, N.J.: Princeton University Press, 1956.

Hugon, A. R. P. Edward. *Logica.* Editio Tertia. Paris: P. Lethielleux, Editor, 1922, Vol. I.

Huppé, Bernard F. and Kaminsky, Jack. *Logic and Language.* New York: Alfred A. Knopf, 1956.

Hutcheson, Francis. *Logicae Compendium.* Argentorate: Stein, 1771.

Hutton, James. *An Investigation of the Principles of Knowledge.* Edinburgh: Publisher Unknown, 1794. 3 vols.

Hyslop, James H. *The Elements Of Logic.* New York: Charles Scribner's Sons, 1892.

Ingleby, C. Mansfield. *Outlines Of Theoretical Logic.* Cambridge: Macmillan And Co., 1856.

Jaccoud, J. B. *Elementa Philosophiae Theoreticae Et Practicae.* Friburgi Helvetiorum: Sumptibus Librariae Academicae, 1892.

Jaffre, P. F. A. *Cours de Philosophie.* Nouvelle Édition. Lyon: Librairie Briday, 1883.

Jamieson, Alexander. *A Grammar Of Logic And Intellectual Philosophy.* New-Haven: A. H. Maltby And Co., 1822.

Jepson, R. W. *Clear Thinking.* Third edition, enlarged, 1937.

Jevons, W. Stanley. *The Elements Of Logic.* Recast by David J. Hill. New York: American Book Company, 1911.

————. *Logic.* New York: D. Appleton And Company, 1877.

————. *The Principles Of Science.* London: Macmillan And Co., 1874, Vol. I.

————. *Studies In Deductive Logic.* Fourth Edition. London: Macmillan And Co., Limited, 1908.

Joachim, Harold H. *Logical Studies.* Oxford: At The Clarendon Press, 1948.

Johnson, W. E. *Logic.* Cambridge: At the University Press, 1921. 3 vols.

Johnstone, Henry W. Jr. *Elementary Deductive Logic.* New York: Thomas Y. Crowell Company, 1954.

Jolivet, Regis. *Traité de Philosophie*. Deuxième édition. Lyon: Emmanuel Vitte, Éditeur, 1945, Vol. I.

Jorgensen, Jorgen. *A Treatise Of Formal Logic*. Copenhagen: Levin Munksgaard, 1931. 3 vols.

Joseph, H. W. B. *An Introduction To Logic*. Second Edition, Revised. Oxford: At the Clarendon Press, 1916.

Jouin, R. P. Ludovico. *Compendium Logicae et Metaphysicae*. Editio Tertia. Neo Eboraci: H. J. Hewitt, 1879.

Joyce, George Hayward. *Principles Of Logic*. Third Edition. London: Longmans, Green And Co., 1923.

Jungius, Joachim. *Logica Hamburgensis*. Ed. Rudolf W. Meyers. Hamburg: In aedibus J. J. Augustin, 1957.

Kant, Immanuel. *Introduction To Logic*. London: Longmans, Green, & Co., 1885. Trans. Thomas Kingsmill Abbott.

Kapp, Ernst. *Greek Foundations Of Traditional Logic*. New York: Columbia University Press, 1942.

Keene, G. B. *Language and Reasoning*. London: D. Van Nostrand Company, 1961.

Keynes, John Neville. *Studies And Exercises In Formal Logic*. Fourth Edition. London: Macmillan And Co., Limited, 1906.

Kidd, Robert Boyd. *A Delineation Of The Primary Principles Of Reasoning*. London: Richard Bentley, 1856.

Kircher, Athanasius, S. J. *Ars Magna Sciendi*. Amstelodami: Apud Joannem Janssonium à Waesburge, 1669.

Kirwan, Richard, Esq. *Logick, Or, An Essay On The Elements, Principles, And Different Modes Of Reasoning*. London: T. Bensley, 1807. 2 vols. in 1.

Kneale, William and Martha. *The Development of Logic*. Oxford: Clarendon Press, 1962.

Kretzmann, Norman. *Elements of Formal Logic*. Indianapolis, Ind.: The Bobbs-Merrill Company, Inc., 1965.

Kreyche, Robert J. *Logic for Undergraduates*. Revised edition. New York: Holt, Rinehart And Winston, 1961.

Krug, Wilhelm Traugott. *System der theoretischen Philosophie*. Konigsberg: A. W. Unzer, 1819.

Lahr, Père Ch. *Cours de Philosophie*. Vingt-sixième édition. Paris: Gabriel Beauchesne Éditeur, 1929, Vol I.

Lalande, André. *VOCABULAIRE Technique et Critique DE LA PHILOSOPHIE*. Neuvième Édition. Paris: Presses Universitaires De France, 1962.

Latta, Robert and Macbeath, Alexander. *The Elements of Logic*. London: Macmillan And Co., Limited, 1929.

Leblanc, Hugues. *An Introduction to Deductive Logic*. New York: John Wiley & Sons, Inc., 1955.

Le Blond, J. M. *Logique et Méthode Chez Aristote*. Paris: Librairie

Philosophique J. Vrin, 1939.

Leechman, Rev. John. *Logic*. Fourth edition. London: William Allan & Co., 1864.

Leibniz, Gottfried Wilhelm. *Nouveau Essais Sur L'Entendement Humain*. Paris: Ernest Flammarion, n. d.

Lemasson, E. *Notions de Logique Formalle*. Paris: Gabriel Beauchesne et ses Fils, 1935.

Leonard, Henry S. *Principles of Right Reason*. New York: Henry Holt And Company, 1957.

Levesque, L'Abbé. *Précis de Philosophie*. Ed. J. De Gigord. Paris: Ancienne Librairie Poussielgue, 1913, Vols. I & II.

Lewis, Charleton T. and Short, Charles. *A Latin Dictionary*. Oxford: At The Clarendon Press, 1958.

Lewis, Clarence I. "Notes on the Logic of Intension", *Structure, Method, and Meaning: Essays in Honor of Henry M. Sheffer*. New York: Liberal Arts Press, 1951.

Liberatori, Matthaeus, S. J. *Institutiones Philosophicae*. Editio Secunda. Romae: Typis Alexandri Befani Et Soc., 1861.

Liddell, Henry George and Scott, Robert. *A Greek-English Lexicon*. Ninth edition. Oxford: At the Clarendon Press, 1958.

Little, Winston W. et al. *Applied Logic*. Boston: Houghton Mifflin Company, 1955.

Lodge, Rupert Clendon. *An Introduction to Modern Logic*. Minneapolis: The Perine Book Company, 1920.

Lortie, Stanislaus A. *Elementa Philosophiae Christianae Ad Mentem S. Thomae Aquinatis Exposita*. Quarta Editio. Quebeci: Ex typographia L'Action Sociale Ltée, 1921, Vol. I.

Lossada, Luis de. *Institutiones Dialecticae*. Salmanticae: Ex Typographia Francisci Garcia Onorato, 1721.

Lotze, Hermann. *Outlines Of Logic And Of Encyclopaedia Of Philosophy*. Second Edition. Boston: Ginn & Company, 1881. Trans. George T. Ladd.

Louis of Poissy, Brother. *Elementary Course Of Christian Philosophy*. Second edition, revised. New York: O'Shea & Company, 1893.

Luce, A. A. *Teach Yourself Logic To Think More Clearly*. New York: Association Press, 1958.

Luquet, G. H. *Éléments de Logique Formelle*. Paris: Felix Alcan, 1909.

Mace, C. A. *The Principles Of Logic*. London: Longmans, Green And Co., 1933.

MacKaye, James. *The Logic Of Language*. Hanover, N. H. Dartmouth College Publications, 1939.

MacLeane, Douglas. *Reason, Thought And Language*. London: Henry Frowde, 1906.

Mahan, Rev. Asa. *The Science Of Logic*. New York: A. S. Barnes & Co., 1857.

Mahony, Michael J. *Essentials Of Formal Logic.* New York: The Encyclopedia Press, Inc., 1918.

Mancini, P. Fr. Hieronymus Maria. *Elementa Philosophiae Ad Mentem D. Thomae Aquinatis.* Romae: Ex Typographia Polyglotta, 1898, Vol. I.

Mander, A. E. *Clearer Thinking.* London: Watts & Co., 1936.

——. *Logic — For The Millions.* New York: Philosophical Library, 1947.

Mansel, Henry Longueville. *Prolegomena Logica: An Inquiry Into The Psychological Character Of Logical Processes.* Boston: Gould And Lincoln, 1860.

Maria, Michaele de, S. J. *Philosophia Peripatetico-Scholastica Ex Fontibus Aristotelis Et S. Thomae Aquinatis.* Editio Quarta. Romae: Ex Pontificia Officina Typographica, 1913, Vol. I.

Maritain, Jacques. *Formal Logic.* New York: Sheed & Ward, 1937. Trans. Imelda Choquette.

——. *An Introduction To Logic.* New York: Sheed & Ward, 1937. Trans. Imelda Choquette.

Maurus, Sylvester, S. J. *Aristotelis Opera Omnia.* Ed Franciscus Ehrle, S. J. Parisiis: P. Lethielleux, 1886. 4 vols. This treatise was originally published by Sylvester Maurus in 1668.

McCall, Raymond J. *Basic Logic.* New York: Barnes & Noble, Inc., 1947.

McClure, Matthew Thomson. *An Introduction To The Logic Of Reflection.* New York: Henry Holt And Company, 1925.

McCosh, James. *The Laws of Discursive Thought.* New York: Charles Scribner's Sons, 1891.

McGovern, Rev. Thomas. *The Division of Logic.* Quebec: Librairie Philosophique M. Doyon, 1956.

McGregor, P. *A System Of Logic.* New York: Harper & Brothers, 1862.

McLaughlin, Joseph. *An Outline And Manual Of Logic.* Milwaukee: Marquette University Press, 1932.

McNair, George Hastings. *A Class Room Logic.* New York: The Ethlas Press, 1914.

Mellone, Sydney Herbert. *An Introductory Text-Book Of Logic.* Nineteenth edition. Edinburgh: William Blackwood & Sons Ltd., 1937.

Mendive, P. Joseph, S. J. *Institutiones Philosophiae Scholasticae.* Vallisoleti: Ex Typographia Viduae De Cuesta Et Fil., 1886.

Mening, Carolus. *Elementa Logicae.* St. Louis: B. Herder Book Co., 1924.

Mercier, Charles. *A New Logic.* London: William Heinemann, 1912.

Mercier, D. *Elements Of Logic.* Third Edition. New York: The Manhattanville Press, 1912. Trans. Ewan Macpherson.

——. *Logique.* Troisième Édition. Louvain: Institut Supérieur De Philosophie, 1902.

Merguet, H. *Lexikon Zu Den Philosophischen Schriften Cicero's.* Jean: Verlag Von Gustav Fischer, 1887, Vol. I.

Meyerson, Émile. *Du Cheminement de la Pensée.* Paris: Librairie Felix Alcan, 1931. 3 vols.

Miano, Vincentius. *Introduction in Philosophiam et Logica.* Romae: Societa Editrice Internazionale, 1961.

Migne, J. P. *Patrologiae Cursus Completus,* Series Graeca. Parisiis: Bibliothecae Cleri Universale, 1860, Vol. XCIV.

———. *Patrologiae Cursus Completus,* Series Graeca. Parisiis: Bibliothecae Cleri Universale, 1885, Vol. CXLII.

———. *Patrologiae Cursus Completus,* Series Latina. Parisiis: Bibliothecae Cleri Universale, 1850, Vol. LXXXII.

———. *Patrologiae Cursus Completus,* Series Latina. Parisiis: Bibliothecae Cleri Universale, 1891, Vol. LXIV.

Mill, James. *Analysis of the Phenomena of the Human Mind.* London: Baldwin and Cradock, 1829. 2 vols.

Mill, John Stuart. *A System of Logic, Ratiocinative and Inductive.* Eighth Edition. New York: Harper & Brothers, 1879.

Miller, James Wilkinson. *The Structure Of Aristotelian Logic.* London: Kegan, et al., 1938.

Minio-Paluello, L. *Twelfth Century Logic.* Romae: Edizioni Di Storia E Letteratura, 1958.

Minto, William. *Logic Inductive and Deductive.* New York: Charles Scribner's Sons, 1893.

Moberly, C. E. *Lectures on Logic.* Oxford: John Henry Parker, 1848.

Molesworth, Vol. *Landmarks In Logic.* Australia: The Law Book Co. Of Australasia Pty Ltd., 1958.

Monaco, Nicolaus, *Praelectiones Logicae Dialecticae Et Critices.* Romae: Ex Officina Libraria Giachetti, Filli Et So., 1910.

Monck, W. H. S. *An Introduction To Logic.* Dublin: Hodges, et al., 1880.

Mourant, John A. *Formal Logic.* New York: The Macmillan Company, 1963.

Munro, H. H. *A Manual Of Logic.* Glasgow: Maurice Ogle And Son, 1850.

Munzi, Attilius. *Logica.* Romae: Apud Aedes Universitatis Gregorianae, 1920.

Musschembroek, Peter van. *Institutiones Logicae.* Venetiis: Ex Typographia Remondiniana, 1763.

Neil, Samuel. *The Art of Reasoning.* London: Walton and Maberly, 1853.

Newton, John. *The English Academy: Or, A Brief Introduction To The Seven Liberal Arts.* London: W. Godbid, 1677.

Nicole, Pierre (1625-1695). *La Logique ou l'Art de Penser.* Paris: Chez Savoye, 1775.

Norris, John. *An Essay towards the Theory of the ideal or intelligible World.* London: Printed for S. Manship, at the Ship in Cornhill, near the Royal Exchange, 1704. 2 vols.

234

Northrop, F. S. C. *The Logic Of The Sciences And The Humanities.* New York: The Macmillan Company, 1947.

Oesterle, John A. *Logic.* Ninth Printing. Englewood Cliffs: Prentice-Hall, Inc., 1959.

Ogden, Charles Kay and Richards, I. A. *The Meaning Of Meaning.* New York: Harcourt Brace & Co., 1923.

Oldfield, Joshua. *An Essay towards the Improvement Of Reason; in the Pursuit of Learning And Conduct of Life.* London: Bible and Three Crowns, 1707.

The Oxford English Dictionary. Oxford: At The Clarendon Press, 1961. Vol. II.

Ozell, John. *Logic.* London: At the Ship in Pater-noster-row, 1717.

Parker, Francis H. and Veatch, Henry B. *Logic as a Human Instrument.* New York: Harper & Brothers, 1959.

Parker, S. E. *Logic.* Philadelphia: Robert Davis, 1837.

Pater, W. A. de. *Les Topiques D'Aristote Et La Dialectique Platonicienne.* Fribourg, Suisse: Editions St. Paul, 1965.

Patterson, Charles H. *Principles of Correct Thinking.* New York: Longmans, Green And Co., 1937.

Peirce, C. S. "Upon Logical Comprehension and Extension," *Proceedings Of The American Academy Of Arts And Sciences.* Boston And Cambridge: Welch, Bigelow, And Company, November 13, 1867, Vol. II, pp. 416-32.

―――――. *Studies in Loyic.* Boston: Little, Brown, And Company, 1883.

Pellissier, Pierre A. *Précis d'un Cours Élémentaire de Logique.* Deuxième édition. Paris: Auguste Durand, Libraire, 1860.

Perrard, J. F. *Logique Classique d'après les Principes de Philosophie de Laromiguière.* Troisième édition. Paris: Librairie de Périsse Frères, 1865.

Pesch, Tilmanus. S. J. *Institutiones Logicae et Ontologicae.* Editio altera a Carolo Frick, S. J. Friburgi Brisgoviae: B. Herder, 1914.

Piaget, Jean. *Traité De Logique.* Paris: Librairie Armand Colin, 1949.

Pieralisi, P. Venceslao. *Della Filosofia Razionale Speculativa.* Romae: Tipografia Della Pace, 1876.

Poland, William. *The Laws Of Thought Or Formal Logic.* New York: Silver, Burdett & Co., 1892.

Prantl, Dr. Carl. *Geschichte Der Logik Im Abendlande.* Leipzig: Verlag Von S. Hirzel, 1867. 4 vols.

Prazak, Milos. *Language And Logic.* New York: Philosophical Library, 1963.

Prior, A. N. *Formal Logic.* Oxford: At The Clarendon Press, 1955.

Prisco, Joseph. *Philosophie Spéculative selon la Doctrine Angélique de Saint Thomas D'Aquin.* Paris: Librairie De H. Oudin Frères, 1877. Traduit de l'Italien par Prosper-Pierre Huchedé.

Prot, Marcel. *Langage et Logique.* Paris: Hermann & Cie, Éditeurs, 1949.

235

Purchotius, V. Cl. Edmundus. *Exercitationes Scolasticae.* Editio tertia. Lugduni: Apud Antonium Boudet, 1711.

————. *Institutiones Philosophicae.* Editio tertia. Parisiis: Apud Joanem Baptistam Coignard, 1711, Vol. I.

Quine, Willard Van Orman. *From A Logical Point Of View.* Cambridge, Mass.: Harvard University Press, 1953.

Rabier, Élie. *Leçons de Philosophie.* Cinquième Édition. Paris: Librairie Hachette et Cie, 1903, Vol. II.

Rattier, M. *Manuel Élémentaire de Philosophie.* Paris: Gaume Frères, 1844.

Read, Carveth. *Logic Deductive And Inductive.* Third Edition. London: Alexander Morning, Limited, 1906.

Regius, Johannes. *Institutionum Logicarum Epitome.* Franequerae: Apud Franciscum Halman, 1705.

Reid, Thomas. *Analysis of Aristotle's Logic.* Second edition. Edinburgh: Printed for William Creech; and sold by J. Murray, Fleet-Street, London, 1806.

Reiffenberg, Le Baron de. *Principes de Logique.* Bruxelles: Louis Hauman Et Cie, 1833.

Reinhold, Ernst. *Die Logik oder allgemeine Denkformenlehre dargestellt.* Jena: Erdterfchen Buchhandlung, 1827.

Reinstadler, Dr. Seb. *Elementa Philosophiae Scholasticae.* Editio septima et octava. Friburgi Brisgoviae B. Herder, 1931, Vol. I.

Reis, Lincoln. *The Predicables and the Predicaments in the Totius Summa Logicae Aristotelis.* New York: Columbia University, 1936.

Reiser, Oliver L. *Humanistic Logic for the Mind in Action.* New York: Thomas Y. Crowell Company, 1930.

Remer, Vincentius, S. J. *Summa Praelectionum Philosophiae Scholasticae.* Prati: Ex Officina Libraria Giachetti, Filii Et Soc., 1895, Vol. I.

Renouvier, Ch. *Traité de Logique Générale et de Logique Formelle.* Paris: Libraire Armand Colin, 1912. 2 vols.

Resa, Alexander John. *The Essentials Of Practical Logic.* Chicago: Champlin-Shealy Co., 1943.

Rescher, Nicholas. *The Development Of Arabic Logic.* Liverpool: C. Tingling & Co., 1964.

Rickaby, John, S. J. *The First Principles Of Knowledge.* Fourth Edition. New York: Longmans, Green, And Co., 1901.

Rieber, Charles H. *Footnotes To Formal Logic.* Berkeley: University Of California Press, 1918.

Ritter, Dr. Heinrich. *System der Logik und der Metaphysik.* Göttingen: Berlag Dieterich'fchen Buchhandlung, 1856. 2 vols.

Robert, Abbé Arthur. *Leçons de Logique.* Québec: Imp. de l'Action Sociale Limitée, 1914.

Robinson, Daniel Sommer. *Illustrations Of The Methods Of Reasoning.* New York: D. Appleton And Company, 1924.

236

Roure, Marie-Louise. *Logique et Métalogique*. Paris: Emmanuel Vitte, Éditeur, 1957.

Roy, Bhola Nath. *Textbook Of Deductive Logic*. Fourteenth edition. Calcutta: S. C. Sarkar & Sons Ltd., 1949.

Ruby, Lionel. *The Art Of Making Sense*. Philadelphia: J. B. Lippincott Company, 1954.

————. *Logic, An Introduction*. Chicago: J. B. Lippincott Company, 1950.

Ruchlis, Hy. *Clear Thinking*. New York: Harper & Row, 1962.

Ruffin, J. N. *Great Logicians*. New York: S. Werner & Co., 1926.

Russell, John Edward. *An Elementary Logic*. New York: The Macmillan Company, 1906.

Saint-Hilaire, J. Barthélemy. *De la Logique d'Aristote*. Paris: Chez Ladrange, Librairie, 1838. 2 vols.

Salmon, Wesley C. *Logic*. Ed. Elizabeth and Monroe Beardsley. Englewood Cliffs, N.J.: Prentice-Hall, 1963.

Sanseverino, Cajetano. *Philosophia Christiana*. Neapoli: Apud Officinam Bibliothecae Catholicae Scriptorum, 1878.

Sauri. *Élémens de Logique*. Paris: Chez Froullé, 1794, Vol. I.

Schiller, F. C. S. *Formal Logic*. London: Macmillan And Co., Limited, 1912.

————. *Logic for Use*. London: G. Bell & Sons Ltd., 1929.

Schipper, Edith W. and Howard, Deton T. *Logic for Use*. Ann Arbor, Mich.: Edward Brothers, Inc. 1950.

Schipper, Edith W. and Schuh, Edward. *Principles of Applied Logic*. Dubuque, Iowa: Wm. C. Brown Company, 1956.

Scholz, Heinrich. *Concise History Of Logic*. New York: Philosophical Library, Inc., 1961. Trans. from the German by Kurt F. Leidecker.

Schulze, Gottlob E. *Grundsätze der allgemeinen Logik*. Göttingen: Vandenhoek and Ruprecht, 1822.

Schuyler, A. *The Principles of Logic*. Cincinnati: Wilson, Hinkle & Co., 1869.

Searles, Herbert L. *Logic and Scientific Methods*. Second Edition. New York: The Ronald Press Company, 1956.

Sellars, R. W. *The Essentials Of Logic*. Boston: Houghton Mifflin Company, 1917.

Sharvy, Robert. *Logic: An Outline*. Patterson, New Jersey: Littlefield Adams & Co., 1962.

Shaw, Charles Gray. *Logic In Theory And Practice*. London: Sir Isaac Pitman & Sons, Ltd., 1935.

Shedden, Thomas. *The Elements Of Logic*. London: Longman, Green, Longman, Roberts, & Green, 1864.

Sicard, R. A. *Élémens de Grammaire Générale Appliqués à la Langue Française*. Seconde Édition. Paris: Chez Deterville, 1801, Vol. I.

237

Sidgwick, Alfred. *The Application Of Logic.* London: Macmillan And Co., Limited, 1910.

————. *Distinction And The Criticism Of Beliefs.* London: Longmans, Green, And Co., 1892.

————. *The Use Of Words In Reasoning.* London: Adam And Charles Black, 1901.

Sigwart, Dr. Christoph. *Logic.* Second Edition. London: Swan Sonnenschein & Co., 1895. 2 vols. Trans. Helen Dendy.

Simmons, Edward D. *The Scientific Art Of Logic.* Milwaukee: The Bruce Publishing Company, 1961.

Sinclair, William Angus. *The Traditional Formal Logic.* Fifth Edition. London: Methuen & Co., Ltd., 1959.

Smart, B. H. *Practical Logic.* London: G. And W. B. Whittaker, 1823.

Smith, George H. *Logic.* New York: G. P. Putnam's Sons, 1901.

Smith, Henry Bradford. *A First Book In Logic.* New York: F. S. Crofts & Co., 1938.

Smith, Vincent Edward. *The Elements Of Logic.* Milwaukee: The Bruce Publishing Company, 1957.

Snyder, Alice D. *Coleridge On Logic And Learning.* New Haven: Yale University Press, 1929.

Solly, Thomas. Esq. *A Syllabus Of Logic.* Cambridge: J & J. J. Deighton, 1839.

Sortais, Gaston. *Manuel de Philosophie.* Sixième Édition. Paris: P. Lethielleux, 1907.

Spalding, William. *An Introduction To Logical Science.* Edinburgh: Adam And Charles Black, 1857.

Squadranus, Ireneus. *Cursus specialis logicam Aristotelis.* Romae: ?, 1932-33.

Stanghetti, Joseph. *Logica.* Romae: Ex Officina Typographica Buona Stampa, 1929.

Stebbing, L. Susan. *Logic in Practice.* London: Methuen & Co., Ltd., 1934.

————. *A Modern Elementary Logic.* London: Methuen & Co., Ltd., 1943.

————. *Modern Introduction To Logic.* London: Methuen & Co., Ltd., 1930.

Steele, Sir Richard. *A Grammar Of The English Tongue.* The fourth edition, corrected. London: J. Roberts et al, 1721.

Stephanus, Robertus. *Theasaurus Linguae Latinae.* Basiliae: Typis et impensis E. & J. R. Thurnisiorum Fratr., 1740, Vol. I.

Strawson, P. F. *Introduction to Logical Theory.* London: Methuen & Co., Ltd., 1952.

Sugiura, Sadajiro. *Hindu Logic As Preserved In China And Japan.* Ed. Edgar A. Singer, Jr. Boston: Ginn & Co., 1900.

Sullivan, Daniel J. *Fundamentals Of Logic.* New York: McGraw-Hill Book Company, Inc., 1963.

Suppes, Patrick. *Introduction to Logic.* Princeton, New Jersey: Van Nostrand Co., 1957.

Swabey, Marie C. *Logic and Nature.* New York: The New York University Press, 1930.

Tagart, Edward. *Remarks On Mathematical Or Demonstrative Reasoning.* London: John Green, 1837.

Tappan, Henry P. *Elements of Logic.* New York: D. Appleton And Company, 1871.

Taylor, William J. *Elementary Logic.* New York: Charles Scribner's Sons, 1909.

Templin, Olin and McCraken, Anna. *A Guide to Thinking.* Garden City, N.Y.: Doubleday, Page & Company, 1927.

Thomson, William. *An Outline Of The Necessary Laws Of Thought.* Third Edition. London: Longman, Brown, Green And Longmans, 1854.

Thouless, Robert H. *How To Think Straight.* New York: Simon And Schuster, 1939.

————. *Straight and Crooked Thinking.* London: Hodder And Stoughton Limited, 1930.

Thynne, William. *A Compendium of Logic.* Third edition. Dublin: J. D. Scott And Co., 1835.

Tigert, Jno. J. *Handbook of Logic.* Nashville, Tenn.: Southern Methodist Publishing House, 1885.

Tissot, J. *Mélanges de Logique d'Emmanuel Kant.* Paris: Librairie Philosophique De Ladrange, 1862.

Tongiorgi, Salvator. *Institutiones Philosophicae.* Neo Eboraci: Typis Joannis M. Shea, 1864.

Toohey, John J. *An Elementary Handbook of Logic.* Second edition. New York: Schwartz, Kirwin & Fauss, 1924.

————. *An Elementary Handbook of Logic.* Third edition. New York: Appleton-Century-Crofts, Inc., 1948.

True, Charles K. *The Elements of Logic.* Third edition, revised. New York: Carlton & Porter, 1861.

Turner, William. *History of Philosophy.* Boston: Ginn And Company, 1929.

————. *Lessons In Logic.* Washington, D. C.: Catholic Education Press, 1911.

Turrell, Henry J. *A Manual Of Logic.* London: Rivingtons, 1870.

Uccello, R. P. Seb., S. S. S. *Philosophia Scholastica Ad Mentem Sancti Thomae.* Augustae Taurinorum: Sumptibus et typis Petri Marietti, 1921, Vol. I.

Ueberweg, Dr. Friedrich. *System Of Logic.* London: Longmans, Green, And Co., 1871. Trans. Thomas M. Lindsay.

Urraburu, P. Joannes Josephus. *Institutiones Philosophicae*. Parisiis: P. Lethielleux, 1890, Vol. I.

Vacherot, E. *Histoire Critique de L'École d'Alexandre*. Paris: Librairie Philosophique de Ladrange, 1846. 3 vols.

Van De Woestyne, P. F. Zachariam. *Cursus Philosophicus*. Mechliniae: Typographia S. Francisci, 1921, Vol. I.

Van Laer, P. Henry. *Philosophy of Science*. Second Edition. Pittsburgh: Duquesne University Press, 1963, Part One.

Varvello, Rev. Francis. *Minor Logic*. San Francisco, Calif.: University Of San Francisco Press, 1933. Trans. and supplemented by Arthur D. Fearon.

Veatch, Henry Babcock. *Intentional Logic*. New Haven: Yale University Press, 1952.

Veitch, John. *Institutes Of Logic*. Edinburgh: William Blackwood And Sons, 1885.

Venn, John. *The Principles Of Empirical Or Inductive Logic*. Second Edition. London: Macmillan And Co., Limited, 1907.

Vidyabhusana, Satis Chandra. *A History Of Indian Logic*. Calcutta: Baptist Mission Press, 1921.

Walch, John George. *Parerga Academica*. Lipsiae: John Friederick Gleditsch, 1721.

Walcott, Gregory Dexter. *An Elementary Logic*. New York: Harcourt, Brace And Company, 1931.

Wallis, John. *Institutio Logicae*. Editio tertia. Oxford: Leon Lichfield, 1702. This book was first printed on Nov. 30, 1686.

Walsh, Joseph B. *Logic*. New York: Fordham University Press, 1940.

Watts, Isaac. *Logick: Or, The Right Use Of Reason In The Enquiry After Truth*. Fourth Edition. London: Printed for Emmanuel Matthews, at the Bible in Pater-noster-Row, 1731.

Werkmeister, W. H. *An Introduction To Critical Thinking*. Lincoln, Nebraska: Johnsen Publishing Company, 1957.

Westlund, Jacob. *Outlines of Logic*. Topeka, Kansas: Crane & Co., 1896.

Whately, Richard. *Elements of Logic*. New York: William Jackson, 1836.

———. *Elements Of Logic*. Ninth edition, revised. London: John W. Parker, 1848.

Wheelwright, Philip. *Valid Thinking*. New York: The Odyssey Press, 1962.

Willcox, James M. *Logic*. Philadelphia: Porter And Coates, 1875.

Willems, C. *Institutiones Philosophicae*. Tertia Editio. Treveris: Ex Officina Ad S. Paulum, 1915, Vol. I.

Williams, Henry Horace. *The Evolution Of Logic*. Durham, N. C.: Christian & King Printing Company, 1925.

———. *Logic For Living*. Ed. Jane Ross Hammer. New York: Philosophical Library, 1951.

240

Wilson, D. D. *An Elementary Treatise on Logic.* New York: D. Appleton And Company, 1856.

Wolf, A. *Textbook Of Logic.* 2nd. Edition. New York: The Macmillan Company, 1936.

Wood, Frederick T. *Training in Thought and Expression.* London: Macmillan And Co., Limited, 1940.

Woolley, J. *An Introduction to Logic.* Oxford: John Henry Parker, 1840.

Wright, George Henrik von. *Logical Studies.* London: Routledge And Kegan Paul, 1957.

Wright, Sir Almroth E. *Alethetropic Logic.* London: William Heinemann Ltd., 1953. Alethetropic Logic is a logic which searches for truth; which concerns itself with truth.

————. *Prolegomena To The Logic Which Searches For Truth.* London: William Heinemann Ltd., 1941.

Wuellner, Bernard. *Dictionary Of Scholastic Philosophy.* Milwaukee: The Bruce Publishing Company, 1956.

Wyclif, John. *De Logica.* Ed. Michael Henry Dziewicki. London: Trubner & Co., 1893. 3 vols.

Yamunacharya, M. *An Introduction to Logic and Scientific Method.* Mysore: H. Venkataramish & Sons, 1953.

Zigliara, F. Thomas Maria. *Summa Philosophica.* Tertia Editio. Paris: Gabriel Beauchesne & Cie, Editeurs, 1880.

ADDENDA

Agricola, Rudolphus. *De Inventione Dialectica Lucubrationes.* Nieuwkoop: B. de Graaf, 1967.

Blundeville, Thomas. *The Art Of Logike (1599).* Menston, England: The Scolar Press Limited, 1967.

De Rijk, L. M. *Logica Modernorum.* Assen: Van Gorcum & Comp., 1967, vols. I, II.

Good, Thomas. *A Brief English Tract Of Logick (1677).* Leeds, England: The Scolar Press Limited, 1967.

Risse, Wilhelm. *Bibliographia Logica.* Germany, Georg Olms Verlagsbuchhandlung Hildesheim, 1965, band I.

Schmidt, Robert W., S.J. *The Domain Of Logic According To Saint Thomas Aquinas.* The Hague: Martinus Nijhoff, 1966.

FOOTNOTES TO CHAPTER I

1. Noah K. Davis, *The Theory Of Thought, A Treatise On Deductive Logic* (New York: Harper & Brothers, 1880), p. 35.

2. Heinrich Scholz, *Concise History of Logic*, trans. from the German by Kurt F. Leidecker (New York: Philosophical Library, Inc., 1961), pp. 42-43. The words 'scope' and 'content' are used as synonyms for 'extension' and 'comprehension'.

3. Augustus De Morgan, *Syllabus Of A Proposed System Of Logic* (London: Walton And Maberly, 1860), p. 61. Cf. Francis Hutcheson (p. 11 of this study) who also distinguishes between the logical whole and metaphysical whole.

4. Antoine Arnauld and M. Nicole, *The Port Royal Logic*, trans. Thomas Spencer Baynes (Edinburgh: Oliver and Boyd, 1865), Intro., p. xxxiii. This statement was later reiterated by James McCosh, *The Laws Of Discursive Thought* (New York: Charles Scribner's Sons, 1891), p. 27: "The Distinction between the Extension and Comprehension of a Notion, though stated earlier, was introduced formally into logic in *La Logique ou l'Art de Penser,* by Arnauld and Nicole (1662 A.D.)."

5. Cf. Chapter II of this treatise.

6. Cf. Richard Whately, *Elements Of Logic* (Ninth edition, revised; London: John W. Parker, 1848), p. 128.

7. Cf. Sir William Hamilton, *Lectures on Logic* (Third edition, rev.; Edinburgh and London: William Blackwood and Sons, 1874), Vol. I, p. 119.

8. Monroe C. Beardsley, *Thinking Straight* (Englewood Cliffs, N.J.: Prentice-Hall, Inc., 1958), p. 200.

9. Antoine Arnauld et M. Nicole, *Logique de Port-Royal* (Paris: Librairie De l. Hachette et Cie, 1869), p. 55: "Mais quand nous parlons ici de mots généraux, nous entendons les univoques qui sont joints à des idées universelles et générales. Or, dans ces idées universelles, il y a deux choses qu'il est très important de bien distinguer, *la compréhension et l'étendue.*

J'appelle *compréhension* de l'idée, les attributs qu'elle renferme en soi, et qu'on ne peut lui ôter sans la détruire, comme la compréhension de l'idée du triangle enferme extension, figure, trois lignes, trois angles, et l'égalité de ces trois angles à deux droits, etc.

J'appelle *étendue* de l'idée les sujets à qui cette idée convient; ce qu'on appelle aussi les inférieurs d'un terme général, qui a leur égard, est appelé supérieur, comme l'idée du triangle en général s'étend à toutes les diverses espèces de triangle.

Mais, quoique l'idée générale s'étende indistinctement à tous les sujets à qui elle convient, c'est-à-dire a tous ses inférieurs, et que le nom commun les signifie tous, il y a néanmoins cette différence entre les attributs qu'elle comprend et les sujets auxquels elle s'étend, qu'on, ne peut lui ôter aucun de ses attributs sans la détruire, comme nous avons déjà dit; au lieu qu'on peut la resserrer, quant à son étendue, ne l'appliquant qu'á quelqu'un des sujets auxquels elle convient, sans que pour cela on la détruise." These definitions are quoted by John Ozell in his *Logic* (London: At the Ship in Paternoster-row, 1717), pp. 58-59. However, he substitutes the word 'extend' for 'extension'. They are also quoted by Pierre Nicole (1625-1695), *La Logique ou l'Art de Penser* (Paris: Chez Savoye, 1775), Part I, Chap. VI, p. 31.

10. Cf. William Kneale and Martha Kneale, *The Development Of Logic* (Oxford: At the Clarendon Press, 1962), p. 318.

11. Cf. H. W. B. Joseph, *An Introduction To Logic* (Oxford: At the Clarendon Press, 1916), p. 144.

12. *Ibid.*, p. 146. Cf. L. S. Stebbing, *Modern Introduction To Logic* (London: Methuen & Co., Ltd., 1930), pp. 28-29.

13. Cf. p. 160 ff. of this study.

14. From now on, all of the authors cited in this chapter will be presented in a strictly chronological order. Only one exception will be made to this mode of procedure. A certain group of logicians belonging to the German school of logic will be treated separately in order to call attention in bold relief to how they agree and disagree with each other.

15. Richard Crakanthorpe, *Logicae Libri Quinque* (Oxoniae: L. Lichfield & H. Hall, 1677), Liber I, Cap. III. De Genere, p. 4: "*Genus est universale quod praedicatur* (actu vel aptitudine) *de differentibus Specie in Quid*: ut animal de homine et bruto: color de albedine et nigredine." A similar definition is found in a later publication by William Brattle, *Compendium Logicae* (Boston ?, 1735), p. 21: "Genus est Universale quod de pluribus, Specie distinctis, in Quaestione *Quid Res Sit*: praedicatur."

16. *Ibid.*, p. 8: "*Species est universale quod subjicitur Generi*: ut Homo, Brutum, Albedo . . . ."

17. Cf. John Wallis, *Institutio Logicae* (Editio tertia; Oxoniae: Leon Lichfield, 1702), p. 14. This book was first printed on November 30, 1686.

18. Cf. *Ibid.*, p. 16.

19. Cf. Joh. Bapt. Du Hamel, *Philosophia* (Editio quinta; Amstaelodami: G. Gallet, 1700), Vol. I, p. 121.

20. *Ibid.*, p. 119: "Genus definiri solet universale, quod praedicatur de multis specie differentibus in quid incomplete."

21. *Ibid.*, p. 121: "[Species infima est] id quod praedicatur de multis numero differentibus in quid complete."

22. John Norris, *An Essay towards the Theory of the ideal or intelligible World* (London: Printed for S. Manship, at the Ship in Cornhill, near the Royal Exchange, 1704), Vol. II, Part II, Sect. 7, p. 178.

23. Johannes Regius, *Institutionum Logicarum Epitome* (Franequerae: Apud Franciscum Halman, 1705), p. 21: "Tota natura generis est in specie; sed tota natura speciei non est in genere."

24. *Ibid.*, p. 22: "Genus latius patet quam species."

25. Joshua Oldfield, *An Essay towards the Improvement Of Reason; in the Pursuit of Learning And Conduct of Life* (London: Bible and Three Crowns, 1707), pp. 70-71. Inasmuch as this author uses the words 'extension' and 'comprehension' explicitly, he disproves De Morgan's contention that this distinction is one of recent origin (Cf. p. 2 of this study).

26. V. Cl. Edmundus Purchotius, *Institutiones Philosophiae* (Editio tertia; Paris: Apud Joannem Baptistam Coignard, 1711), Vol. I, p. 60: "Per *comprehensionem* ideae intelliguntur *ea attributa, quae in rei cujusdam idea sic continentur, ut sine illis stare non possit istius rei idea*: v.g. esse *compositum ex mente et corpore,* sic continetur in hominis idea, ut aliter homo intelligi non possit. Sic esse *rotundum* in idea circuli ita includitur ut sine hoc attributo comprehendi nequeat circulus.

Per *extensionem* idea intelliguntur *subjecta quibus ista idea convenire potest,* ut idea hominis competit Socrati, Aristoteli, et caeteris; idea circuli, cuilibet circulo; idea trianguli, cuilibet triangulo potest aptari." For similar definitions of comprehension and extension, consult this author's *Exercitationes Scolasticae* (Editio tertia; Lugduni: Apud Antonium Boudet, 1711), pp. 10-11.

27. Jean Pierre de Crousaz, *A New Treatise Of The Art Of Thinking* (London: Printed for Tho. Woodward at the Half-Moon over-against St. Dunstan's Church in Fleet-Street, 1724), Vol. II, p. 87. This book was originally written in French by the same author.

28. Jean Pierre de Crousaz, *Examen du Pyrrhonisme* (A la Haye: Chez Pierre de Hondt, 1733), p. 365b: "Nous avons des Idées générales, c'est à dire des Idées applicables à un grand nombre des choses. Lorsque ces choses auxquelles on applique un Idée générale font différentes entr'elles, on les appelle *espèces* par rapport à cette idée générale qu'on leur applique, et qui s'appelle *genre;* et on trouve également dans chacune des espèces tout ce que cette générale renferme, et outre cela quelque chose de plus. Ainsi j'ai une Idée générale qui répond au mot de Figure. J'applique cette Idée à une surface fermée de lignes *courbes.* J'ai donc *figure rectiligne,* et *figure curviligne.* Chacune de ces espèces est figure autant que l'autre: mais dans chacune je trouve quelque chose, que je ne trouve pas dans l'autre. Voilà de quelle manière un *genre* se distingue dans ses espèces, et de quelle manière chaque Espèce contient le Genre avec quelque chose de plus."

245

29. Isaac Watts, *Logick: Or, The Right Use Of Reason In The Enquiry After Truth* (The Fourth Edition, Corrected; London: Printed for Emmanuel Matthews, at the Bible in Pater-noster-Row, 1731), p. 37.

30. Cf. p. 5 of this treatise.

31. Peter Van Musschembroek, *Institutiones Logicae* (Venetiis: Ex Typographia Remondiniana, 1763), p. 31: "*Species* est idea universalis formata iterum ex modis iis, in quibus individua conveniunt, veluti Paulus, Titius, conveniunt in eo ut sint Jureconsulti, vel Eruditi, vel nati in eadem regione, vel ejusdem religionis, vel donati mente rationali et corpore, unde formatur idea quaedam universalis Jurisperitorum, Eruditorum, Civium, Fratrum, Hominis."

32. Emile Meyerson, *Du Cheminement de la Pensée* (Paris: Librairie Felix Alcan, 1931), Vol. III, p. 826: "L'animal comprend plus d'individus que l'homme mais l'homme comprend plus d'idées ou plus de formalités; l'un a plus d'exemples, l'autre plus de degrés de realité; l'un a plus d'extension, l'autre plus d'intension." This same passage is also cited by André Lalande in his *Vocabulaire Technique et Critique de la Philosophie* (Neuvième édition; Paris: Presses Universitaires de France, 1962), p. 528. The earliest edition of Leibniz' collected works is that of Raspe (Leipzig and Amsterdam, 1765). Even though he is German, Leibniz' remarks on extension and intension are more in keeping with the French school than the later German school.

33. According to I. M. Bochenski, Leibniz was aware of this distinction, and yet he did not refer to it in traditional terminology. Cf. p. 72 of this treatise.

34. Louis Couturat, *La Logique de Leibniz* (Hildesheim: Georg Olms Verlagsbuchhandlung, 1961), p. 444: "On peut dire, en gros, qu'au point de l'extension le sujet est contenu dans le predicat, tandis qu'au point de vue de la compréhension il le contient. En d'autres termes, le predicat est à la fois plus général et plus abstrait que le sujet."

35. Francis Hutcheson, *Logicae Compendium* (Argentorate: Stein, 1771), Ch. V, p. 20: "Totum Logicum sive extensio ideae declaratur per Divisionem, quae est 'enumeratio plurium, quae in communis ideae aut nominis extensione continentur'." Here appears one of the earliest identifications of extension with the *Totum Logicum*. The history of such identification cannot be considered in this treatise.

36. *Ibid.,* Ch. VI, p. 20: "Totum Metaphysicum, aut comprehensio ideae complexae, declaratur per Definitionem; quae est 'oratio explicans simpliciores ideas, quae in complexa conjunguntur'." This assertion is also an open refutation of De Morgan's declaration that the distinction was introduced in the nineteenth century (Cf. p. 2 of this study).

37. St. Thomas, In V *Metaph.,* lect. 21, n. 1094: "*Secundo modo ea dicuntur partes, in quae dividitur aliquid sine quantitate: et per hunc modum species dicuntur esse partes generis. Dividitur enim in species,*

non sicut quantitas, in partes quantitatis. Nam tota quantitas non est in una suarum partium. Genus autem est in qualibet specierum."

38. *Ibid.*, n. 1096: "*Quarto modo* dicuntur partes, quae ponuntur in definitione cuiuslibet rei, quae sunt partes rationis sicut animal et bipes sunt partes hominis."

39. Dominicus Angeloni, *Institutiones Logicae* (Neapoli: Ex Typographia Raymundiana, 1772), Liber I, p. 18: "In ideis universalibus considerandae sunt, *comprehensio,* et *extensio.* Comprehensio ideae est omnium, quae in ipsa idea continentur, aggregatum. Sic ideae corporis comprehensio est, extensum esse, solidum, divisible, mobile, caeteraque, quae in corpore comprehenduntur; ideae trianguli comprehensio est, habere tria latera spatium comprehendentia. Extensio ideae est subjectorum omnium, quibus idea illa convenit, aggregatum. Sic extensio ideae corporis est omne corpus; extensio ideae trianguli est omne triangulum. Comprehensio semper ad ea refertur, quae idea ipsa continet; extensio vero refertur ad objecta, quibus convenire intelligitur idea."

40. Alexander Gottlieb Baumgarten, *Acroasis Logica* (Halae Magdeburgae: C. H. Hemmerde, 1773), §§56, 57, p. 19: "NOTIO pluribus commune repraesentat (§51.): hinc notam plurium' (§54.): hinc alios conceptus ingreditur, et in aliis continetur (§55.). Quos ingreditur, seu in quibus continetur, illos SUB SE CONTINET (complectitur, comprehendit). Conceptus sub notione contenti ad eamdem referuntur.

CONCEPTUS alium sub se continens est respectu ipsius SUPERIOR (transcendentalis). CONCEPTUS sub alio contentus est respectu ipsius INFERIOR. Ergo omnis notio est respectu aliquorum conceptuum conceptus superior (§56.). Complexus inferiorum sub illa contentorum est illius ambitus."

41. Author Unknown, *Logic, Ontology And The Art Of Poetry* (Being The Fourth And Fifth Volumes Of The Circle Of The Sciences; London: Printed for T. Carnan, and F. Newberry, at Number 65, in St. Paul's Church Yard, 1776), p. 8.

42. Antonio Genovesi, *Elementorum Artis Logico-Criticae* (Editio novissima; Venetiis: Apud Remondini, 1794), Liber II, cap. XIII, p. 150: "*Species* ergo significant ideas, quae comprehendunt communia individuis: genera ideas, quae complectuntur communia speciebus. Quod si fuerit plura genera habentia quasdam proprietates communes, tum eae proprietates communes generaliori idea et vocabulo complectuntur."

43. *Ibid.*, Liber II, cap. II, p. 95: "Genus est notio maxime communis, quae alias notiones minus communes ab se propagatas comprehendit, deque illis enunciatur."

44. William Best, *A Concise System of Logics* (New York: Printed by Samuel Campbell, 1796), p. 16.

45. *Ibid.*

46. *Ibid.*, p. 22.

47. *Ibid.*, p. 23.

48. Immanuel Kant, *Introduction To Logic*, trans. Thomas Kingsmill Abbott (London: Longmans, Green, & Co., 1885), p. 30.

49. John Andrews, *A Compend Of Logick* (Philadelphia: Budd and Bartram, 1801), pp. 31-32. He considers Duncan's *Logick* to be the best of those logical works which he has perused.

50. William Duncan, *The Elements Of Logic* (New York: L. Nicols & Co., 1802), pp. 53-54.

51. Thomas Reid, *Analysis of Aristotle's Logic* (Second edition; Edinburgh: Printed for William Creech; and sold by J. Murray, Fleet-Street, London, 1806), pp. 21-22.

52. Cf. *Ibid.*, p. 23.

53. Cf. Richard Kirwan, Esq., *Logick, Or, An Essay On The Elements, Principles, And Different Modes Of Reasoning* (London: T. Bensley, 1807), Vol. I, pp. 6-7.

54. Georg Wilhelm Friedrich Hegel, *The Logic Of Hegel*, trans. William Wallace and quoted in *The Encyclopaedia Of The Philosophical Science* (Second edition; London: Oxford University Press, 1950), p. 187. Hegel's *Logik* (*Wissenschaft der Logik*) was published in 1816. Wallace's first edition of Hegel's *Logik* appeared in 1892.

55. *Ibid.*, p. 188.

56. Levi Hedge, *Elements Of Logick or A Summary Of The General Principles And Different Modes Of Reasoning* (Fourth edition; Boston: Cummings, Hilliard & Co., 1824), p. 35.

57. *Ibid.*, pp. 36-37.

58. Le Baron de Reiffenberg, *Principes de Logique* (Bruxelles: Louis Hauman Et Cie, 1833), p. 14: "*L'extension*, c'est le nombre de tous les individus auxquels l'idée convient. La totalité extensive est *l'omnis* des Latins.

"*La compréhension*, c'est l'assemblage de toutes les idées particulières qui composent l'idée dont on s'occupe. La totalité compréhensive s'exprime en latin par *totus*."

59. Sir William Hamilton, *op. cit.*, pp. 140-41. His *Lectures on Logic* were delivered in 1837-38, and were first published in 1859-60. Cf. Henry Day, *Elements of Logic* (New York: Charles Scribner And Company, 1867), p. 73.

60. Aristotle, *Categ.*, c. 3, 1b.

61. Sir William Hamilton, *op. cit.*, p. 144.

62. Daniel Stahl, *Expositionis Regularum Philosophicarum* (Oxoniae: J. Webb, 1663), tix. xi., reg. 5, p. 363: "Quidquid est partis, est quoque pars totius." Hamilton used the London edition of 1658.

63. Cf. William Kneale and Martha Kneale, *op. cit.*, p. 318.

64. Cf. William Turner, *Lessons In Logic* (Washington, D.C.: Catholic Education Press, 1911), p. 42.

65. W. Stanley Jevons, *Studies In Deductive Logic* (Fourth edition; London: Macmillan And Co., Limited, 1908), p. 130.

66. *Ibid.*, p. 131.
67. *Ibid.*
68. S. E. Parker, *Logic* (Philadelphia: Robert Davis, 1837), p. 62.
69. Thomas Solly, Esq., *A Syllabus Of Logic* (Cambridge: J. & J. J. Deighton, 1839), pp. 20-21.
70. John Stuart Mill, *A System Of Logic, Ratiocinative and Inductive* (Eighth edition; New York: Harper & Brothers, 1879), pp. 34-36. This text was first published in 1843.
71. F. H. Bradley, *The Principles of Logic* (Second edition; London: Oxford University Press, 1928), Vol. I, p. 169.
72. Cf. H. W. B. Joseph, *op. cit.*, p. 149.
73. L. S. Stebbing, *op. cit.*, p. 32.
74. William Minto, *Logic Inductive and Deductive* (New York: Charles Scribner's Sons, 1893), p. 47.
75. H. W. B. Joseph, *op. cit.*, p. 157.
76. Cf. *Ibid.*, pp. 150-55; George Hayward Joyce, *Principles Of Logic* (Third Edition; London: Longmans, Green And Co., 1923), pp. 30-31; L. S. Stebbing, *op. cit.*, pp. 30-32; F. H. Bradley, *op. cit.*, Vol. I, p. 59.
77. Antoine Arnauld et M. Nicole, *op. cit.*, p. 42: "Les noms qui signifient les choses comme modifiées, marquant premièrement et directement la chose, quoique plus confusément, et indirectement le mode, quoique plus distinctement, sont appelés *adjectifs* ou *connotatifs;* comme rond, dur, juste, prudent."
78. M. Rattier, *Manuel Élémentaire de Philosophie* (Paris: Gaume Frères, 1844), p. 162: "L'ensemble des parties d'un *complexe* constitue ce que les logiciens appelaient *la compréhension* de l'idée. L'idée est plus ou moins compréhensive, selon que son objet renferme un plus ou moins grand nombre d'éléments unis ou impliqués les uns dans les autres, c'est-à-dire existant au même point de l'espace et du temps."
79. *Ibid.*, p. 164: "Le nombre des êtres dont la réunion forme une *classe* détermine ce qu'on appelle *l'extension* de l'idée. L'idée est d'autant plus extensive, que le genre contient plus d'espèces et l'espèce plus d'individus."
80. William Thomson, *An Outline Of The Necessary Laws Of Thought* (Third edition; London: Longman, Brown, Green And Longmans, 1854), p. 103.
81. *Ibid.*, p. 105.
82. *Ibid.*, p. 106.
83. Sir William Hamilton, *op. cit.*, p. 162.
84. *Ibid.*, p. 164. Cf. *Logic, Ontology, and the Art of Poetry* by an unknown author (London: Printed for T. Carnan, and F. Newberry, Number 65, in St. Paul's Church Yard, 1776), p. 9: "A *clear* or *distinct* idea, is that which fully represents the object to the mind, so as plainly to distinguish it from every other subject." This author does not oppose clearness to distinction.

249

85. St. Augustine, *Confessiones,* XI, 14: "Quid ergo est tempus? Si nemo ex me quaerat, scio: si quaerenti explicari velim, nescio." Cf. Aloysius Antonius Vernius, *De Re Logica* (Roma: In officina viduae Josephi De Orga, 1369), pp. 67-69; Peter Van Mussembroek, *op. cit.,* pp. 16-20; Jean Pierre de Crousaz, *A New Treatise Of The Art Of Thinking* (London: Printed for Tho. Woodward at the Half-Moon over-against St. Dunstan's Church in Fleet-Street, 1724), Vol. II, pp. 1-5; Dr. Friedrich Ueberweg, *System Of Logic,* trans. Thomas M. Lindsay (London: Longmans, Green, And Co., 1871), p. 125.

86. Antoine Arnauld et M. Nicole, *op. cit.,* p. 68: "On peut distinguer dans une idée la clarté d'avec la distinction, et l'obscurité d'avec la confusion; car on peut dire qu'une idée nous est claire quand elle nous frappe vivement, quoiqu'elle ne soit point distincte, comme l'idée de la douleur nous frappe très vivement, et, selon cela, peut être appelée claire; et néanmoins elle est fort confuse, en ce qu'elle nous représente la douleur comme dans la main blessée, quoiqu'elle ne soit que dans notre esprit."

87. René Descartes, *Les Principes de la Philosophie* (Paris: Victor Cousin, 1824), Part I, §45-46: "Ce que c'est qu'une perception claire et distincte. Qu'elle peut être claire sans être distincte, mais non au contraire."

88. Gottfried Wilhelm Leibniz, *Nouveau Essais Sur L'Entendement Humain* (Paris: Ernest Flammarion, N. D.), L. II, c. 29: "J'ai coutume de suivre ici le langage de M. Descartes, chez qui une idée pourra être claire et confuse en même temps: et telles sont les idées des qualités sensibles affectées aux organes, comme celle de la couleur ou de la chaleur. Elles sont claires, car on les reconnaît et on les discerne aisément les unes des autres; mais elles ne sont point distinctes, parce qu'on ne distingue pas ce qu'elles renferment."

89. William Barron, *Elements Of Logic,* ed. and compiled by Rev. James R. Boyd (New York: A. S. Barnes & Co., 1856), p. 29.

90. Cf. Augustus De Morgan, *op. cit.,* p. 61.

91. Cf. *Ibid.,* p. 59.

92. *Ibid.,* pp. 62-63. The author is quoting in this passage Aristotle, *Metaph.* V, c. 25, 1023b24-25.

93. Henry Longueville Mansel, *Prolegomena Logica: An Inquiry Into The Psychological Character Of Logical Processes* (Boston: Gould And Lincoln, 1860), p. 170.

94. Rev. John Leechman, *Logic* (Fourth edition; London: William Allan & Co., 1864), p. 33.

95. Cf. Thomas Shedden, *The Elements Of Logic* (London: Longman, Green, et al., 1864), p. 42.

96. Cf. *Ibid.,* p. 50.

97. *Ibid.,* p. 10.

98. Francis Bowen, *A Treatise On Logic, Or, The Laws Of Pure*

Thought (Cambridge: Sever And Francis, 1865), p. 66.

99. *Ibid.*, p. 67.

100. *Ibid.*, pp. 67-68.

101. Cf. S. H. Emmens, Esq., *A Treatise On Logic* (London: Virtue Brothers & Co., 1865), p. 18.

102. Cf. Henry N. Day, *The Logic Of Sir William Hamilton* (Cincinnati: Moore, Wilstach & Baldwin, 1865), p. 60.

103. Cf. W. Stanley Jevons, *The Principles Of Science* (London: Macmillan And Co., 1874), p. 31.

104. *Ibid.*

105. George Hayward Joyce, *op. cit.*, p. 27. Cf. André Lalande, *op. cit.*, p. 173.

106. W. Stanley Jevons, *Logic* (New York: D. Appleton & Company, 1877), p. 35.

107. Ralph M. Eaton, *op. cit.*, p. 262.

108. James M. Willcox, *Logic* (Philadelphia: Porter And Coates, 1875), pp. 34-35.

109. P. Venceslao Pieralisi, *Della Filosofia Razionale Speculativa* (Roma: Tipografia Della Pace, 1876), p. 110: "*Comprensione* d'un'idea si vuole indicare il numero delle idee o note semplici che concorrono a costituire l'esser suo; e nelle quali, quando siano più, potrebbe essere mentalmente risoluta. — La diversità di queste note fa diversa dalle altre l'idea stessa; il diverso numero la fa di maggiore o minore comprensione. — Da questo diverso numero le idee prendono denominazione diversa per rapporto alla comprensione loro.

Per *extensione*, ambito, sfera, d'un'idea si vuol denotare il numero degli individui da essa rappresentati. Sono poi rappresentati da un'idea tutti quegli esseri individui (non in collezione, ma ciascuno da sè), i quali hanno nell'esser loro tutte quelle forme, note o ragioni che sono rappresentate dalle semplici nozione che concorrono a formare la comprensione di quell'idea."

110. Joseph Prisco, *Philosophie Spéculative selon la Doctrine Angélique de Saint Thomas D'Quin*, trad. de l'Italien par Prosper-Pierre Huchedé (Paris: Librairie De H. Oudin Frères, 1877), pp. 25-26: "Il résulte qu'entre les concepts de genre, d'espèce, d'individu, il y a une contenance opposée et réciproque. Le genre contient l'espèce, et l'espèce contient l'individu, comme le supérieur contient l'inférieur. Mais, d'un autre côte, l'individu renferme le contenu du concept spécifique ou générique. Par exemple, dans l'individu humain se trouve l'humanité, et dans l'humanité l'animalité. Cette contenance opposée et réciproque des concepts donne lieu à *la compréhension* et à *l'extension*.

On entend par *compréhension* d'un concept la totalité des éléments qu'il contient *en soi;* et par *l'extension* la totalité des sujets qu'il contient *sous soi.*"

111. Cajetano Sanseverino, *Philosophia Christiana* (Neapoli: Apud

Officinam Bibliothecae Catholicae Scriptorum, 1878), pp. 233-34: "Iam-vero, complexus, et ambitus notionis contrarie se habent, quia, quo maior est eius complexus, eo minor est ambitus, et contra ea, quo maior est ambitus, eo minor est complexus. 'In quolibet genere,' ait S. Thomas, 'quanto aliquid est prius, tanto est simplicius, et in paucioribus con-sistens.' Cuius rei ratio . . . est, quod differentia, eo ipso quod essen-tiam in genere inchoatam perficiens constituit speciem, ipsum genus dividit, ex quo efficitur, ut quaelibet specierum, in quas genus dividitur, habeat aliquid quod generi non inest, scilicet differentiam, sed non ambiat, uti genus, speciem contrariam. Hinc cuilibet speciei aliquid inest, quod non inest generi, scilicet differentia, sed quaelibet species pauciora, quam genus, sibi subiecta habet. Ex. gr. complexus hominis maior, quam animalis est, quia homini animal per rationem perfectum inest, sed minor est ambitus, quia animal non solum notionem hominis, sed etiam belluae ambit."

112. J. H. Gilmore, *Outlines Of Logic* (New York: D. Appleton And Company, 1879), p. 37. This same thought is expressed by a French Logician. Cf. Louis Couturat, *La Logique de Leibniz* (Hildesheim: Georg Olms Verlagsbuchhandlung, 1961), p. 444.

113. R. P. Ludovicus Jouin, S. J., *Compendium Logicae Et Metaphy-sicae* (Editio tertia; Neo Eboraci: H. J. Hewitt, 1879), p. 11: "In qualibet idea universali considerandae sunt *extensio* et *comprehensio*. Haec est collectio proprietatum quas idea universalis in se complectitur; illa est multitudo objectorum aut individuorum de quibus idea illa praedicari potest; haec objecta vocantur ideae *inferiora* seu *subjecta*. Sic idea 'hominis' complectitur notas substantiae viventis, sentientis, et rationalis; haec est eius comprehensio. Sed individua de quibus idea haec praedicari potest, ut 'Petrus,' 'Paulus,' constituunt eius extensionem."

114. Cf. Alexander Bain, *Logic* (London: Longmans, Green, & Co., 1879), Vol. I, pp. 50-51.

115. Noah K. Davis, *op. cit.*, pp. 38-39.

116. F. Thomas Maria Zigliara, *Summa Philosophica* (Editio Tertia; Paris: Gabriel Beauchesne & Cie, Éditeurs, 1880), pp. 16-17: "Res quibus communis est idea universalis *inferiores et subiectae. — Patet autem huius-modi *inferiora* in se habere et quidquid *universalis* natura habet, et *alia quaedam*. Unde universale potius est *extensione* suis inferioribus; sed haec *comprehensione* potiora sunt ipso universali."

117. Cf. F. H. Bradley, *op. cit.*, Vol. I, p. 168. This book was first published in 1883.

118. *Ibid.*

119. Cf. Bernard Bosanquet, "Logic As The Science Of Knowledge", *Essays In Philosophical Criticism,* ed. Andrew Seth and R. B. Haldane (London: Longmans, Green, And Co., 1883), p. 83.

120. *Ibid.*

121. Bernard Bosanquet, *Knowledge And Reality* (London: Kegan

Paul, Trench & Co., 1885), pp. 63-64. This book is a criticism of F. H. Bradley's *Principles Of Logic*.

122. John Neville Keynes, *Studies And Exercises In Formal Logic* (Fourth edition; London: Macmillan And Co., 1906), p. 22. This text was originally published in 1884.

123. *Ibid.*

124. Cf. *Ibid.*, pp. 23-24; André Lalande, *op. cit.*, p. 528.

125. *Ibid.*, pp. 24-25; Cf. André Lalande, *op. cit.*, p. 173.

126. Cf. *Ibid.*, p. 26.

127. Cf. *Ibid.*, pp. 29-30.

128. Cf. *Ibid.*, pp. 41-42.

129. Cf. *Ibid.*, p. 27; André Lalande, *op. cit.*, p. 528.

130. Jacques Maritain, *Formal Logic*, trans. Imelda Choquette (New York: Sheed & Ward, 1937), p. 24.

131. Cf. L. S. Stebbing, *op. cit.*, p. 29.

132. Heinrich Scholz, *op. cit.*, p. 48.

133. Jno. J. Tigert, *Handbook of Logic* (Nashville, Tenn.: Southern Methodist Publishing House, 1885), p. 51.

134. *Ibid.*, p. 52.

135. John Veitch, *Institutes Of Logic* (Edinburgh: William Blackwood And Sons, 1885), p. 100.

136. Charles Coppens, *Logic and Mental Philosophy* (New York: Kirwin & Fauss, 1891), p. 16.

137. Herman Lotze, *Outlines Of Logic And Of Encyclopaedia Of Philosophy*, trans. and ed. by George T. Ladd (Second edition; Boston: Ginn & Company, 1887), p. 20. Lotze's contributions to logic are considered to be less valuable than his contributions to the other branches of philosophy.

138. Richard F. Clarke, S. J., *Logic* (New York: Benziger Brothers, 1889), p. 281.

139. P. Joannes Josephus Urraburu, S. J., *Institutiones Philosophicae* (Paris: P. Lethielleux, 1890), p. 121: "Comprehensio ideae vel conceptus est complexio notarum, quae in illa relucent. Extensio vero est multitudo subjectorum, de quibus idea quaelibet enuntiari potest." Cf. T. K. Abbott, *The Elements Of Logic* (Fourth edition; London: Thomas Nelson And Sons, Ltd., 1951), p. 5.

140. James H. Hyslop, *The Elements Of Logic* (New York: Charles Scribner's Sons, 1892), p. 72.

141. Cf. *Ibid.*, p. 94.

142. Alfred Sidgwick, *Distinction And The Criticism Of Beliefs* (London: Longmans, Green, And Co., 1892), p. 100. Cf. *The Use Of Words In Reasoning* (London: Adam And Charles Black, 1901), pp. 244-58, and *The Application Of Logic* (London: Macmillan And Co., Limited, 1910), pp. 245-47, by the same author.

143. William Minto, *Logic Inductive and Deductive* (New York:

253

Charles Scribner's Sons, 1893), p. 45. This text contains an interesting section on the history of the word 'connotative'. Cf. pp. 46-48.

144. Élie Blanc, *Traité de Philosophie Scolastique* (Nouvelle édition; Lyon: Emmanuel Vitte, 1893), Vol. I, pp. 60-61: "Le genre contient l'espèce et réciproquement, suivant le point de vue auquel on se place. Le genre s'étend à plus d'individus que l'espèce; mais il comprend moins de notes ou d'éléments. Ainsi l'idée d'animal (genre) s'étend aux hommes et aux bêtes; mais elle est moins riche que l'idée d'homme (espèce) si on l'analyse, puisque l'homme possède tous les attributs de l'animalité, et ceux de la raison en plus. En un mot, le genre a plus *d'extension* que l'espèce, mais il a moins de *compréhension*."

145. Brother Louis Of Poissy, *Elementary Course Of Christian Philosophy* (Second edition, revised; New York: O'Shea & Company, 1893), p. 9.

146. Thomas Fowler, *Logic Deductive And Inductive* (Tenth edition; Oxford: At The Clarendon Press, 1895), p. 19.

147. Dr. Christoph von Sigwart, *Logic,* trans. Helen Dendy (Second edition; London: Swan Sonnenschein & Co., 1895), Vol. I, p. 269.

148. *Ibid.,* p. 271.

149. Cf. George H. Smith, *Logic* (New York: G. P. Putnam's Sons, 1901), p. 39.

150. Cf. John Rickaby, S. J. *The First Principles Of Knowledge* (Fourth edition; New York: Longmans, Green, And Co., 1901), p. 18.

151. D. Mercier, *Cours de Philosophie* (Troisième édition; Louvain: Institut Supérieur de Philosophie, 1902), p. 93: "Tout métaphysique qui comprend la corporéité, la vie, la sensibilité, la raison . . . [tout logique] qui embrasse tous les hommes passés, présents, à venir ou même simplement possibles. . . ." Cf. D. Mercier, *Elements Of Logic,* trans. Ewan Macpherson (Third edition; New York: The Manhattanville Press, 1912), pp. 16-17. Aldrich speaks of genus as a logical whole when he talks about extension, and species as a metaphysical whole when he talks about comprehension. Cf. Henry Aldrich, *Artis Logicae Rudimenta* (Fourth edition; London: W. Baxter, 1828), p. 51.

152. Élie Rabier, *Leçons de Philosophie* (Cinquième Édition; Paris: Librairie Hachette et Cie., 1903, Vol. II, p. 23: "Les rapports d'inclusion ou d'exclusion entre les idées résultent de la compréhension et de l'extension réciproques des idées.

La compréhension d'une idée est *la somme des caractères* qu'elle enferme. *L'extension* d'une idée est *la somme des êtres* dans lesquels cette somme de caractères se trouve realisée. La compréhension d'une idée est donc l'ensemble des attributs dont elle est le sujet (ex.: L'homme est animal, bimane, raisonnable, etc.); l'extension d'une idée est l'ensemble des sujets dont elle est l'attribut (ex.: Les Européens, les Africains, les Océaniens, les Américains sont hommes).

La compréhension est *la matière* propre du concept; l'extension, c'est *la circonscription* ou la sphère d'application du concept."

153. Herbert Austin Aikins, *Principles Of Logic* (2nd. edition; New York: H. Holt & Co., 1904), p. 60.

154. John Grier Hibben, *Logic Deductive And Inductive* (New York: Charles Scribner's Sons, 1905), p. 42.

155. John Venn, *The Principles Of Empirical Or Inductive Logic* (Second edition; London: Macmillan And Co., 1907), p. 178.

156. Cf. W. R. Boyce Gibson, *The Problem Of Logic* (London: Adam And Charles Black, 1908), p. 72.

157. *Ibid.*

158. Joseph Gredt, O. S. B., *Elementa Philosophiae Aristotelico-Thomisticae* (Editio secunda; Friburgi Brisgoviae: Herder &. Co., 1909), Vol. I, p. 12: "Comprehensio conceptus est complexio notarum, quae conceptum constituunt; extensio est complexio omnium objectorum, quorum imago est conceptus." His fifth edition (1929) contains the same wording for these two definitions.

159. Cf. John Dewey, *Logic, The Theory Of Inquiry* (New York: Henry Holt And Company, 1938), p. 359.

160. *Ibid.*, p. 362.

161. John Dewey, *How We Think* (Boston: D. C. Heath & Co., 1910), p. 131.

162. Nicolaus Monaco, *Praelectiones Logicae Dialecticae Et Critices* (Roma: Ex Officina Libraria Giachetti, Filli Et So., 1910), p. 70: "*Complexus perfectionum* (seu *notarum*, ut aiunt), *quas terminus de re significata refert.*" Cf. Kenneth F. Dougherty, *Logic* (Peekskill, N. Y.: Graymoor Press, 1956), p. 35.

163. *Ibid.*: "Numerus rerum seu subjectorum, quibus terminus attribui potest."

164. Cf. *Ibid.*, p. 69.

165. Cf. William Turner, *op. cit.*, p. 41.

166. *Ibid.*, p. 42.

167. Cf. Robert Adamson, *A Short History Of Logic*, ed. W. R. Sorley (Edinburgh: William Blackwood And Sons, 1911), p. 254.

168. F. C. S. Schiller, *Formal Logic* (London: Macmillan And Co., Limited, 1912), p. 36.

169. L'Abbé Levesque, *Précis de Philosophie*, ed. J. De Gigord (Paris: Ancienne Librairie Poussielgue, 1913), Vol. I, p. 252: "On réduit communément à trois groupes toutes les conceptions humaines: substances, modes et relations. *Porphyre* le premier a classé les universaux ou idées générales et it les ramenait à cinq en les considérant soit au point de vue de l'extension: ce qui donne le genre et l'espèce, soit au point de vue de la compréhension: d'ou résultent la différence, le propre et l'accident."

170. L'Abbé Arthur Robert, *Leçons de Logique* (Quebec: Imp. de l'Action Sociale Limitée, 1914), p. 15: "La compréhension ou le contenu

de l'idée est *l'ensemble des éléments que comprend ou que contient une idée . . . .* L'extension de l'idée est *l'ensemble des individus auxquels l'idée est attribuable."*

171. Tilmanus Pesch, S. J., *Institutiones Logicae et Ontologicae* (Editio altera a Carolo Frick, S. J.; Friburgi Bisgoviae: B. Herder, 1914), p. 51: "Collectio illarum notarum, quas conceptus rei continet, complexus vel *comprehensio* conceptus appellatur. A qua comprehensione distinguitur *ambitus* vel *extensio* conceptus, quae est maior minorve numerus subiectorum, quibus aliquis conceptus applicari potest."

172. C. Willems, *Institutiones Philosophicae* (Tertia Editio; Treveris: Ex Officina Ad S. Paulum, 1915), Vol. I, Liber I, c. 1, pp. 17-18: "Simplici apprehensione peracta, mens potest redire in illum actum suum idque *reflexione* vel *psychologica* vel *ontologica* vel *logica:* prima considerat actum subiective, i.e. tanquam affectionem mentis, eius naturam et originem, unde pertinet ad psychologiam; altera considerat ipsum *obiectum* cognitionis idque formale, i.e. comprehensionem conceptus; logica tandem reflexio directe *modum* cognitionis, eius obiectum materiale, i.e. extensionem conceptus respicit.

1. Si *comprehensio* consideratur, per reflexionem ontologicam (a) conceptus primo confusus et obscurus perficitur, ita ut fiat clarus et distinctus sicut obiectum procul visum eo melius cognoscitur, quo propius illud spectamus; (b) notae conceptum constituentes distinguuntur essentiales et accidentales, ita ut conceptus primo confusus fiat distinctus et ad perfectionem definitionis scientificae evehatur.

2. Si vero consideratur *obiectum materiale* sive *extensio,* per reflexionem logicam, apparet conceptum non solum aptum esse ad obiectum aliquod praesens exprimendum, sed, quia universalis est, infinita eum eiusdem naturae individua exhibere posse, unde conceptus per abstractionem directam a re sensibili formatus, iam *in se vel potentia* universalis (universale directum), per mentis reflexionem ontologicam vel potius logicam *actu* extenditur et fit *universale reflexum."*

173. Aristotle, *Phys.,* IV, c. 3, 210a17-19.

174. Cf. St. Thomas, In IV *Phys.,* lect. 4, n. 435.

175. H. W. B. Joseph, *op. cit.,* p. 136.

176. *Ibid.*

177. *Ibid.*

178. Cf. *Ibid.,* p. 146.

179. R. W. Sellars, *The Essentials Of Logic* (Boston: Houghton Mifflin Company, 1917), p. 39.

180. Attilius Munzi, *Logica* (Roma: Apud Aedes Universitatis Gregorianae, 1920), p. 22: "Comprehensio termini in genere est ea quam accepimus ex definitione Aristotelis: nempe intelligibilitas contenta in eo in quod resolvitur propositio; extensio, omne id quod fungi potest munere subjecti vel praedicati in aliqua propositione."

181. Cf. Edmond Goblot, *Traité de Logique* (Deuxième édition; Paris: Librairie Armand Colin, 1920), pp. 110-13.

182. *Ibid.*, p. 103: "L'extension ou dénotation d'un terme est le nombre des individus contenus dans le genre, c'est-à-dire des jugements possibles dont il est l'attribut, sa compréhension ou connotation est le nombre des qualités communes aux individus du genre, c'est-à-dire des jugements possibles dont il est le sujet. Si un terme est général, c'est-à-dire s'il est un concept, sa dénotation est infinie; s'il est singulier, sa connotation est infinie."

183. *Ibid.*, p. 113: "Un vertébré n'est pas un animal qui n'a ni poil, ni plumes, ni écailles, c'est un animal dont les appendices tégumentaires peuvent avoir les formes poil, plumes, écailles." The italics are mine.

184. St. Albert, *Commentaria In De Praedicabilibus*, ed. Ludovicus Vivès, Paris, 1890, Tr. IV, c. 1, p. 75: "Differentia non est in genere nisi potestate." Cf. Tr. III, c. 2, p. 61. (The text of St. Albert has been transcribed from the original mimeographed by Michel Doyon, 1215, Chemin Ste — Foy, Quebec, Canada, 1951).

185. Edmond Goblet, *op. cit.*, pp. 203-04: "Si par compréhension de l'idée on entend tout ce qui peut en être affirmé avec vérité. . . ."

186. Cf. André Lalande, *op. cit.*, p. 173.

187. Cf. Edmond Goblot, *op. cit.*, p. 115.

188. R. P. Seb. Uccello, S. S. S., *Philosophia Scholastica Ad Mentem Sancti Thomas* (Augustae Taurinorum: Sumptibus et typis Petri Marietti, 1921), Vol. I, p. 16: "Complexio, vero, vel summa notarum, quibus constant aliqua idea, dicitur ejus COMPREHENSIO. . . . Summa autem vel complexio entium quae aliqua idea manifestari possunt, dicitur huius ideae EXTENSIO.

Comprehensio et extensio ideae vere ad eius naturam pertinent quia:

(a) Comprehensio est aliquid ideae intrinsecum; revera, si ad idea "homo" aliquam notam v.g., "rationalitas" tollas, hominis essentiam evertes.

(b) Extensio, quamquam est aliquid ideae extrinsecum, idea enim maneret eadem etiam si unum tantum subiectum extaret cui conveniret. tamen capacitatem, seu aptitudinem per se dicit ad sui extensionem, sola excepta idea "Deus" quae uni enti tantum conveniri potest."

189. W. E. Johnson, *Logic* (Cambridge: At the University Press, 1921), Vol. I, p. 100.

190. Cf. George Hayward Joyce, *op. cit.*, p. 22.

191. *Ibid.*, p. 27.

192. *Ibid.*

193. Cf. *Ibid.*, p. 29. Here is an appropriate place to quote two linguists who are highly read even by logicians today. Ogden and Richards view the words 'denotation' and 'connotation', which are used by many logicians. as something artificial. These two authors insist that "no word has any denotation apart from some reference which it symbolizes . . . The

257

connotation is a selection of properties or adjectives; but properties are not to be found by themselves anywhere, they are fictitious or nominal entities which we are led to feign through the influence of the bad analogy by which we treat certain parts of our symbols as though they were nouns". Charles Kay Ogden, and I. A. Richards, *The Meaning Of Meaning* (New York: Harcourt Brace & Co., 1923), p. 308.

194. Cf. H. E. Cunningham, *Textbook Of Logic* (New York: The Macmillan Company, 1924), p. 27.

195. John J. Toohey, S. J., *An Elementary Handbook of Logic* (Second edition; New York: Schwartz, Kirwin & Fauss, 1924), p. 4. Similar definitions of comprehension and extension are given by P. Joseph Mendive, S. J., *Institutiones Philosophiae Scholasticae* (Vallisoleti: Ex Typographia Vidua De Cuesta Et Fil, 1886), p. 31. Cf. Père Ch. Lahr, S. J., *Cours de Philosophie* (Vingt-sixième édition; Paris: Gabriel Beauchesne, 1929), Vol. I, p. 492.

196. Cf. *Ibid.* (New York: Appleton-Century-Crofts, Inc., 1948), p. 6.

197. Pio De Mandato, *Institutiones Philosophicae* (Editio quarta; Roma: Pontificia Universitas Gregoriana, 1925), p. 32: "*Extensio termini est ejus amplitudo respectu eorum de quibus praedicari potest.*" Cf. Roland Houde and Jerome J. Fischer, *Handbook Of Logic* (Second printing; Dubuque: Wm. C. Brown Company, 1954), pp. 22-24.

198. *Ibid.* "*Comprehensio termini* est complexus notarum, quas terminus de re significata refert."

199. Carolus Frick, S. J., *Cursus Philosophicus* (Editio sexta emendata; Friburgi Brisgoviae; Herder & Co., 1925), Vol. I, p. 11: "Extensio (ambitus, amplitudo) est capacitas ideae plura vel pauciora objecta repraesentandi."

200. *Ibid.*: "Complexio notarum, quae idea (subjectiva) exprimuntur et ideam (objectivam) constituunt."

201. Cf. Mathew Thompson McClure, *An Introduction To The Logic Of Reflection* (New York: Henry Holt And Company, 1925), p. 161.

202. *Ibid.,* p. 163.

203. *Ibid.,* p. 165.

204. *Ibid.,* p. 169.

205. Thomas Crumley, C. S. C., *Logic: Deductive And Inductive* (New York: The Macmillan Company, 1926), p. 44.

206. Mortimer J. Adler, *Dialectic* (New York: Harcourt, Brace & Company, Inc., 1927), p. 85.

207. *Ibid.*

208. Robert Latta and Alexander Macbeath, *The Elements Of Logic* (London: Macmillan and Co., Limited, 1929), p. 47.

209. W. H. Forbes and Dennis Hird, *Palestra Logica* (Fifth edition; Oxford: J. Thornton & Son, 1929), pp. 30-31.

210. Federigo Enriques, *The Historic Development Of Logic,* trans. Jerome Rosenthal (New York: Henry Holt And Company, 1929), p. 45.

This author considers logic to be a part of psychology.

211. Emile Meyerson, *Du Cheminement de la Pensée* (Paris: Librairie Felix Alcan, 1931), Vol. III, p. 826: "Qu'un terme soit inclus dans un autre en tant que tout, a le même sens que pour cet autre d'être attribué au premier tout entier."

212. Jorgen Jorgensen, *A Treatise Of Formal Logic* (Copenhagen: Levin Munksgaard, 1931), Vol. I, pp. 149-50. Scholz calls the German mathematician Gottlob Frege (1848-1925) the greatest genius of modern logic in the nineteenth century. Cf. Heinrich Scholz, *op. cit.*, p. 58.

213. *Ibid.*, Vol. II, p. 3.

214. *Ibid.*

215. Cf. Ralph M. Eaton, *op. cit.*, p. 235.

216. *Ibid.*, p. 241.

217. Cf. *Ibid.*, p. 242.

218. Cf. Charles Gray Shaw, *Logic In Theory And Practice* (London: Sir Isaac Pitman & Sons, Ltd., 1935), p. 45.

219. *Ibid.*, p. 48.

220. *Ibid.*, p. 50.

221. Jacques Maritain, *op. cit.*, p. 21.

222. *Ibid.*, p. 27.

223. Henricus Grenier, *Cursus Philosophiae* (Quebec: L'Action Sociale Ltée, 1937), Vol. I, p. 35: "Comprehensio conceptus est collectio notarum quae conceptum constituunt. . . . Extensio conceptus est collectio individuarum et generaliter objectorum quibus conceptus universalis convenit." For similar definitions, consult Regis Jolivet, *Traité de Philosophiae* (Deuxième édition; Lyon: Emmanuel Vitte, 1945), Vol. I, p. 60; J. B. Bouvier, *Institutiones Philosophicae* (Duodecima editio; Parisiis: Apud Méquigon Juniorem, 185), p. 30.

224. Cf. F. Gonseth, *Qu'est-ce que la Logique?* (Paris: Herman & Cie, Éditeurs, 1937), p. 19.

225. D. Luther Evans and Walter S. Gamertsfelder, *Logic: Theoretical And Applied* (New York: Doubleday, Doran & Company, Inc., 1937), p. 121.

226. Cf. Peter Coffey, *The Science Of Logic* (Second edition; New York: Peter Smith, 1938), Vol. I, p. 48.

227. *Ibid.*, p. 172.

228. Henry Bradford Smith, *A First Book In Logic* (New York: F. S. Crofts & Co., 1938), p. 19.

229. Albert Myrton Frye and Albert William Levi, *Rational Belief* (New York: Harcourt, Brace & World, Inc., 1941), p. 66.

230. Celestine N. Bittle, *The Science Of Correct Thinking* (Fifth printing; Milwaukee: The Bruce Publishing Company, 1941), p. 28.

231. L. Susan Stebbing, *A Modern Elementary Logic* (London: Metheun & Co., Ltd., 1943), p. 101.

232. *Ibid.*, p. 104.

233. Cf. *Ibid.*

234. L. S. Stebbing, *Modern Introduction To Logic* (London: Methuen & Co., Ltd., 1930), p. 29.

235. Cf. Alburey Castell, *A College Logic* (Eight edition; New York: The Macmillan Company, 1944), p. 78.

236. *Ibid.*, p. 79.

237. Cf. Max Black, *Critical Thinking* (New York: Prentice-Hall, Inc., 1946), p. 176.

238. Morris R. Cohen and Ernest Nagel, *An Introduction to Logic and Scientific Method* (Third edition; London: Routledge & Kegan Ltd., 1951), p. 31.

239. Cf. Morris R. Cohen, *A Preface to Logic* (Fourth printing; New York: Henry Holt And Company, 1946), p. 71.

240. Raymond J. McCall, *Basic Logic* (New York: Barnes & Noble, Inc., 1947), p. 15.

241. *Ibid.*, p. 24.

242. Sylvester J. Hartman, *Fundamentals of Logic* (St. Louis: B. Herder Book Co., 1949), pp. 22-23.

243. St. Thomas, *Ia-IIae*, p. 52, a. 3: "Similitudo autem et dissimilitudo non solum attenditur secundum qualitatem eandem vel diversam, sed etiam secundum eundem vel diversum participationis modum. Est enim dissimile non solum nigrum albo, sed etiam minus album magis albo; nam etiam motus fit a minus albo in magis album, tanquam ex opposito in oppositum, ut dicitur in *V Phys.*"

244. Thomas Gilby, O. P., *Barbara Celarent* (London: Longmans Green And Co., 1949), pp. 64-65. Cf. p. 64 for his reference to the *Summa Theologiae*.

245. Cf. Paul Henle et al., *Structure, Method And Meaning* (New York: The Liberal Arts Press, 1951), p. 27.

246. Cf. Francis H. Parker and Henry B. Veatch, *Logic as a Human Instrument* (New York: Harper & Brothers, 1959), p. 56; Henry B. Veatch, *Intentional Logic* (New Haven: Yale University Press, 1952), p. 408.

247. Francis H. Parker and Henry B. Veatch, *op. cit.*, p. 60.

248. Willard Van Orman Quine, *From A Logical Point Of View* (Cambridge, Mass.: Harvard University Press, 1953), p. 22.

249. Henry W. Johnstone, Jr., *Elementary Deductive Logic* (New York: Thomas Y. Crowell Company, 1954), pp. 218-19.

250. Herbert L. Searles, *Logic and Scientific Method* (Second edition; New York: The Ronald Press Company, 1956), p. 47.

251. Wilbur Samuel Howell, *Logic and Rhetoric in England, 1500-1700* (Princeton, N. J.: Princeton University Press, 1956), pp. 353-54.

252. Cf. Maylon H. Hepp, *Thinking Things Through* (New York: Charles Scribner's Sons, 1956), pp. 50-52.

253. Cf. *Ibid.*, p. 51.

254. Edith W. Schipper and Edward Schuh, *Principles of Applied Logic* (Dubuque, Iowa: Wm. C. Brown Company, 1956), p. 14.

255. Vincent Edward Smith, *The Elements Of Logic* (Milwaukee: The Bruce Publishing Company, 1957), p. 36.

256. Andrew H. Bachhuber, S.J., *Introduction To Logic* (New York: Appleton-Century-Crofts, Inc., 1957), p. 17.

257. *Ibid.,* pp. 18-19.

258. *Ibid.,* p. 19.

259. John W. Blythe, *A Modern Introduction To Logic* (Boston: Houghton Mifflin Company, 1957), p. 47.

260. James Edwin Creighton and Harold R. Smart, *An Introductory Logic* (Twenty-Fourth printing; New York: The Macmillan Company, 1958), pp. 69-70. Cf. James Edwin Creighton, *An Introductory Logic* (Fifth Edition; New York: The Macmillan Company, 1932), pp. 69-70.

261. Cf. *Ibid.*

262. Monroe C. Beardsley, *op. cit.,* p. 200. Cf. Henry Aldrich, *op. cit.,* p. 47: he uses comprehension in the same manner when he speaks of "genus comprehending horses, cows, lions, ..." Edward J. Hamilton asserts that genus "comprehends oaks, beeches, maples, etc.," (sense of extension), and that species "comprehends genus together with a difference" (sense of intension), Edward John Hamilton, *The Modalist* (Boston: Ginn & Co., 1891), pp. 53-54.

263. Cf. Monroe C. Beardsley, *Practical Logic* (New York: Prentice-Hall, Inc., 1950), pp. 64-65.

264. St. Thomas, *Ia*, q. 12, a. 7, ad 1: "Comprehensio dicitur dupliciter, Uno modo, inclusio comprehensi in comprehendente. . . . Alio modo comprehensio nihil aliud nominat quam tentationem alicuius rei quae iam praesentialiter habetur; sicut aliquis consequens aliquem, dicitur eum comprehendere quando tenet eum." Cf. *Ia-Ilae*, q. 4, a. 3, ad 1; Cicero, "Academ. Priorum", *Opera*, ed. C. F. A. Nobbe (Lipsiae: Ex Officina Car. Tauchnitii, 1828), Vol. I, L. II, c. 10/31, p. 39.

265. Bernard Wuellner, S. J., *Dictionary Of Scholastic Philosophy* (Milwaukee: The Bruce Publishing Company, 1956), p. 25.

266. Cf. Daniel J. Sullivan's remarks on the overlapping of meaning to be found in the words 'comprehension' and 'extension' on p. 73 of this treatise.

267. Vol Molesworth, *Landmarks In Logic* (Australia: The Law Book Co. of Australia Pty Ltd., 1958), p. 79.

268. Irving M. Copi, *Introduction to Logic* (Second edition; New York; The Macmillan Company, 1961), p. 109.

269. Cf. I. M. Bochenski, *A History Of Formal Logic,* trans. and ed. by Ivo Thomas (South Bend: University of Notre Dame, 1961), p. 258.

270. Cf. *Ibid.,* p. 259.

271. *Ibid.*

272. Romane Clark and Paul Welsh, *Introduction to Logic* (Princeton, New Jersey: D. Van Nostrand Company, Inc., 1962), p. 154.

273. Cf. John A. Mourant, *Formal Logic* (New York: The Macmillan Company, 1963), p. 36.

274. *Ibid.*

275. *Ibid.*, p. 37.

276. Daniel J. Sullivan, *Fundamentals of Logic* (New York: McGraw-Hill Book Company, Inc., 1963), p. 34.

277. Samuel S. S. Browne, *Fundamentals of Deductive Logic* (Dubuque: Iowa: Wm. C. Brown Company, 1964), p. 25.

278. *Ibid.*, p. 26.

279. Cf. Wilhelm Traugott Krug, *System der theoretischen Philosophie* (Konigsberg: A. W. Unzer, 1819), p. 76.

280. Cf. *Ibid.*, p. 77.

281. Cf. *Ibid.*

282. Cf. Gottlob E. Schulze, *Grundsätze der allgemeinen Logik* (Göttingen: Vandenhoeck und Ruprecht, 1822), pp. 50-51.

283. Cf. Jakob Friedrich Fries, *Grundris der Logik* (3rd. edition; Heidelberg: Winter, 1827), pp. 26-27. He includes only 'actual' things or representations under extension.

284. Cf. Ernst Reinhold, *Die Logik oder die allgemeine Denkformenlehre dargestellt* (Jena: Erdterfchen Buchhandlung, 1827), p. 115. He limits extension to individual representations.

285. Cf. Wilhelm Esser, *System der Logik* (Münster: Theissingschen Buchhandlung, 1830), p. 74. He includes merely 'possible' things as well as actual things under extension.

286. Cf. Karl Fischer, *Grundzüge der Systems der Philosophie* (Erlangen: Berlag von Gender & Zimmer, 1848), p. 113.

287. Cf. Dr. Heinrich Ritter, *System der Logik und der Metaphysik* (Göttingen: Berlag der Dieterich'fchen Buchhandlung, 1856), p. 17. He assigns extension to merely 'possible' things as well as to actual things.

288. Cf. *Ibid.*, p. 19.

289. Cf. Moritz Wilhelm Drobisch, *Neue Darstellung Der Logik* (Leipzig: Leopold Voss, 1863), p. 28.

290. Cf. *Ibid.*, p. 29.

291. Dr. Friedrich Ueberweg, *op. cit.*, p. 126.

292. *Ibid.*, p. 130.

293. Cf. Appendix II which contains a resume of the different terminology and meanings studied in Chapter I of this treatise.

FOOTNOTES TO CHAPTER II

1. Petrus Gassendus, *Opera Omnia* (Lugduni: Sumptibus Laurentii Anisson, & Joan. Bapt. Devent, 1658), Vol. I, Pars II, Canon XVI, p. 105: *"Quidquid convenit Generi, Speciei etiam convenit; ut, quia convenit*

Animali esse sensu praeditum, id Homini etiam convenit."

2. *Ibid.*: "*Quod omnibus speciebus convenit, generi conveniet;* ut quia Prudentia, Justitia, Fortitudo, Temperantia amabiles sunt; et Virtus amabilis erit."

3. F. P. Burgersdijck, *Institutionum Logicarum* (London: Ex officina Rogeri Danielis, 1651), Liber I, Cap. XI, p. 40: "Cum autem genus dicitur de *pluribus* praedicari, distinguitur ab individuis. Cum dicitur praedicari de pluribus *specie differentibus*, distinguitur a speciebus, quae praedicentur de pluribus numero differentibus."

4. *Ibid.*, p. 45: "Genus latius sit sua specie, et species individuo. . . ." Valla reiterates this thought from the viewpoint of predication: "Genus is that which is predicated of its species. . . . Species is that which is predicated of its individuals." Cf. Lorenzo Valla, *Dialectice* (Parisiis: In edibus Ascensianis, 1509), Liber I, Fo. XIX: "Genus est id quod de suis speciebus praedicatur. . . . Species est quod praedicatur de suis individuis."

5. *Ibid.*,: "Species includit genus suum, et praeter genus, differentiam essentialem. . . ."

6. R. P. Roderico De Arriaga, *Cursus Philosophicus* (Paris: Apud Jacobum Quesnel, 1639), Liber Tertius, Disputatio Septima, Sectio II, p. 113: "Species subjicibilis, quae correlativa est Generis, definitur esse, *quae sub genere continetur.*"

7. *Ibid.*, Sectio III, p. 115: "Species praedicabilis . . . est: *quae de pluribus differentibus numero in eo, quod quid complete praedicatur . . . .*" Cf. Petrus Fonseca, S. J., *Institutionum Dialecticarum* (Coloniae: Apud Petrum Cholinum, 1616), Liber II, Caput IV, p. 65.

8. Cf. pp. 82-83 of this study.

9. Cf. Daniel Stahl, *op. cit.*, tit. xii, p. 375. Thomas Spencer Baynes in his introduction to the translation of the *Port Royal Logic*, p. xxxiii (footnote), refers to the 1635 edition of Stahl's *Regulae Philosophicae*. Sir William Hamilton in his *Lectures on Logic*, p. 141 (footnote), mentions the 1658 edition of Stahl's treatise.

10. Cf. *Ibid.*, pp. 375-78: "Reg. 1, genus praedicatur de omnibus speciebus sub se contentis . . . . reg. 2, quicquid praedicatur de genere, praedicatur etiam de specie . . . . reg. 3, genus est prius specie. . . ."

11. Cf. p. 51 of this study which enumerates some of the different ways in which one thing can be said to be in another.

12. *Ibid.*, p. 380: "Genus est latius specie." Stahl acknowledges the fact that this rule is derived from Aristotle, *Top.*, IV, c. 1, § 9.

13. *Ibid.*, p. 380: "Species est collectiva multorum in unam naturam, et adhuc magis genus. Porphyrius cap. de genere et specie §37."

14. *Ibid.*: "Omnia individua unius speciei conveniunt in ipsius speciei natura: ut, omnia individua humana in natura humana. Sed in natura generis conveniunt individua non solum unius speciei, sed omnium specierum talis generis: ut, omnes homines et omnia bruta in natura animalis.

Et hinc est, quod species dicitur collectiva multorum in unam naturam, genus autem magis."

15. Cf. *Ibid.,* p. 381.

16. In his commentary on the seventh rule (cf. *Ibid.,* pp. 382-83), Stahl repeats the word *comprehensio* several times. However, in that context, *comprehensio* comports a traditional meaning which can be traced back to Cicero and which names the activity of our intellect understanding and grasping things.

17. Cf. John of St. Thomas, O. P., "Ars Logica Seu De forma Et Materia Ratiocinandi", *Cursus Philosophicus Thomisticus,* ed. P. Beatus Reiser, O. S. B. (Nova editio; Taurini: Marietti, 1948), Log. II, Prooemium, q. 7, a. 1, Vol. I, p. 387. The second part of his *Ars Logica* was first published in 1632.

18. *Ibid.,* p. 390: "Quod genus comparatur ad speciem ut quid formalius, quatenus est minus contractum."

19. *Ibid.:* "Consequenter genus praedicatur etiam de pluribus numero differentibus, non tamen sicut species infima, quae immediate de illis praedicatur."

20. *Ibid.,* a. 2, p. 398: "Ex modo concipiendi . . . ex parte rei conceptae et significatae."

21. *Ibid.,* q. 8, a. 2, p. 411: "Species enim subicibilis dicitur, quae sub assignato genere collocatur, vel de quo genus praedicatur in quid."

22. Cf. *Ibid.,* q. 10, a. 2, pp. 441-42: "Differentia est id quo species genus excedit."

23. Pierre Du Moulin, *The Elements Of Logick,* trans. from the French by Nathanael De-Lavvne (London: Printed by I. Dawson for Nicholas Bourne, 1624), Book II, Chapter 2, pp. 33-34.

24. *Ibid.,* Chapter 3, p. 36.

25. *Ibid.,* pp. 37-38.

26. Cosmus (Medionalensis) Alamannius, *Summa Totius Philosophiae S. Thomae* (Ticini: Excudebat Jo. Baptista Rubeus, 1624), Pars Prima, Quaestio Tertia, Articulus II, p. 63: "Praeterea animal in quantum est genus est in plus, quam homo, et leo, de quibus praedicatur; sed esse in plus est dicere, et continere totum, quod dicit homo, et leo, et quaecunque alia species, ergo genus continet totum, quod dicunt species, et per consequens differentias."

27. *Ibid.,* ad 6, p. 67: "Species dicitur abundare a genere per differentiam, non quia haec non contineatur in genere confuse, et indistincte, sed quia species abundat, idest excedit in suo significato etiam illud, quod explicite significat differentia."

28. P. Raphaele Aversa, A. Sanseverino, *Logica* (Romae: Apud Jacobum Muscardum, 1623), Tractatus Primus, c. 9, p. 10: "Generis nomen tripliciter accipitur, quae dici solet triplex acceptio generis, et sumitur ex Aristot., *Metaphy.* V, c.28. Primo dicitur genus collectio multorum aliquo modo se habentium ad unum. . . ."

29. Aristotle, *Metaphy.* V, c. 28, 1024a29.

30. P. Raphaele Aversa A. Sanseverino, *op. cit.*, c. 10, p. 11: "Species quatenus praedicabilis definitur, quae de pluribus et differentibus numero praedicatur in quid."

31. *Ibid.*, c. 10, p. 13: "Species constat ex genere et differentia, v. g. homo ex animali et rationali. Hoc ergo modo definitur differentia quatenus constitutiva speciei."

32. Petrus Molinaeus, *Elementa Logica* (Bremae: Apud Thomam Villerianum, 1619), p. 41: "Genus continet potentia omnes species. Species continet actu genus nam animal est in definitione hominis."

33. Petrus Fonseca, *Isagoge Philosophica* (Coloniae: Apud Petrum Cholinum, 1616), Caput III, p. 571: "Atque ut ex universalibus quaedam minus universalia sunt, ut homo, et albedo; quaedam magis universalia, ut animal et color; quaedam maxime, ut substantia et qualitas. . . ." His preface to this text is dated 1591.

34. *Ibid.*, Caput VIII, p. 597: "Denique; ut ascendendo a speciebus ad genera, et ab individuis ad species ex multis unum colligimus, ita descendendo a generibus ad species, et a speciebus ad individua, ex uno multa facimus, Participatione enim speciei multi homines unus homo sunt. . . ."

35. *Ibid.*, Caput IX, p. 600: "Dicitur quoque differentia specifica id, quo species genus excedit. Quo eodem pacto dici potest differentia individualis esse id, quo individuum excedit infimam speciem. Ut namque homo in sua essentia communi hoc amplius habet, quam animal, quod sit rationis particeps; ita Socrates in essentia sua singulari, hoc superat essentiam hominis communis, quod sic hic singularis, ac determinatus."

36. Paulus Barbus Soncinas, O. P., *Quaestiones Metaphysicales Acutissimae* (Venetiis: Apud Haeredem Hieronymi Scoti, 1587), Liber IV, q. 1, p. 2: "Conceptus nam specificus, puta hominis, . . . est comprehendere indifferentes [sic; the text should read indifferenter] omnes homines, et ratione huius indifferentis comprehensionis, est confusus. . . . Conceptus autem genericus majorem habet confusionem, quia comprehendit indifferenter plures species."

37. Dudley Fenner, *The Artes Of Logike And Rhetorike* (Middelburg?: R. Schilders?, 1584), Book I, Chapter 5. No pages or symbols are listed in this text.

38. D. Franciscus Toletus, S. J., *Commentaria In Universam Aristotelis Logicam* (Venetiis: Apud Iuntas, 1576), p. 20: "Genus enim est universalius, cum comprehendat sub se multas Species."

39. *Ibid.*, p. 27: " . . . id quod est magis unum, quod dicitur magis collectivum intensive: altero modo id quod plura comprehendit, et sic dicitur magis collectivum extensive. Juxta hoc intellige minus universale esse magis collectivum intensive, quia magis sunt unum, quae in minus universali conveniunt, quam quae solum in magis universali: at magis universale est magis collectivum extensive, quia sub se plura continet, et sic loquitur Porphyrius."

40. *Ibid.*, p. 37 verso: "Differunt autem primo, quod Genus continet

Speciem; Species autem non continet Genus: hoc intellige quantum ad potestatem, idest Genus continet Speciem, et omnia, quae in potentia Speciei sunt [e.g.] Individua; at Species continet quidem Generis naturam, sed non potestatem, quia non comprehendit omnia, sub Genere continentur: et hinc est, Genus de pluribus quam Species praedicetur."

41. Francis Titelmannus, *De Consideratione Dialectica* (Venetiis: Apud Franciscum, Gasparem Bindonum & Fratres, 1571), Liber I, Cap. XVIII, p. 39: "Sic animal abundat supra genus suum corpus animatum, per differentiam sensible, et ita in reliquis omnibus. Quidquid enim habet genus, habet etiam generis ipsius species, et ultra totum hoc habet species differentiam in se, ut essentialem sui partem, quam sic non habet genus. Unde consequitur per differentiam omnem constitutivam, speciem abundare prae suo genere."

42. Thomas Wilson, *The Rule Of Reason* (London: Ihon Kingston, 1567), p. B iii verso.

43. *Ibid.*, p. 4.

44. *Ibid.*, p. 4 verso.

45. Rudolf Agricola, *De Inventione Dialectica* (Coloniae: Martinus Gymnicus, 1548), Liber I, p. 40: "Genus est quod de pluribus specie differentibus, in quid est praedicatur: ut quaerenti, quid est homo? quid asinus est? quid est bos; bene respondetur, homo est animal, asinus est animal, bos est animal. Species, in quam sub se comprehensam dividitur genus: ut homo est species animalis. Comprehenditur enim sub animali." One of the earliest texts in Mexico adds nothing worthwhile to this historical survey (Cf. Alonso de la Veracruz, *Dialectica Resolutio* [Mexici: Excudebat Joannes Paulus Brissensis, 1554], Liber Praedicabilium, quaestio quarta, Capitulum primum, p. 11 verso, Capitulum II, p. 13, and Capitulum V, p. 23 verso).

46. *Ibid.*, p. 46: "Genus autem id est . . . duas aut plures complectitur partes. . . . Virtus est genus quoddam: complectitur enim plures partes, hoc est, species, nempe prudentiam, justiciam, fortitudinem et temperantiam. . . . Rursum, genus est animal: duas anim partes complectitur, hominem et brutum, quae partes etsi specie sunt differentes, tamen communione quadam ipsius generis. . . ."

47. Cf. Philipp Melanchthon, *Compendiaria Dialectices* (? : Apud Inclytam Basilieam, 1521), Liber I.

48. Sir William Hamilton cites this reference in his *Lectures on Logic*, p. 141 (footnote). He quotes the 1579 edition of Cajetan's *In Porphyrii Praedicabilia*. The latter treatise was first published in 1496. Thomas Spencer Baynes also mentions in his translation of the *Port Royal Logic*, p. xxxii (introduction), that the distinction of comprehension and extension was indicated by Cajetan as early as 1496.

49. Thomas de Vio Cardinalis Cajetanus, *Commentaria In Porphyrii Isagogen Ad Praedicamenta Aristotelis*. ed. P. Isnardus M. Marega (Romae: Apud Institutum Angelicum, 1934), Capitulum I, p. 25: "Ad hoc

breviter dicitur, quod esse magis collectivum multorum potest intelligi dupliciter. Uno modo intensive; et sic species est magis collectiva, quia magis unit adunata, et ratio adducta probat. Alio modo extensive; et sic genus est magis collectivum, quia multo plura sub sua adunatione cadunt, quam sub speciei ambitu. Unde species et genus se habent sicut duo duces, quorum alter habet exercitum parvum, sed valde unanimem, alter exercitum magnum, sed diversarum factionum. Ille enim magis colligit intensive, hic extensive."

50. *Ibid.,* p. 26: "Genus est magis collectivum, quam species, ita quod illud est maius quod continet omnia, quae continet alterum et ultra illa aliqua alia, sicut animal est maius homine; illud vero minus, quod non continet quidquid alterum ambit, ut homo respectu animalis. . . ."

51. *Ibid.,* p. 31: "Quod totum dicitur dupliciter, scilicet totum universale et totum diffinible. Et similiter pars dicitur dupliciter, scilicet pars subjectiva et pars diffinitiva. Totum universale vocatur superius respectu inferiorum, quae partes eius subjectivae dicuntur. Totum autem diffinibile vocatur id, quod diffinitur respecʋu partium suae diffinitionis, quae partes diffinitivae dicuntur.

Differt autem tantum alter istorum modorum dicere aliquid totum aut partem, ut id, quod totum uno modo est, pars sit ejusdem altero modo, et e converso. Superius enim respectu inferioris est totum universale, quia continet in potestate sua illud et alia et praedicatur de eis; et est pars diffinitiva ejusdem, quia continetur actu et intrinsece in diffinitione illius; et consequenter inferius respectu superioris totum est diffinibile et pars est subjectiva."

52. *Ibid.,* Capitulum II, p. 40: "Species abundat a genere per differentiam, et non altero tantum, quoniam species nihil includit, quo careat genus, nisi differentiam; et proxima causa, quod species plus includat, quam genus, est ipsa differentia. . . ."

53. *Ibid.,* p. 41: "Species abundat a genere, quia actualiter plus habet in se, quam genus in se actualiter habeat. Species enim habet in se actu differentiam, quam genus actu non habet. . . ."

54. Aloysius Antonius Verneus, *De Re Logica* (Romae: In officina viduae Josephi De Orga, 1369), L. III, c. 5, p. 81: *"Petrus* plures ideas comprehendat, quam *homo,* vere dico, *Petrus est homo:* quod valet, *in Petro dantur praedicata similia aliis hominibus."* William of Ockham does not provide his reader with anything new pertaining to the notions of extension and comprehension in relation to genus and species. Cf. William Ockham, *Summa Logicae,* ed. Philotheus Boehner, O. F. M. (St. Bonaventure, N. Y.: The Franciscan Institute, 1951), Capitulum 20 "De Genere", Capitulum 21 "De Specie", Capitulum 22 "De Comparatione Generis ad Speciem". No page numbers are recorded in this text.

55. Further elaboration will be made upon this expression *genus est latius specie* with reference to the words *'latitudo', 'ampliatio',* and *'extensio'* when this particular point is discussed in Chapter III.

267

56. Pseudo-Thomas, *De Totius Logicae Aristotelis Summa*. Cf. St. Thomas Aquinas, *Opera Omnia* (Parmae: Petri Fiaccadori, 1864), Vol. XVII, Opusculum XLIV, c. 3, p. 56: "Quod omnis forma sub se habens multa, idest, quae universaliter sumitur, habet quamdam latitudinem: nam invenitur in pluribus et dicitur de pluribus." Pseudo-Thomas is an unknown author of the fourteenth century.

57. *Ibid*.: "Secundum gradus formales, quorum unus secundum se nobilior et perfectior est altero; et haec, ut dictum est, latitudo generis est, sub quo sunt diversi gradus formales specifice differentes." The translation of Lincoln Reis, *The Predicables and The Predicaments in the Totius Logicae Aristotelis* (New York: Columbia University, 1936) is unacceptable on account of its over-simplification.

58. *Ibid*., c. 4, p. 57: "Differentia est qua species abundat a genere: quia species abundat, idest excedit in suo significato etiam illud quod explicite significant differentia."

59. Joannis Duns Scotus, "In Universam Logicam Quaestiones." *Opera Omnia* (Parisii: Apud Ludovicum Vivès, 1891), Vol. I, Q. XVII, p. 248: "Dico enim quod in fundamentis est majus Universale Genus quam Species. Similiter in intentionibus, quia praedicatur de differentibus specie, et numero: Species autem de differentibus numero tantum: et ita habet plura supposita, non tamen in actu *exercitio*, imo pauciora."

60. *Ibid*., Q. XVIII, p. 252: "*Genus requirere multas species* potest intelligi dupliciter. Uno modo in actu, vel in potentia: alio modo in aptitudine. . . ." The word *aptitudo* was used by Peter of Spain and was commonly employed at the University of Sienna prior to 1250.

61. *Ibid*.: "*Aptitudo est inclinatio alicujus in aliquid secundum se, vel potius non repugnantia*, ut patet in homine ad ridendum, et in superficie ad albedinem. Potentia autem dicit ordinem ad actum."

62. *Ibid*., Q. XVIII, p. 255: "Genus habet se, in una etiam specie, ut potentiale, et contrahibile, et actuale, et per consequens minus habens de entitate, et actuali, atque essentiali intelligibilitate, quam species cujus est."

63. *Ibid*., Q. XXV, p. 308: "Genus continet actualiter potentialiter, id est, indeterminate differentias, quas Species determinate continet."

64. In II *Post Analyt*., lect. 13, n. 529: "Circa primum considerandum est quod ea quae praedicantur in eo quod quid est, oportet quod semper et universaliter praedicentur, ut supra habitum est: et ideo accipiens ea quae praedicantur de unoquoque ut semper, dicit quod inter ea quaedam inveniuntur quae extenduntur in plus quam id cui insunt; non tamen ita quod inveniantur extra genus illud.

Et exponit quid sit esse *in plus*, et dicit quod in plus esse dicuntur quaecunque universaliter insunt alicui, non tamen ei soli, sed etiam alii. Datur autem per hoc intelligi aliud membrum oppositum, quia scilicet est aliquid quod extenditur in plus, et est extra genus."

65. *Ibid*., n. 532.

66. Cf. *Ibid*., lect. 19, n. 578-79.

67. In I *Sent*., d. 28, q. 1, a. 1, ob. 3: "Quanto enim homo est in

paucioribus quam animal, tanto magis negatio animalis de paucioribus praedicatur quam negatio hominis."

68. Kenneth F. Dougherty, *Logic* (Peekskill, New York: Graymoor Press, 1956), p. 35.

69. *De Ver.*, q. 8, a. 3, ad 4: "Res comprehenditur cuius definitio cognoscitur, si tamen ipsa definitio comprehendatur."

70. In XI *Metaph.*, lect. 1, n. 2172: "Est autem veritas quod universalia sunt principia, scilicet in cognoscendo; et sic genera magis sunt principia, quia simpliciora. Et quod dividantur in plura quam species, hoc est, quia continent plura in potentia. Sed species continent plura in actu. Unde sunt magis divisibiles per modum resolutionis compositi in simplicia." This same idea is repeated in *Ia*, q. 85, a. 3, ad 2.

71. Cf. Petrus Hispanus, *Summulae Logicales,* ed. I. M. Bochenski, O.P. (Romae: Domus Editorialis Marietti, 1947), Tr. II, p. 17, 2.07, p. 21, 2.17. R. Stapper believes that Peter of Spain completed the *Summulae Logicales* at the University of Siena sometime between 1246 and 1250. Cf. R. Stapper, *Papst Johannes XXI in Kirchengeschichtliche Studien*, IV, 1898. The author, Petrus Hispanus, is recorded under *John XXI* in the bibliography.

72. St. Albert, *Commentaria In De Praedicabilibus* (Parisiis: Ludovicus Vivès, 1890), Tr. VI, c. 5, p. 181: "Genera quidem abundant de speciebus in continentia earum quae sub genere sunt specierum: quia secundum ambitum communitatis species non continent genera. Species vero constitutae abundant a generibus continentia propriarum differentiarum, per quas constituuntur. . . ."

73. *Ibid., Commentaria In Posteriora Analytica Aristotelis* (Parisiis: Ludovicus Vivès, 1890), Vol. II, Tr. IV, c. 1, p. 73: "Eorum quae insunt unicuique ut praedicata substantialia, quaedam secundum communitatem et ambitum suae praedicationis extenduntur in plus quam sit communitas subjecti vel speciei quae diffinienda est: . . . ."

74. Cf. *Ibid., Commentaria In De Praedicabilibus*, Tr. III, c. 3, p. 65b: "Quia de potestate et ambitu naturali animalis est et de aptitudine generis, quod dividatur oppositis differentiis."

75. *Ibid., Commentaria In Praedicamenta Aristotelis* (Parisiis: Ludovicus Vivès, 1890), Tr. II, c. 8, p. 51: "Tam enim species quam genus qualitate differentiae determinantur, sed genus per suam qualitatem determinatur ad significandum plus quam species, quia genus sua qualitate determinat sibi subjecta differentia specie et numero, qualitas autem quae speciei communitatem determinat, non determinat speciem nisi ad hoc ut contineat differentia solo numero."

76. *Ibid., Commentaria in De Praedicabilibus*. Tr. IV, c. 6, p. 100: "Magis autem est collectivum et adunativum genus, quam species, in hoc quod plura colligit quam species, etsi etiam species magis secundum intentionem sit una. quam forma generis: minus enim a se distant et magis unum sunt quae sunt unum in specie, quam ea quae sunt unum in genere,

cum plura uniat in se et colligat genus quam species: unit enim et colligit multas species et omnia quae in speciebus colliguntur."

77. *Ibid.,* p. 101: "Collectio enim incipit a multis, et terminatur ad unum: adunatio incipit ab uno, et terminatur ad multa, quae in uno uniuntur."

78. Cf. p. 2, of this treatise.

79. Cf. S. R. E. Cardinalis S. Bonaventurae, *Opera Omnia,* ed. A. C. Peltier (Parisiis: Ludovicus Vivès, 1867). 15 vols.

80. Cf. Antonius de Carpenedulo Marc, O. M. C., *Summa Totius Dialecticae Ad Mentem S. Bonaventurae* (Romae: Apud Andream Phraeum, 1634), Lib. III, Tr. II, c. 1, p. 198. c. 8, p. 208.

81. Nicephorus Blemmida, *Epitomes Logicae Prooemium.* Cf. *MG,* Vol. CXLII, c. 12, p. 767: "Differentia est qua species superat genus, Homo enim superat animal per rationale. Animal enim actu neque rationale est neque irrationale; quoniam idem opposita habent. Potestate tamen animal et rationale exsistit et irrationale, omnesque habet sub se (constitutas) differentias."

82. Joannis Saresberiensis Episcopi Carnotensis, *Metalogicon,* ed. Clemens C. I. Webb (Oxonii: E. Typographeo Clarendoniano, 1929), L. IIII, pp. 103-104 text 880d-881a): "Item in Elenchis: ˙Homo et omne commune non hoc aliquid, sed quale quid, (vel) ad aliquid vel aliquo modo vel huiusmodi quid significat. Et post pauca: Manifestum quoniam non dandum hoc aliquid esse quod communiter praedicatur de omnibus, sed aut quale aut ad aliquid aut quantum aut talium quid significare. Profecto quod non est hoc aliquid, significatione expressa non potest explanari quid sid. [The meaning of the preceding sentence is not altogether clear. However, such lack of understanding does not seem to derogate from the importance of the whole paragraph]. Existentium enim a natura certus est finis, et singula suis ab invicem proprietatibus discreta sunt, sed eorumdem est plerumque minus finita cognitio et quodammodo conceptio vaga. Nec istis prejudicat quod fere in omnium ore celebre est, aliud scilicet esse quod appellativa significant et aliud esse quod nominant. Nominantur singularia, sed universalia significantur." The *Metalogicon* of John of Salisbury was completed in 1159.

83. Cf. Petrus Abaelardus, *Dialectica,* ed. L. M. De Rijk (Assen: Van Gorcum & Co., 1956), Tr. I, Liber Partium, Vol. III, p. 112, line 22-p. 114, line 15. Abaelard considers *denotare* and *exprimere* as synonyms for *significare.*

84. St. John Damascene, *Dialectica.* Cf. *MG,* Vol. XCIV, c. 9, p. 559: "Itaque genus est id cui species subjicitur [est item genus, quod dividitur in species]. Nam genus in species dividitur, latiusque patet quam species, ac species complectitur, iisque superius est."

Ibid.: "Ut idem genus de specie, ita species praedicatur de individuis. Liquet autem genus quidem esse specie generalius, ac speciem individuis."

Ibid., c. 15, p. 578: "Omne praedicatum, aut latius patent quam subjectum, aut aeque; minus autem late, nunquam. . . . Latius porro patent superiora: minus late inferiora."

270

Ibid., p. 579: "Generum de speciebus, et differentiarum de speciebus, ac specierum de individuis praedicatio latior dicitur; propriorum autem, aequa."

85. *Ibid.*, 20, 586: "Quod genus universalius sit quam species: quod species differentiis abundet prae genere. . . ."

86. An. Manlius Severinus Boetius, *In Porphyrium Dialogi*, trans. Victorinus Cf. *ML*, Vol. LXIV, Dialogus I, p. 24: "Nam et genus speciebus principium est, et plurimarum in se specierum collectivum est."

87. *Ibid.*, p. 45: "Genus enim cum unum sit, plurimarum specierum progenitivum est. Namque sub uno genere plures species inveniuntur. . . . Genus autem plurimas colligit res, sicut ipsum a plurimis iterum speciebus dividitur. . . . Est igitur genus collectivum specierum suarum et quodammodo adunativum. Species vero divisae generis quodammodo et multiplicativae. Igitur quicunque ad magis genera ascendit, omnem specierum multitudinem per genera colligit adunatque."

88. Ibid., p. 61. "Omne quod genus est, plures sub se species continet; omne vero quod species sub se plures habet, differentias habet. Genus enim, id est animal, in hoc homine, id est specie, superabundat et superest, quod homo solum homo est. Animal vero non solum homo, sed etiam bos vel avis, vel alia hujusmodi. Species vero in eo superant genera sua, quod eas differentias quas species in actu habent, eas genera non habent. . . . Atque ideo species quae est homo, vel alia species, sicut est equus, a genere suo animali in hoc abundant supersunt, quod animal ipsum per se neque rationale neque irrationale est."

89. An. Manlius Severinus Boetius, *In Porphyrium Commentariorum*. Cf. *ML*, Vol. LXIV, Lib. III, p. 112: "Species vero et genera collectiva, species quidem individuorum collectiva atque adunativa. . . . Species autem singularem particularemque multitudinem ab singularitatis deducit unitatem, igitur plus genus adunativum est quam species."

90. *Ibid.*, p. 113: "Nomen generis toti convenit speciei: non enim coaequatur, solum speciei generis magnitudo, verumetiam speciem ipsam supervadit. Idcirco igitur omnis homo animal est, quoniam intra animalis vocabulum et homo et caetera animalia continentur. At vero nullus dixerit, Omne animal homo est; non enim pervenit ad totum animal hominis nomen, quia cum sit minus, nullo modo generis vocabulo coaequatur. Itaque quae majora sunt de minoribus praedicantur, quae vero minora sunt, non convertuntur ut de majoribus praedicentur."

91. *Ibid.*, Lib. IV, p. 125: "Differentia specifica est qua abundat species a genere, fit enim genus animal, species homo: habet igitur homo differentias in se, quae ipsum constituunt rationale atque mortale. . . ." Cf. *In Porphyrium Dialogi* in *ML*, Vol. LXIV, Dialogus II, p. 52: "Quare quoniam species actu differentias continet, genus vero potestate, species a genere merito differentiis abundare dicuntur."

92. *Ibid.*, Lib. V, p. 142: "Genera supervadunt species suas . . .; species vero genera differentiarum pluralitate. Animal enim quod est genus, supervadit hominem, quod est species, quia non hominem solum continet,

271

verumetiam bovem, equum aliasque species. . . . Species vero ut homo supervadit genus, ut animal multitudine differentiarum."

93. Cf. Ammonius Hermeae, *In Porphyrii Isagogen Sive V Voces*, ed. Adolfus Busse (Berolini: Typis et impensis Georgii Reimeri, 1891), Vol. IV, Pars III, p. 98, 4.14.

94. Ammonius Hermeae, *In Quinque Porphyrii Voces Commentarium* (Venetiis: Apud Hieronymum Scotum, 1542), p. 28: "Res quo magis compositae sunt, magis coarctantur; simpliciora vero dilatantur, et super pluribus extenduntur, utpote quae rerum omnium primo, universalique principio sunt proximiora. Atque idcirco animal ipsum per se, pluribus, rationale vero adunctum paucioribus accommodatur; rationale vero animal mortali adnexum pauciora etiam comprehendit si insuper grammaticum addideris, multo pauciora continebit. Quare deficientes definitiones rem faciunt abundare, abundantes vere rem faciunt deficere."

95. *Ibid.*, p. 36: "Species individua singulatim tantum, genus vero & species, & individua comprehendit: Ab inferiori quidem, vel ab individuis ad generalissima conscendentibus multitudine res coangustantur, potentia tamen augentur. Species quoad multitudinem individuis sunt pauciores, potentia tamen & accretione superabundant, eodem pacto speciebus genera, donec ad unum generalissimum devenerimus. Id quoque jure factum censetur quoniam una tantum rerum omnium causa est, & origo, propterea quae huic proximiora sunt, multitudine coarctantur, potentia vero augentur. Quae vero longinquiora, numero augentur potentia diminuuntur."

96. Ibid., p. 37: "Genus, inquit [Porphyrius] aliquod semper de specie praedicatur, ut animal de homine, et de animali substantia, verum species amplius de genere non praedicatur. . . . Hinc igitur genera semper de speciebus praedicari manifestum est, species de generibus nunquam."

97. Aristotle, *Metaph.* V, c. 26, 1023b29-34: "Universale quidem enim et quod totaliter, dicitur ut aliquid ens unum sicut universale, quasi multa continens, quia praedicatur de unoquoque, et unum omnia sunt et unumquodque: ut homo, et equus, et Deus, quia omnia animalia."

98. Sir William Hamilton, *Lectures on Logic* (Third edition; London: William Blackwood and Sons, 1874), Vol. I, pp. 296-97.

99. Jacques Maritain, *Formal Logic,* trans. Imelda Choquette (New York: Sheed & Ward, 1937), p. 120.

100. Kenneth F. Dougherty, *op. cit.,* pp. 36-37. Cf. Vincent Edward Smith, *op. cit.,* p. 37; Thomas Crumley, *op. cit.,* p. 44.

101. Cf. Sir William Hamilton, *op. cit.,* p. 141.

102. Cf. *Porphyrii Isagoge Et In Aristotelis Categorias Commentarium.* ed. Adolfus Busse (Berolini: Typis et impensis Georgii Reimeri, 1887). Vol. IV, Pars I.

103. Cf. Ammonius Hermeae, *In Porphyrii Isagogen Sive V Voces,* ed. Adolfus Buses (Berolini: Typis et impensis Georgii Reimeri, 1891), Vol. IV, Pars III, p. 97, 9 sq. Cf. Ammonius, *In Aristotelis Categorias Commentarius,* ed. Adolfus Busse (Berolini: Typis et Impensis Georgii Reimeri, 1895), Vol. IV, Pars IV, p. 43, 4.

104. Antoine Arnauld and M. Nicole, *The Port Royal Logic*, trans. Thomas Spencer Baynes (Edinburgh: Oliver and Boyd, 1865), Intro., p. xxxiii.

105. C. S. Peirce, "Upon Logical Comprehension and Extension", *Proceedings Of The American Academy Of Arts And Sciences* (Boston and Cambridge: Welch, Bigelow, And Company, 1868), Vol. II, p. 417. In a footnote Peirce mentions that Porphyry appears to refer to the doctrine of extension and comprehension as an ancient one.

106. Cf. Porphyry, "The Introduction Of Porphyry", *The Organon, Or Logical Treatises Of Aristotle*, trans. Octavius Freire Owen (London: Henry G. Bohen, 1853), Vol. II, pp. 609-33.

107. Cf. Porphyre, *Isagoge*, trans. by J. Tricot (Paris: Librairie Philosophique J. Vrin, 1947).

108. Cf. *Porphyrii Introductio In Aristotelis Categorias*, trans. a Boethio, ed. Adolfus Busse (Berolini: Typis et impensis Georgii Reimeri, 1887), Vol. IV, Pars I, pp. 25-51.

109. An attempt will be made to explain the use of the word 'extension' in this chapter because *de facto* the translators use the word in English and French. A doctrinal justification will be attempted in Part II of this treatise.

110. Octavius Freire Owen, *op. cit.*, Vol. II, c. 2, p. 610.
J. Tricot, *op. cit.*, c. 1, p. 13: "Le genre, en effet, se dit, d'abord, d'une collection d'individus se comportant d'une certaine façon par rapport à un seul être et par rapport entre eux."
An. Manl. Sev. Boetius, *op. cit.*, p. 26, 1-3: "Genus enim dicitur et aliquorum quodammodo se habentium ad unum aliquid et ad se invicem collectio, ..."

111. Octavius Freire Owen, *op. cit.*, c. 2, p. 611.
J. Tricot, *op. cit.*, c. 1, p. 13: "Genre est pris encore en un autre sens: c'est le point de départ de la génération de chaque chose, qu'il s'agisse soit du générateur lui-même, soit du lieu où une chose a été engendrée."
An. Manl. Sev. Boetius, *op. cit.*, p. 26, 8-10: "Dicitur autem et aliter rursus genus, quod est uniuscuiusque generationis principium vel ab eo qui genuit vel a loco in quo quis genitus est."

112. Octavius Freire Owen, *op. cit.*, c. 2, p. 611-12.
J. Tricot, *op. cit.*, 2, p. 14-15: "Il y a encore un autre sens de genre, c'est ce sous quoi est rangée l'espèce, et ce nom lui a sans doute été donné pour sa ressemblance avec les cas précédents: le genre en ce sens, en effet, est une sorte de principe pour toutes les espèces qui lui sont subordonées, et il semble aussi contenir toute la multitude rangée sous lui.

Le genre est donc pris en trois sens, et c'est le troisième dont il est traité chez les philosophes: c'est lui qu'ils ont décrit quand ils ont défini le genre en disant qu'il est l'attribut essentiel applicable à une pluralité de choses différant entre elles spécifiquement, comme l'animal par exemple."

An. Manl. Sev. Boetius, *op. cit.*, p. 26, 19—p. 27, 2: "Aliter autem rursus genus dicitur, cui supponitur species, ad horum fortasse similitudinem dictum. Etenim principium quoddam est huiusmodi genus earum quae sub ipso sunt specierum, videturque etiam multitudinem continere omnem quae sub eo est.

Tripliciter igitur cum genus dicatur, de tertio apud philosophos sermo est. Quod etiam describentes adsignaverunt genus esse dicentes, quod de pluribus et differentibus specie in eo quod quid sit praedicatur ut animal."

113. Octavius Freire Owen, *op. cit.*, c. 2, p. 615.

J. Tricot, *op. cit.*, c. 5, pp. 20-21: "De son côte, le terme spécialissime n'a, lui aussi, qu'une seule face: il n'a de rapport qu'avec les termes placés avant lui et dont il est espèce, tandis qu'il soutient avec les termes qui viennent après lui un rapport toujours le même, et il est appelé aussi espèce des individus. Mail il est dit, d'une part, espèce des individus en ce qu'il les contient, et, d'autre part, en sens contraire, espèce des termes antérieurs à lui en ce qu'il est contenu par eux.

On définit donc le genre le plus général de la manière suivante: ce qui, étant genre, n'est past espèce, et encore: ce au-dessus de quoi il ne saurait y avoir d'autre genre supérieur."

An. Manl. Sev. Boetius, *op. cit.*, p. 30, 16-22: "Et specialissimum autem unam habet habitudinem, eam quae est ad superiora, quorum est species, eam vero quae est ad posteriora non habet, sed etiam individuorum species dicitur, sed species quidem individuorum velut ea continens, species autem superiorum, velut quae ab eis contineatur.

Determinant ergo generalissimum ita, quod cum genus sit non est species, et rursus, supra quod non erit aliud superveniens genus; . . . ."

114. Octavius Freire Owen, *op. cit.*, c. 2, p. 616.

J. Tricot, *op. cit.*, c. 6, p. 23: "Quand on descend aux espèces spécialissimes, la division procède nécessairement dans le sens de la multiplicité; quand, au contraire, on remonte aux genres les plus généraux, on réduit nécessairement la multiplicité à l'unité: l'espèce, en effet, et plus encore le genre. . . ."

An. Manl. Sev. Boetius, *op. cit.*, p. 32, 1-4: "Descendentibus igitur ad specialissima necesse est dividentem per multitudinem ire, ascendentibus vero ad generalissima necesse est colligere multitudinem. Collectivum enim multorum in unam naturam species est et magis id quod genus est. . . ."

115. Octavius Freire Owen, *op. cit.*, c. 2, p. 616.

J. Tricot, *op. cit.*, c. 7, p. 24: "Le genre est toujours attribueé à l'espère, et tous les termes supérieurs aux termes inférieurs, l'espèce, par contre, n'est attribuée ni au genre inmédiat, ni aux genres supérieurs, et cela faute de réciprocation. Ce qui'il faut, en effet, c'est ou bien que des termes également extensifs soient attribués à des termes également extensifs, comme 'ce qui hennit' à cheval, ou bien des termes plus extensifs à des termes moins extensifs, comme l'animal à l'homme; mais pour l'attribution de termes moins extensifs à des termes plus extensifs, il n'en est plus de même et on ne peut plus dire que l'animal est homme, comme on peut dire que l'homme est animal."

An. Manl. Sev. Boetius, *op. cit.*, p. 32, 11-17: "Genus quidem semper de specie praedicatur et omnia superiora de inferioribus, species autem neque de proximo sibi genere neque de superioribus, neque enim convertitur. Oportet autem aequa de aequis praedicari, ut hinnibile de equo, aut maiora de minoribus, ut animal de homine; minora vero de maioribus minime, neque enim animal dicis esse hominem quemadmodum hominem dicis esse animal."

116. Octavius Freire Owen, *op. cit.*, c. 2, p. 617.

J. Tricot, *op. cit.*, c. 7, pp. 24-25: "Ainsi donc comme les termes supérieurs sont toujours attributs des termes subordonnés, l'espèce sera attribuée à l'individu, le genre le sera a l'espèce et a l'individu, et le genre le plus général au genre ou aux genres (s'il y a plusieurs termes moyens et subordonnés), ainsi qu'a l'espèce et a l'individu. Le genre le plus général s'applique à tous les genres qui lui sont subordonnés, ainsi qu'aux espèces et aux individus; le genre placé avant l'espèce spécialissime, à toutes les espèces spécialissimes et aux individus; l'espèce qui n'est qu'espèce, à tous les individus; et l'individu, à un seul être particulier. On appelle individu Socrate, ou cette chose blanche que voici, ou ce fils de Sophronisque qui s'approche, en supposant que Socrate fût le seul fils de Sophronisque. Les êtres de cette sorte sont appelés individus, parce que chacun d'eux est composé de particularités dont la réunion ne saurait être jamais la même dans un autre être: les particularités propres à Socrate ne sauraient être les mêmes pour chacun autre être particulier, ..."

An. Manl. Sev. Boetius, *op. cit.*, p. 32, 21-p. 33, 7: "Semper igitur superioribus de inferioribus praedicatis species quidem de individuo praedicabitur, genus autem et de specie et de individuo, generalissimum autem et de genere et de generibus, si plura sint media et subalterna, et de specie et de individuo. Dicitur enim generalissimum quidem de omnibus sub se generibus speciebusque et de individuis, genus autem, quod ante specialissimum est, de omnibus specialissimis et de individuis, solum autem species de omnibus individuis, individuum autem de uno solo particulari. Individuum autem dicitur Socrates et hoc album et hic veniens, ut Sophronisci filius, si solus ei Socrates sit filius. Individua ergo dicuntur huiusmodi, quoniam ex proprietatibus consistit unumquodque eorum, quarum collectio numquam in alio eadem erit. Socratis enim proprietates nunquam in alio quolibet erunt particularium, ..."

117. Octavius Freire Owen, *op. cit.*, c. 2, pp. 617-18.

J. Tricot, *op. cit.*, cc. 7-8, p. 25: "Ainsi donc, l'individu est contenu par l'espèce, et l'espèce par le genre: le genre est un tout, et l'individu une partie, l'espèce est à la fois tout et partie, mais partie d'une autre chose, tandis que le tout n'est pas le tout d'une autre chose, mais il est en d'autres choses, car le tout est dans les parties."

An. Manl. Sev. Boetius, *op. cit.,* p. 33, 10-14: "Continetur igitur individuum quidem sub specie, species autem sub genere; totum enim quiddam est genus, individuum autem pars, species vero et totum et pars, sed pars quidem alterius, totum autem non alterius sed aliis; partibus enim totum est."

118. Octavius Freire Owen, op. cit., p. 618. "Genus is a whole in *predication,* containing under it various subjective species; species is a whole in *definition,* containing genus and differentia, as parts of the essence; the former may be called 'Totum Universale', the latter 'Totum Essentiale', (cf. Crakanthorpe, *Logica,* lib. ii, ch. 5): sometimes the distinction is expressed by the terms, *'whole of extension'* and *'whole of comprehension'.* Port Royal *Log.,* part i, ch. 6. Species contain genus by implication, genus contains species by comprehension, so also in this latter sense, does species contain 'individuals', yet it is a *less full and complete* term than that of 'individual'. Vide Whately, *Log.* ii, ch. 5, sec. 3; Wallis, lib. i. 4; Abelard *de Gen. et Spec.;* Hill's *Log.* vol. i."

119. Octavius Freire Owen, *op. cit.,* c. 3, p. 621.

J. Tricot, *op. cit.,* c. 11, p. 30: "La différence est ce par quoi l'espèce l'emporte en compréhension sur le genre. L'homme, par exemple, a en plus de l'animal le raisonnable et le mortel; l'animal, en effet, n'est rien de tout cela, car alors d'où les espèces tireraient-elles leurs différences? Ill n'a pas non plus en lui toutes es différences opposées, car le même sujet recevrait en même temps les opposées, mais il possède en puissance seulement, comme on a raison de le dire, toutes les différences qui lui sont subordonées, et il n'en possède aucune en acte. . . . ."

An. Manl. Sev. Boetius, *op. cit.,* p. 36, 20-p. 27, 3.: "Differentia est qua abundat species a genere. Homo enim ab animali plus habet rationale et mortale, animal enim neque ipsum nihil horum est, nam unde habebunt species differentias? neque enim omnes oppositas habet, nam in eodem simul habebunt opposita, sed, quemadmodum probant, potestate quidem omnes habet sub se differentias, actu vero nullam."

120. Octavius Freire Owen, *op. cit.,* c. 7, pp. 624-25.

J. Tricot, *op. cit.,* c. 14, p. 35: "Un caractère commun au genre et à la différence, c'est de contenir des espèces: car la différence enveloppe aussi les espèces, bien qu'elle ne contienne pas toutes celles que renferme le genre. En effet, le raisonnable, quoiqu'il n'enveloppe pas les êtres non-raisonnables, comme le fait le vivant, renferme du moins l'homme et le dieu, qui en sont des espèces."

An. Manl. Sev. Boetius, *op. cit.,* p. 40, 18-22: "Commune autem generi et differentiae continentia specierum. Continet enim et differentia species, etsi non omnes quot genera. Rationale enim etiamsi non continet ea quae sunt inrationabilia, ut genus, quemadmodum animal, sed continet hominem et deum, quae sunt species."

121. Octavius Freire Owen. *op. cit.*, c. 7, p. 625.

J. Tricot, *op. cit.*, c. 14, p. 36: "Un caractère propre du genre, c'est d'être attribué à un plus grand nombre de termes que la différence, l'espèce, le propre et l'accident: l'animal est attribué à l'homme, au cheval, à l'oiseau, au serpent; le quadrupède, aux seuls animaux ayant quatre pieds; l'homme n'est attribué qu'aux individus; capable de hennir, au cheval seulement et aux chevaux particuliers; et, pareillement, l'accident à des termes moins nombreux."

An. Manl. Sev. Boetius, *op. cit.*, p. 41, 14-18: "Proprium autem generis est de pluribus praedicari, quam differentia et species et proprium et accidens; animal enim de homine et equo et ave et serpente, quadrupes vero de solis quattour pedes habentibus, homo vero de solis individuis et hinnibile de equo et de his qui sunt particulares et accidens similiter de paucioribus."

122. Octavius Freire Owen, *op. cit.*, c. 8, p. 626.

J. Tricot, *op. cit.*, c. 15, p. 38: "Genre et espèce diffèrent en ce que le genre contient les espèces, tandis que les espèces sont contenues dans le genre et ne le contiennent pas: car le genre a plus d'extension que l'espèce."

An. Manl. Sev. Boetius, *op. cit.*, p. 42, 22-p. 43, 2: "Different autem eo quod genus quidem continent species sub se, species vero continentur et non continent genera, in pluribus enim genus quam species est."

123. Octavius Freire Owen, *op. cit.*, c. 8, p. 626.

J. Tricot, *op. cit.*, c. 15, p. 38: "De plus, les genres ont une extension plus grande, parce qu'ils embrassent les espèces qui leur sont subordonnées, et les espèces une compréhension plus grande que les genres, en raison de leurs différences propres."

An. Manl. Sev. Boetius, *op. cit.*, p. 43, 7-9: "Amplius quidem genera abundant earum quae sub ipsis sunt specierum continentia, species vero a generibus abundant propriis differentiis."

124. Marcus Fabius Quintilianus, *De Institutione Oratoria* (Lipsiae: Sumptibus et typis Caroli Tauchnitii, 1829), Vol. I, L. V, c. 10, pp. 254-55: "Genus ad propagandam speciem minimum valet, plurimum ad refellendam. Itaque non, quia est arbor, platanus est; at, quod non est arbor, utique platanus non est: nec, quod non est virtus, utique potest esse justitia. . . . Numquam itaque tolletur a specie genus, nisi omnes species, quae sunt generi subjectae, removeantur: hoc modo, *Quod neque immortale est, neque mortale, animal non est.*"

125. Lucius Annaeus Seneca, *Opera Omnia* (Lipsiae: Sumptibus et typis Car. Tauchnitii, 1832), Vol. III, Ep. LVIII, p. 138. "Nunc enim primum illud genus quaerimus, ex quo ceterae species suspensae sunt, a quo nascitur omnis divisio, quo univers a comprehensa sunt. Invenietur autem, si coeperimus singula retro legere: sic enim perducemur ad primum. Homo species est, ut Aristotelis ait: equus species est, canis species:

ergo commune aliquod quaerendum est his omnibus vinculum, quod illa complectatur, et sub se habeat."

126. Cicero "De Inventione", *Opera,* ed. Aldus Pius Mannuccius (Venetiis: Carolum Emmanuelem, 1583), Liber I, p. 40: "Nam genus est, quod plures partes amplectitur, ut animal: pars est, quae subest generi, ut equus." In his *Commentary on Cicero's Topics,* Boethius employs the Latin word *maius* to indicate that genus is larger than species, and the word *ambitus* to point out the scope or breadth of the genus. Cf. Cicero, "Topica", *Opera,* Liber II, p. 154. His use of the Latin word would represent then an evolution in the meaning of this term, for there is no evidence that Cicero himself used the word *ambitus* with a strictly logical sense. Cf. H. Merguet, *Lexikon Zu Den Philosophischen Schriften Cicero's* (Jena: Verlag Von Gustav Fischer, 1887), Vol. I, p. 152.

127. Aristotle, *Top.,* I, c. 5. Cf. *The Organon Or Logical Treatises Of Aristotle,* trans. Octavius Freire Owen (London: G. Bell And Sons, Limited, 1910), Vol. II, p. 364.

128. Aristotelis, *Opera Omnia Graece Et Latine* (Parisiis: Editoribus Firmin - Didot Et Sociis, 1927), Vol. I, p. 175. 8-9: «Γένος δ' ἐστὶ τὸ κατὰ πλειόνων καὶ διαφερόντων τῷ εἴδει ἐν τῷ τὶ ἐστὶ κατηγορούμενον».

"Genus vero est id, quod de pluribus et specie differentibus ratione ejus quid sit praedicatur."

129. Aristotle, *Top.,* II, c. 2, p. 386.
Aristotelis, *Opera Omnia Graece Et Latine,* p. 187. 21-23: «Ἄλλος τὸ ἐπιθλέπειν οἷς ὑπάρχειν ἢ πᾶσιν ἢ μηδενὶ εἴρηται. Σκοπεῖν δὲ κατ' εἴδη καὶ μὴ ἐν τοῖς ἀπείροις ὁδῷ γὰρ μᾶλλον καὶ ἐν ἐλάττοσιν ἡ σκέψις».

"Alius *locus,* ut videamus *de iis,* quibus aut omnibus, aut quorum nulli *aliquid* inesse dictum est. Considerare vero *nos oportet* secundum species, nec in infinitis: sic enim via certiori *progredimur,* et in paucioribus *versatur* consideratio."

130. Aristotelis, *Opera Omnia Graece Et Latine,* p. 206. 26-30: «Ὅρος δὲ τοῦ μετέχειν τὸ ἐπιδέχεσθαι τὸν τοῦ μετεχομένου λόγον. Δῆλον οὖν ὅτι τὰ μὲν εἴδη μετέχει τῶν γενῶν, τὰ δὲ γένη τῶν εἰδῶν οὔ. Τὸ μὲν γὰρ εἶδος ἐπιδέχεται τὸν τοῦ γένους λόγον, τὸ δὲ γένος τὸν τοῦ εἴδους οὔ».

"Definitio autem participandi est, recipere ejus definitionem, quod communicatur. Patet igitur, species quidem participes esse generum; genera vero specierum non *similiter;* nam species quidem recipit definitionem generis; genus autem non *recipit* speciei *definitionem.*"

131. Aristotle, *Top.,* IV, c. 1, p. 420.

132. Aristotle, *Top.,* IV, c. 1, pp. 421-22. In his translation, Ross speaks of genus having a wider 'denotation' than the species or the difference. Cf. *The Works Of Aristotle,* ed. and trans. W. D. Ross (London: Oxford University Press, 1950), Vol. I.
Aristotelis, *Opera Omnia Graece Et Latine,* p. 207. 7-8, 15-18:

278

«ἐπὶ πλέον γὰρ ἀεὶ τὸ γένος τοῦ εἴδους λέγεται. . . . Στοιχεῖον δὲ πρὸς ἄπαντα τὰ τοιαῦτα τὸ ἐπὶ πλέον τὸ γένος ἢ τὸ εἶδος, καὶ τὴν διαφορὰν λέγεσθαι ἐπ᾽ ἔλαττον γὰρ καὶ ἡ διαφορὰ τοῦ γένους λέγεται».

"Nam genus semper latius patet, quam species. . . . Elementum vero omnium hujusmodi *locorum* est, quod genus latius pateat, quam species et differentia; nam et differentia de paucioribus dicitur, quam genus." While the Latin word employed to designate the wider extension of the genus is *latius*, the Greek words used by Aristotle are ἐπὶ πλέον.

Tricot includes in his translation of the *Topics* a citation made by one of Aristotle's Greek commentators concerning the greater extension of the genus: "The genus having more of a relation with accident than property or definition have with accident: the genus and accident have a greater extension than the subject [species], whereas the property and definition have the same extension as the subject." Cf. J. Tricot's translation *Les Topiques*, Vol. I, p. 54, footnote: "Le genre ayant plus de rapport avec l'accident que n'en ont le propre ou la définition: le genre et l'accident ont une extension plus grande que le sujet, tandis que le propre et la définition ont la même extension que lui." Tricot cites as his reference Alexandre D'Aphrodise, *In Aristotelis Topicorum libros octo Commentaria*, ed. M. Wallies, Berlin, 1891 (Coll. Ac. Berol., II, 2), 136. 3.

133. Aristotle, *Top.*, IV, c. 2, p. 425.
Aristotelis, *Opera Omnia Graece Et Latine*, p. 209. 7-11:
«Οὐδὲ δοκεῖ μετέχειν ἡ διαφορὰ τοῦ γένους πᾶν γὰρ τὸ μετέχον τοῦ γένους ἢ εἶδος ἢ ἄτομόν ἐστιν ἡ δὲ διαφορὰ οὔτε εἶδος οὔτε ἄτομόν ἐστιν. Δῆλον οὖν ὅτι οὐ μετέχει τοῦ γένους ἡ διαφορά, . . .»
"Omne enim particeps generis aut species, aut individuum est; differentia vero neque species, neque individuum est. Patet igitur, non participem esse generis differentiam."

134. Aristotelis, *Opera Omnia Graece Et Latine*, p. 209. 36-37:
«ἐπὶ πλέον τε γὰρ τὸ γένος τῆς διαφορᾶς δεῖ λέγεσθαι, . . .»
"Nam et de pluribus genus dici oportet, quam differentiam, ..."
135. Aristotle, *Top.*, IV, c. 2, p. 426.
136. Aristotle, *Top.*, IV, c. 4, p. 431.
Aristotelis, *Opera Omnia Graece Et Latine*, p. 213. 4-5:
«πάλιν εἰ μὴ πρὸς ἴσα τὸ εἶδος καὶ τὸ γένος λέγεται».
"Rursus, an non ad totidem genus et species referantur."
137. Aristotle, *Top.*, IV, c. 5, p. 435.
Aristotelis, *Opera Omnia Graece Et Latine*, pp. 214. 49—p. 215. 1:
«Πάλιν εἰ κατά τι τὸ εἶδος τοῦ εἰρημένοι γένους μετέχει οὐ δοκεῖ γὰρ κατά τι μετέχεσθαι τὸ γένος οὐ γάρ ἐστιν ὁ ἄνθρωπος κατά τι ζῷον, οὐδ᾽ ἡ γραμματικὴ κατά τι ἐπιστήμη. . . .»
"Porro *videndum est,* an ex parte species dicti generis particeps sit; non videtur enim genus ex parte communicari; nam non est homo ex parte animal, neque grammatica ex parte scientia; . . . ."
138. Aristotle, *Top.*, IV, c. 6, p. 438. In a marginal annotation, Owen

279

comments "to a less extent 'than genus' ". W. D. Ross substitutes the words 'narrower range' for 'less extent'.

Aristotelis, *Opera Omnia Graece Et Latine*, p. 216. 46-49:

«Συμβαίνει οὖν κατὰ πάντων, ὧν τὸ γένος κατηγορεῖται, καὶ τὸ εἶδος κατηγορεῖσθαι, ἐπειδὴ τὸ ὄν καὶ τὸ ἓν κατὰ πάντων ἁπλῶς κατηγορεῖται, δέον ἐπ' ἔλαττον τὸ εἶδος κατηγορεῖσθαι».

"Accidit igitur, de omnibus, de quibus genus praedicatur, etiam speciem praedicari, siquidem et ens et unum de omnibus simpliciter praedicantur: oportet autem de paucioribus speciem praedicari."

139. Aristotelis, *Opera Omnia Graece Et Latine*, p. 218. 13:

«Τὸ γένος ἐπὶ πλέον λέγεται τῆς διαφορᾶς, . . .»

"Genus de pluribus dicitur, quam differentia; . . . ."

140. Aristotle, *Top.*, IV, c. 6, p. 441.

141. Aristotelis, *Opera Omnia Graece Et Latine*, p. 243. 24-28:

«Ἔτι εἰ κατηγορεῖται τοῦ γένους ἡ διαφορὰ ἢ τὸ εἶδος ἢ τῶν κάτωθεν τι τοῦ εἴδους, οὐχ ἂν εἴν ὡρισμένος οὐδὲν γὰρ τῶν εἰρημένων ἐνδέχεται τοῦ γένους κατηγορεῖσθαι, ἐπειδὴ τὸ γένος ἐπὶ πλεῖστον πάντων λέγεται».

"Porro, si de genere praedicatur differentia, aut species, aut aliquid speciei subjectum; non fuerit *recte* definitum. Nihil enim ex dictis de genere praedicari potest; quoniam genus latius, quam omnia, patet."

142. Aristotle, *Top.*, VI, c. 6, p. 482.

143. Aristotle, *Categ.* c. 5, 2b19-21. Cf. *The Works Of Aristotle*, ed. and trans. W. D. Ross (First edition; London: Oxford University Press, 1950).

Aristotelis, *Opera Omnia Graece Et Latine*, p. 3. 39-41:

«Ὑπόκειται γὰρ τὸ εἶδος τῷ γένει τὰ μὲν γὰρ γένη κατὰ τῶν εἰδῶν κατηγορεῖται, τὰ δὲ εἴδη κατὰ τῶν γενῶν οὐχ ἀντιστρέφει. . . .»

"Nam species generi subjicitur; genera enim de speciebus praedicantur; species autem non vicissim de generibus; . . . ."

144. Cf. Henry George Liddell and Robert Scott, *A Greek-English Lexicon* (Ninth edition; Oxford: At The Clarendon Press, 1958), p. 1378.

145. Aristotle, *Categ.* c. 3, 3b21-23. Cf. W. D. Ross edition. Another English translation reads as follows: "Still a wider limit is made by genus than by species, for whoever speaks of 'animal', comprehends more than he who speaks of 'man'." Cf. *The Organon Or The Logical Treatises Of Aristotle*, trans. Octavius Freire Owen, Vol. I, p. 12.

Cf. Aristotle, *Organon*, I. Catégories, trans. J. Tricot (Paris: Librairie Philosophique J. Vrin, 1959), p. 15: "La détermination a d'ailleurs une plus grande extension dans le cas du genre que dans le cas de l'espèce, car le terme *animal* embrasse un plus grand nombre d'êtres que le terme *homme*."

Aristotelis, *Opera Omnia Graece Et Latine*, p. 5. 15-18:

«Ἐπὶ πλεῖον δὲ τῷ γένει ἢ τῷ εἴδει τὸν ἀφορισμὸν ποιεῖται ὁ γὰρ ζῷον εἰπών ἐπὶ πλεῖον περιλαμβάνει ἢ ὁ τὸν ἄνθρωπον».

280

"Amplior autem genere denotatio fit, quam specie; animal enim dicens plura comprehendit, quam *dicens* hominem."

146. The modern translators disagree with Bonitz who states that the expressions ποιεῖσθαι τὸν ἀφορισμὸν ἐπὶ πλεῖον and ἐπὶ πλεῖον περιλαμβάνει are synonymous. Cf. H. Bonitz, *Index Aristotelicus* (Secunda editio; Graz: Akademische Druck-U. Verlagsanstalt, 1955), p. 129.

147. Cf. Henry George Liddell and Robert Scott, *op. cit.*, p. 292, who suggest 'determination' as the appropriate translation for this word in 3b22. In Latin, Boethius translated that word by *determinatio*. This particular Greek word is only found once in Aristotle's writings.

148. Cf. *Ibid.*, p. 1415a: πλέον (look under πλεῖων) means more in number, size, extent, etc.

149. Aristotle, *Post. Analyt.*, II, c. 13, 96a24-26. Cf. W. D. Ross edition. Aristotelis, *Opera Omnia Graece Et Latine*, p. 164. 39-42: «τῶν δὴ ὑπαρχόντων ἀεὶ ἑκάστῳ ἔνια ἐπεκτείνει ἐπὶ πλέον, οὐ μέντοι ἔξω τοῦ γένους. Λέγω δὲ ἐπὶ πλέον ὑπάρχειν, ὅσα ὑπάρχει μὲν ἑκάστῳ καθόλου, οὐ μὲν ἀλλὰ καὶ ἄλλῳ».

150. Aristotle, *Post. Analyt.*, II, c. 13, 96a24-26. Cf. St. Thomas Aquinas, *In Post. Analyt.*, ed. Spiazzi (Taurini: Marietti, 1953), Liber II, c. 12, 383 bis, p. 376. The medieval translation of Aristotle contains the words *extenduntur in plus,* while a more recent translation substitutes *latius sese extendunt.* Cf. St. Thomas Aquinas, *Opera Omnia* (Parmae: Tipis Petri Fiaccordori, 1852), Vol. XVIII, p. 208. Cf. St. Thomas Aquinas, *In II Post. Analyt.*, lect. 13, n. 529, p. 377 for his commentary on this passage. When St. Albert attempts to interpret this Aristotelian passage, he introduces the word 'breadth' *(ambitus)* which is frequently employed by logicians as a synonym for extension: "That of those things which are present in any thing as substantial predicates, certain ones are extended according to the community and breadth of their predication in more things than are the community of subject or species which must be defined. . . ." Cf. St. Albert, *Commentaria In Posteriora Analytica Aristotelis* (Paris: Ludovicus Vivès, 1890), Liber II, Tr. IV, c.1, p. 73: "Quod eorum quae insunt unicuique ut praedicata substantialia, quaedam secundum communitatem et ambitum suae praedicationis extenduntur in plus quam sit communitas subjecti vel speciei quae diffinienda est. . . ."

151. Cf. Aristotelis, *Opera Omnia Graece Et Latine*, p. 125. 10-19.

152. Cf. W. A. de Pater, *Les Topiques D'Aristote Et La Dialectique Platonicienne* (Fribourg, Suisse: Editions St. Paul, 1965), p. 27.

153. Plato, *Euthyphro*, 12c: «ΣΩ. Οὐκ ἄρ ὀρθῶς ἔχει λέγειν «ἵνα γὰρ δέος ἔνθα καὶ αἰδὼς,» ἀλλ' ἵνα μὲν αἰδώς, ἔνθα καὶ δέος, οὐ μέντοι ἵναγε δέος, πανταχοῦ αἰδώς, ἐπὶ πλέον γὰρ οἶμαι δέος αἰδοῦς».

Cf. Platon, "Euthyphron", *Oeuvres Complètes* (Deuxième édition; Paris: societé D'Édition, 1925), Vol. I, pp. 199-200. In this text, the last sentence of the preceding Greek quotation is translated as follows: "La crainte, à mon avis, s'étend plus loin que le respect," that is, "fear, in my opinion, is extended further than respect."

154. Plato, *Euthyphro*, 5d-e. Cf. *Plato, trans.* Harold North Fowler (London: William Heinemann Ltd., 1943), Vol. I, p. 19.

155. *Ibid.*, 6c-d.

156. *Ibid.*, 7.

157. *Ibid.*, 7: "Excellent, Euthyphro; now you have answered as I asked you to answer."

158. *Ibid.*, 9e.

159. *Ibid.*, 12e.

160. *Ibid.*, 14b.

161. *Ibid.*, 15b.

162. Cf. William Turner, *History of Philosophy* (Boston: Ginn And Company, 1929), p. 39. According to Turner, the few genuine and extant writings of Archytas do not contribute anything to our knowledge of Pythagorian doctrines inasmuch as they bear the imprint of Platonic influence.

163. Archytas, "Les Fragments D'Archytas de Tarente", *Pythagore et la Philosophie Pythagoricienne*, trans. Anthelme Edouard Chaignet (Paris: Didier et Cie, 1873), Vol. I, p. 312: "Cependant l'animal se divise en raisonnable et irraisonnable; l'animal raisonnable en mortel et immortel; le mortel dans les subdivisions enfermées sous l'espèce, telles que homme, boeuf, cheval et le reste."

164. Cf. William Turner, *loc. cit.*, p. 39.

165. Pythagore, *Pythagore et la Philosophie Pythagoricienne*, trans. by Anthelme Edouard Chaignet (Paris: Didier et Cie, 1873), Vol. II, p. 254: "C'est ainsi qu'il emprunte au pythagorisme ce grand et admirable principe, que l'ensemble des êtres, le monde réel des substances, le tout, comme disaient le pythagoriciens, est une progression, forme une série liée dont chaque terme contient tous les termes qui le précèdent, comme, dans le système de la Décade, tout nombre contient les nombres placés au-dessous de lui dans le développement naturel des nombres identiques aux choses."

166. *Ibid.*, p. 259-60: "Bien plus, ces termes sont des termes quantitatifs: ils expriment des quantités, et des quantités de même espèce, de nature à être mesurées par une commune mesure, à être comparées les unes avec les autres. Au fond il est très-exact de dire qu'Aristote les traite comme des nombres. C'est pour cela que les termes peuvent et doivent être considérés comme contenus l'un dans l'autre, comme ayant une quantité susceptible de plus et de moins. Ramené à sa forme la plus simple, le syllogisme n'est qu'une proportion: A est en B; B est en C, et par conséquent, A est necessairement en C. Et les rapports de contenance et de quantité persistent en se renversant, soit qu'on envisage la compréhension, soit qu'on envisage l'extension des termes. Car la compréhension

comme l'extension envellopent l'idée du plus et du moins, de la grandeur, de la quantité. Les deux extrêmes sont à cet egard dans le rapport inverse; le plus grand selon l'extension est le plus petit selon la compréhension; on voit ainsi qu'ils se contiennent tour à tour l'un l'autre: et de même le moyen doit être considéré tour à tour comme contenant chaque extrême, et comme contenu dans chacun d'eux: soit A, B, C. Si B est contenu dans A selon la compréhension, A est contenu dans B selon l'extension; et de même si B contient C, selon l'extension, C contient B selon la compréhension. Il n'y a donc d'après Aristote, dans le syllogisme que des rapports de grandeurs, c'est-à-dire des rapports numeriques."

167. Cf. page 2 of this study.

FOOTNOTES TO CHAPTER III

1. "Commune," *Thesaurus Linguae Latinae*, ed. Academiae Germanicae Berolinensis Gottingensis Lipsiensis Monacensis Vindobonensis (Lipsiae: In Aedibus B. G. Tenubneri, 1906), Vol. V, p. 1969. Henceforth, all references to this text will be abbreviated as TLL.

2. *Ibid.*, p. 1970.
3. *Ibid.*
4. *Ibid.*
5. *Ibid.*, p. 1973.
6. *Ibid.*, p. 1975.
7. *Ibid.*
8. *Ibid.*
9. *Ibid.*
10. *Ibid.*
11. *Ibid.*, p. 1976.
12. *Ibid.*
13. *Ibid.*
14. *Ibid.*, p. 1979.
15. *Ibid.*, p. 1978.
16. *Ibid.*, p. 1977.
17. *Ibid.*
18. *TLL*, Vol. III, p. 2146.
19. Charleton T. Lewis and Charles Short, *A Latin Dictionary* (Oxford: At the Clarendon Press, 1958), p. 394.
20. *TLL*, Vol. III, p. 2146.
21. Charleton T. Lewis and Charles Short, *op. cit.*, p. 394.
22. *Ibid.*
23. *Ibid.*
24. Robertus Stephanus, *Thesaurus Linguae Latinae* (Basiliae: Typis et impensis E. & J. R. Thurnisiorum Fratr., 1740), Vol. I, p. 611.
25. Charleton T. Lewis and Charles Short, *op. cit.*, p. 394.
26. *TLL*, Vol. III, p. 2152.
27. *Ibid.*

28. Guill. Freund et N. Theil, *Grand Dictionnaire de la Langue Latine* (Paris: Librairie de Firmin Didot Frères, Fils et Cie, 1866), Vol. I, p. 572.

29. *TLL*, Vol. III, p. 2151.

30. *Ibid.*, p. 2150.

31. Robertus Stephanus, *op. cit.*, Vol. I, p. 612.

32. *TLL*, Vol. III, p. 2148.

33. *Ibid.*, p. 2149.

34. *Ibid.*, p. 2150.

35. Charleton T. Lewis and Charles Short, *op. cit.*, p. 394.

36. *Ibid.*

37. Robertus Stephanus, *op. cit.*, Vol. I, p. 612.

38. *TLL*, Vol. III, p. 2150.

39. Cf. Guill. Freund et N. Theil, *op. cit.*, Vol. I, p. 572.

40. *Ibid.*

41. Cf. *Dictionaire Étymologique de la Langue Latine* (Quatrième édition; Paris: Librairie C. Koincksieck, 1959), p. 531.

42. *TLL*, Vol. III, p. 2155.

43. *Ibid.*

44. *Ibid.*, p. 2156.

45. *Ibid.*

46. Marcus Tullius Cicero, "The Orator", *Orations*, trans. C. D. Yonge (London: Henry G. Bohn, 1852), Vol. IV, p. 445.

47. *The Oxford English Dictionary* (Oxford: At The Clarendon Press, 1961), Vol. II, p. 741.

48. *Ibid.*

49. St. Albertus Magnus, "Physicorum lib. VIII", *Opera Omnia*, ed. Augustus Borgnet (Parisiis: Apud Ludovicum Vivès, 1890), Vol. III, L. vii, Tr. 1, c. 3, p. 490: "Motus autem [violentus] qui est ad aliud dicitur extensio."

50. *Ia*, q. 14. a. 1: "Cognoscentia a non cognoscentibus in hoc distinguuntur, quia non cognoscentia nihil habent nisi formam suam tantum; sed cognoscens natum est habere forman etiam rei alterius, nam species cogniti est in cognoscente. Unde manifestum est quod natura rei non cognoscentis est magis coarctata et limitata; natura autem rerum cognoscentium habet maiorem amplitudinem et extensionem."

51. Aristotle, *On The Soul*, III, c. 7, 431b21-23.

52. Cf. *Ia*, q. 7, a. 1. This article is an important preliminary to the understanding of *Ia*, q. 14, a. 1.

53. Cf. Aristotle, *On The Soul*, II, c. 12. 424a32.

54. Cf. *Ibid.*, III, c. 4, 429a18-28.

55. *De Ver.*, q. 8, a. 2: "Proprie dicitur comprehendi ab aliquo quod ab eo includitur; dicitur enim aliquis aliquid comprehendere, quando simul ex omnibus partibus apprehendere potest, quod est undique inclusum

habere.

Quod autem includitur ab aliquo, non excedit includens, sed est minus includente, vel saltem aequale. Haec autem ad quantitatem pertinent; unde secundum duplicem quantitatem est *duplex* modus comprehensionis; scilicet secundum quantitatem *dimensivam* et *virtualem*. Secundum dimensivam quidem, ut dolium comprehendit vinum: secundum virtualem autem, ut materia dicitur comprenendere formam, quando nil materiae remanet imperfectum a forma.

Et per hunc modum dicitur aliqua vis cognitiva comprehendere suum cognitum, in quantum scilicet cognitum perfecte substat cognitioni eius; tunc autem a comprehensione deficit, quando cognitum cognitionem excedit.

Hic autem excessus *diversimode* in diversis potentiis considerandus est. In potentiis enim *sensitivis* obiectum comparatur ad potentiam non solum secundum quantitatem virtualem, sed etiam secundum quantitatem dimensivam; eo quod sensibilia movent sensum, utpote in magnitudine existentem, non solum ex vi qualitatis propriorum sensibilium, sed secundum quantitatem dimensivam, ut patet de sensibilibus communibus.

Unde comprehensio sensus potest impediri *dupliciter*. *Uno modo* ex excessu sensibilis secundum quantitatem virtualem; sicut impeditur oculus a comprehensione solis, quia virtus claritatis solis, quae est visibilis, excedit proportionem virtutis visivae quae est in oculo. *Alio modo* propter excessum quantitatis dimensivae; sicut impeditur oculus ne comprehendat totam molem terrae, sed partem eius videt et partem non, quod in primo impedimento non accidebat; simul enim omnes solis partes videntur a nobis, sed non perfecte, sicut visibilis est.

Ad intellectum autem comparatur intelligibile per accidens quidem etiam secundum quantitatem dimensivam, in quantum intellectus a sensu accipit; unde etiam intellectus noster impeditur a comprehensione infiniti secundum quantitatem dimensivam, ita quod aliquid eius est in intellectu et aliquid extra intellectum. Per se autem non comparatur ad intellectum intelligibile secundum quantitatem dimensivam, cum intellectus sit virtus non utens organo corporali; sed per se comparatur ad ipsum, solum secundum quantitatem virtualem. Et ideo in his quae per se intelliguntur sine coniunctione ad sensum, non impeditur comprehensio intellectus nisi propter excessum quantitatis virtualis; quando scilicet quod intelligitur, habet modum intelligendi perfectiorem quam sit modum quo intellectus intelligit; sicut si aliquis cognoscat hanc conclusionem: Triangulum habet tres angulos aequales duobus rectis; per probabilem rationem utpote per auctoritatem, vel quia ita communiter dicitur, non comprehendit ipsam; non quod unam partem eius ignoret, alia scita, sed quia ista conclusio est scibilis per demonstrationem, ad quam cognoscens nondum pervenit, et ideo non comprehendit ipsam, quia non stat perfecte sub cognitione eius."

56. In view of such meanings, one is justified in foreseeing the use of 'extension' to mean 'a stretching out to more and more things' and the

285

use of 'comprehension' to signify 'a constantly improving grasp of the things known'. But more of this later.

57. Cf. among others: Antoine Arnauld et M. Nicole, *op. cit.,* p. 55; Joshua Oldfield, *op. cit.,* pp. 70-71; Edmund Purchotius, *op cit.,* Vol. I, p. 60; Isaac Watts, *op. cit.,* p. 37; Dominicus Angeloni, *op. cit.,* L. I. p. 18; Venceslao Pieralisi, *op. cit.,* p. 110; Tilmanus Pesch, *op. cit.,* p. 51; John J. Toohey, *op cit.,* p. 4; Carolus Frick, *op. cit.,* Vol. I, p. 11; Ch. Lahr, *op. cit.,* Vol. I, p. 492; Jacques Maritain, *op. cit.,* p. 21; Henry Grenier, *op. cit.,* Vol. I, p. 35; Sylvester J. Hartman, *op. cit.,* pp. 22-23; Gottlob E. Schulze, *op. cit.,* pp. 50-51; Ernest Reinhold, *op. cit.,* p. 115; Dr. Friedrich Ueberweg, *op. cit.,* p. 126.

58. *Quodl.* V, q. 5, a. 2, ad 1: "Intellectus intelligit aliquid *dupliciter: uno modo formaliter,* et sic intelligit specie intelligibili qua fit in actu; *alio modo* sicut instrumento quo utitur ad aliud intelligendum: et hoc modo intellectus verbo intelligit, quia format verbum ad hoc quod intelligat rem."

59. *De Pot.,* q. 7, a. 9: "Prima enim intellecta sunt res extra animam, in quae primo intellectus intelligenda fertur. Secunda autem intellecta dicuntur intentiones consequentes modum intelligendi: hoc enim secundo intellectus intelligit in quantum reflectitur supra se ipsum, intelligens se intelligere et modum quo intelligit."

60. In VII *Metaph.,* lect. 17, n. 1658: "Logicus enim considerat modum praedicandi, et non existentiam rei."

61. In IV *Metaph.,* lect. 4, n. 574: "Et huiusmodi, scilicet ens rationis, est proprie subiectum logicae." Cf. In I *Post. Analyt.,* lect. 20, n. 171.

62. St. Albertus Magnus, "Metaphysica", *Opera Omnia,* ed. Bernhardus Geyer (Germania: Monasterium Westfalorum In Aedibus Aschendorff, 1960), Lib. I, Tract, I, p. 3: "Istae igitur tres sunt scientiae speculativae, et non sunt plures, sicut et in *III Libro nostro De Anima* nos dixisse meminimus, quia scientiae logicae non considerant ens vel partem entis aliquam, sed potius intentiones secundas circa res per sermonem positas, per quas viae habentur veniendi de noto ad ignotum secundum syllogismum inferentem vel probantem." Cf. St. Albertus Magnus, *Commentaria In Perhihermenias Aristotelis* (Parisiis: Ludovicus Vivès, 1890), L. I, Tr. 1, c. 1, p. 1.

63. Cf. L'Abbé Levesque, *Précis de Philosophie* (Paris: Ancienne Librairie Poussielgue, 1913), Vol. I, p. 251. He also mentions extension and comprehension in Vol. II, pp. 12-14.

64. Antoine Arnauld and M. Nicole, *op. cit.,* Première Partie, c. 7, p. 62: "En voilà plus qu'il n'en faut touchant les cinq universaux qu'on traite dans l'école avec tant d'étendue. . . ."

65. Cf. Joseph T. Clark, *Conventional Logic and Modern Logic* (Woodstock, Md.: Woodstock College Press, 1952), p. 11; Clarence I. Lewis, "Notes on the Logic of Intension", *Structure, Method, And Meaning:*

Essays in Honor of Henry M. Sheffer (New York: Liberal Arts Press, 1951), pp. 25-26.

66. The division of logic into formal and material need not detain us. For a detailed explanation of such a division propounded by John of St. Thomas and others, consult: Thomas McGovern, *The Division of Logic* (Quebec: Librairie Philosophique M. Doyon, 1956).

67. Cf. In I *Periherm.*, Prooem., n. 1: "Additur autem et tertia operatio. . . ."

68. *Ia*, q. 79, a. 8: "Ratiocinari autem est procedere de uno intellecto ad aliud, ad veritatem intelligibilem cognoscendam." Cf. In I *Post. Analyt.*, Prooem., n. 4.

69. *De Ver.*, q. 8, a. 2, obj. 4: "Praeterea, sicut per demonstrationem scire est perfectissimus modus cognoscendi complexa, ita scire quod quid est, est perfectissimus modus cognoscendi incomplexa. Sed omne complexum quod scitur per demonstrationem, comprehenditur. Ergo omne id de quo scitur quid est, comprehenditur. Sed illi qui vident Deum per essentiam, sciunt de eo quid est, cum nihil aliud sit scire quid est quam scire essentiam rei. Ergo comprehendunt angeli divinam essentiam."

70. *Ibid.*: "Res comprehenditur cuius difinitio cognoscitur, si tamen ipsa definitio comprehendatur. Sed sicut possibile est cognoscere rem sine comprehensione, ita et definitionem ipsius; et sic res ipsa remanet non comprehensa. Angelus autem, quamvis videat aliquo modo quid est Deus, non tamen hoc comprehendit."

71. *Post. Analyt.*, II, c. 17, 99a17-36 (Cf. *The Basic Works of Aristotle*, ed. Richard McKeon, pp. 182-83). The Latin translation by William Moerbek reads as follows: "Habet autem sic consequi causam adinvicem et cuius est causa et in quo est causa. Unumquodque quidem accipienti, cuius est causa *in plus* est; ut quatuor aequales qui sunt extra, *in plus* sunt quam triangulus aut quadrangulus: in omnibus autem et in aeque. Quaecunque enim quatuor rectis aequales qui sunt extra et medium similiter est. Est autem medium ratio primi extremi; ex quo omnes scientiae fiunt per definitiones: ut folio fluere similiter sequitur vitem et *excellit*, et ficum et *excellit;* sed non omnia, sed aequalium est. Si vero accipiat aliquis primum medium, ratio fluendi folium est. Erit enim primum quidem in altera medium, quoniam huiusmodi sunt omnia. Deinde huius medium quoniam succus densatur, aut aliquid aliud huiusmodi. Quid autem est folio fluere? densar in contactu seminis succum. In figuris autem sic assignabit quaerentibus consecutionem causae et cuius est causa: sit enim A quidem in B omni, B autem in unoquoque eorum quae sunt D, *in plus* autem; B quidem universaliter utique in ipsis erit D. Hoc autem dico universale, quod non convertitur: primum autem universale, cui unumquodque quidem non convertitur, omnia autem convertuntur et *excedunt*. In ipsis D igitur causa ipsius A, B est. Oportet itaque A *in plus* quam B *extendi*. Si vero non, quid magis erit causa hoc illius?" (Certain words in this text have been italicized for the sake of emphasis).

287

72. Aristotelis, *Opera Omnia* (Parisiis: Didot Et Sociis, 1627), Vol. I, c. 14, 19, 47, p. 169.

73. H. Bonitz, *Index Aristotelis* (Secunda editio; Gram: Akademische Druck U. Verlagsanstalt, 1955), p. 568.

74. *Ibid.*

75. *Ibid.*, p. 792.

76. *Ibid.*, p. 789.

77. Cf. In II *Post. Analyt.*, lect. 19, n. 578-79.

78. *Ibid.*, lect. 13, n. 529, 530, 532, 533, 535.

79. *Ibid.*, n. 532.

80. *Post. Analyt.*, II, c. 13, 96a24-26: "Eorum igitur quae insunt semper unicuique, quaedam extenduntur in plus, non tamen extra genus: dico autem in plus esse quaecunque insunt quidem unicuique universaliter, at vero et alii." The ancient version of Aristotle contains the words *extenduntur in plus,* while the more recent version *latius sese extendunt.* Cf. St. Thomas Aquinas, *Opera Omnia*, Vol. 18, p. 208.

81. Cf. among others: William Best, *op. cit.*, p. 16; Levi Hedge, *op. cit.*, p. 19; S. E. Parker, *op. cit.*, p. 62; John Leechman, *op. cit.*, p. 33; Brother Louis of Poissy, *op. cit.*, p. 9; Attilius Munzi, *op. cit.*, p. 22; Andrew H. Bachhuber, *op. cit.*, p. 17; Monroe C. Beardsley, *op. cit.*, pp. 53-54.

82. *Prior Analytics,* I, c. 1, 24b16-17. Cf. St. Thomas, In *Periherm.*, lect. 1, n. 5.

83. Thomas of Erfort, *Grammatica Speculativa*, ed. Ludovicus Vivès (Quebec: Librairie Philosophique M. Doyon, 1962), c. 6, n. 7: "*Terminus* vero dicit rationem terminandi resolutiones Syllogismi, quia dialecticus resolvit Syllogismum in Propositiones, et Propositiones in Subjectum, et Praedicatum; quae dicuntur *termini* secundum Logicum."

84. For an interesting and correct use of the word 'extension' in which it is clearly shown how the third operation of the intellect presupposes universal predicability, consult Thomas McGovern's *The Division of Logic*, pp. 126-27. "The Middle, in other words, is contained within the extension of one of the extremes, while containing the other within its own" (p. 127). Father McGovern also quotes St. Albert who explains how this part of logic names things by analogy to continuous quantity.

85. Cf. among others: Louis Couturat, *op. cit.*, p. 444; Francis Bowen, *op. cit.*, pp. 67-68; J. H. Gilmore, *op. cit.*, p. 37; John Rickaby, *op. cit.*, p. 18.

86. In *Post Analyt.*, Prooem., n. 4: "Sunt autem rationis *tres* actus. . . . *Secunda* vero operatio intellectus est compositio vel divisio intellectus, in qua est iam verum vel falsum." Cf. *De Ver.*, q. 14, a. 1; Aristotle, *On Interpretation*, c. 1, 16a10-11; I *Periherm.*, lect. 3, n. 24-25.

87. Judgment names a perfection of knowledge which is consequent to the act of reasoning. It is the result of an enunciation.

88. In *De Trin.*, q. 5, a. 3: "Secunda vero operatio respicit ipsum esse rei, quod quidem resultat ex congregatione principiorum rei in compositis

vel ipsam simplicem naturam rei concomitatur, ut in substantiis simplicibus. Et quia veritas intellectus est ex hoc quod conformatur rei, patet quod secundum hanc secundam operationem intellectus non potest vere abstrahere quod secundum rem coniunctum est, quia in abstrahendo significaretur esse separatio secundum ipsum esse rei, sicut si abstraho hominem ab albedine dicendo: homo non est albus, significo esse separationem in re. Unde si secundum rem homo et albedo non sint separata, erit intellectus falsus. Hac ergo operatione intellectus vere abstrahere non potest nisi ea quae sunt secundum rem separata. . . ." Cf. In III *De Anima*, lect. 11, n. 747; *De Ver.*, q. 14 a. 1.

89. Cf. Footnote #85 on p. 288 of this study.

90. In I *Post. Analyt.*, Prooem., n. 4: "Una enim actio intellectus est intelligentia indivisibilium sive incomplexorum, secundum quam concipit quid est res."

91. Cf. *De Pot.*, q. 8, a 1.

92. In *De Trin.*, q. 5, a. 3: "Prima quidem operatio respicit ipsam naturam rei, secundum quam res intellecta aliquem gradum in entibus obtinet, sive sit res completa, ut totum aliquod, sive res incompleta, ut pars vel accidens."

93. In III *De Anima*, lect. 11, n. 746: ". . . incomplexa non sunt vera neque falsa, tum quia intellectus non decipitur in eo quod quid est. . . ." Cf. Aristotle, *On The Soul*, III, c. 6, 430a26-28.

94. St. Thomas, In III *Phys.*, lect. 5, n. 322: "Sciendum est quod ens dividitur in decem praedicamenta non univoce, sicut genus in species, sed secundum diversum modum essendi. Modi autem essendi proportionales sun modis praedicandi. Praedicando enim aliquid de aliquo altero, dicimus hoc esse illud: unde et decem genera entis dicuntur decem praedicamenta."

95. This paragraph and the next two are a paraphrase of St. Thomas, In II *De Anima*, lect. 12, n. 378: "Universale potest accipi dupliciter. *Uno modo* potest dici universale ipsa natura communis, prout subiacet intentioni universalitatis. *Alio modo* secundum se. Sicut et album potest accipi dupliciter: vel id, cui accidit esse album, vel ipsummet, secundum quod subest albedini. Ista autem natura, cui advenit intentio universalitatis, puta natura hominis, habet duplex esse: unum quidem materiale, secundum quod est in materia naturali; aliud autem immateriale, secundum quod est in intellectu. Secundum igitur quod habet esse in materia naturali, non potest ei advenire intentio universalitatis, quia per materiam individuatur. Advenit igitur ei universalitatis intentio, secundum quod abstrahitur a materia individuali. Non est autem possibile, quod abstrahatur a materia individuali realiter, sicut Platonici posuerunt. Non enim est homo naturalis, id est realis, nisi in his carnibus, et in his ossibus, sicut probat Philosophus in *septimo Metaphysicae*. Relinquitur igitur, quod natura humana non habet esse praeter principia individuantis, nisi tantum in intellectu." Cf. In VII *Metaphy.*, lect. 13, n. 1570; *Ia-IIae*, q. 29, a. 6; *Ia*, q. 85, a. 3, ad 1.

96. Cf. St. Thomas, *Ia*, q. 85, a 3, ad 1: "Uno modo, secundum quod natura universalis consideratur simul cum intentione universalitatis."

97. The first meaning will be used in the next section of this study.

98. Cf. St. Thomas, In I. *Sent.*, d. 7, q. 2, a 1.

99. St. Albertus Magnus, *Commentaria In Praedicamenta Aristotelis* (Parisiis: Ludovicus Vivès, 1890), L. II, Tr. I, c. 1, p. 2: ". . . consistit in decem generibus praedicabilium sive praedicamentorum."

100. Cf. St. Albertus Magnus, *De Praedicabilibus* (Quebec: Les Presses Universitaires Laval, 1951), L. I., Tr. II, c. 1, p. 23.

101. Aristotle, *Categories*, c. 4, 1b25-29. Cf. St. Thomas, In V *Metaphy.*, lect. 9, n. 891-92; In III *Phys.*, lect. 5, n. 322. Edward Brerewood in his *Tractatus Quidam Logici De Praedicabilibus Et Praedicamentis* (Oxoniae: Excudebat Guilielmus Turner, 1631), Tr. 9, Sect. 2, p. 208, defines predicaments as "series generum specierum, et individuorum, secundum sub et supra positorum" (series of genera, species and individuals according to what is positioned below and above).

102. Cf. among others: Immanuel Kant, *op. cit.*, p. 30; Georg Wilhelm Friedrich Hegel, *op. cit.*, p. 187; Sir William Hamilton, *op. cit.*, p. 140-41; Augustus De Morgan, *op. cit.*, p. 61; Francis Bowen, *op. cit.*, p. 66; Henry Day, *op. cit.*, p. 60; Wilhelm Trougott Krug, *op. cit.*, p. 76; Ernst Reinhold, *op. cit.*, p. 115; Wilhelm Esser, *op. cit.*, p. 74.

103. Cf. *Categories*, c. 6, 5a15-36.

104. *Ibid.*, c.6, 5a37-38.

105. Sir William Hamilton, *op. cit.*, p. 141.

106. Porphyry, "The Introduction Of Porphyry", *The Organon, Or Logical Treatises Of Aristotle*, trans. Octavius Freire Owen (London: Henry G. Bohn, 1853), Vol. II, p. 614.

107. St. Albertus Magnus, *De Praedicabilibus* (Quebec: Les Presses Universitaires Laval, 1951), L. I., Tr. II, c. 1, p. 23: "Et sic universale est, quod de sua aptitudine est in multis et de multis." Aristotle defines the universal in *Metaph.*, VII, c. 13, 1038b11: "that is called universal which is such as to belong to more than one thing."

107a. Here the word 'universal' is used according to the first meaning which is explained on p. 159 of this treatise.

108. St. Albertus Magnus, *De Praedicabilibus*, L.I., Tr. II, c. 1, p. 24: "Universale autem sic acceptum prout est praedicabile quod in multis et de multis, aut inest essentialiter, aut accidentaliter: sive ut essentia, sive ut accidens. Si inest ut essentia: aut inest ut tota essentia, aut ut pars essentialis. Si inest ut tota formalis essentia, constat quod est species, quia species totum est formale esse individuorum de quibus praedicatur: quia quidquid est post speciem, est de materia vel individuantibus. Si autem ut pars essentialis: tunc aut est [sic, pars] secundum potentiam in qua est esse per inchoationem, aut est pars secundum actum in quo est esse secundum actum perfectum. Et priori quidem modo est genus, secundo vero modo est differentia. Si vero inest ut accidens: aut inest ut accidens naturae, quod de ipsius naturae aptitudine causatur

et emanat: aut ut accidens commune, quod est accidens individui. Et priori quidem modo est proprium, et secundo modo est accidens vocatum." Cf. *Ibid.*, c. 9, p. 55a.

109. Porphyry, "The Introduction Of Porphyry". Cf. *The Organon, Or Logical Treatises Of Aristotle,* trans. Octavius Freire Owen (London: Henry G. Bohn, 1853), Vol. II, c. 5, p. 623.

110. *Ibid.*

111. *Ibid.*, p. 624.

112. Aristotle, "The Topics", I, c. 5. Cf. *The Organon Or Logical Treatises Of Aristotle,* trans. Octavius Freire Owen (London: G. Bell And Sons, Limited, 1910), Vol. II, p. 365.

113. Cf. among others: James H. Hyslop, *op. cit.,* p. 72; F. H. Bradley, *op. cit.,* pp. 178-79; Abbé Arthur Robert, *op. cit.,* p. 16; L. Susan Stebbing, *A Modern Elementary Logic,* p. 104; Jacques Maritain, *Formal Logic,* pp. 21, 127.

114. Porphyry, *op. cit.,* c. 4, pp. 622-23.

115. Aristotle, *Top.,* I, c. 5, p. 364.

116. Porphyry, *op. cit.,* c. 15, p. 631.

117. Porphyry, *op. cit.,* c. 3, p. 621.

118. *Ibid.*

119. *Ibid.*, p. 622.

120. *Ibid.*

121. *Ibid.*

122. Aristotle, *Top.,* VI, c. 6, p. 480.

123. This statement should suffice to refute those logicians who maintain that extension is signified by nouns and comprehension by adjectives. Cf. Charles Gray Shaw, *op. cit.,* p. 45.

124. Porphyry, *op. cit.,* c. 1, p. 613.

125. *Ibid.*, c. 2, pp. 611-12.

126. Aristotle, *Top.,* I, c. 5, p. 364.

127. Cf. *Ibid.* Cf. Sylvester Maurus, *Aristotelis Opera Omnia,* ed. Franciscus Ehrle, S. J. (Parisiis: P. Lethielleux, 1886), Vol. I, p. 398: "Genus autem est, quod pluribus et differentibus specie attribuitur in quaestione quid est." Because 'extension' is implied by 'many things', it follows that all the predicables imply extension.

128. Porphyry, *op. cit.,* p. 610.

129. *Ibid.*, p. 611.

130. Aristotle, *Top.,* IV, c. 6, p. 438.

131. Porphyry, *op. cit.,* p. 617.

132. *Ibid.*

133. Cf. St. Thomas, In V. *Metaph,* lect. 22, n. 1119-27.

134. Aristotle, *Top.,* IV, c. 1, pp. 421-22. When Ross substitutes the word 'denotation' for 'extension', he seems to falsify the meaning of the text because denotation is in the line of comprehension. Cf. *The Works Of Aristotle,* ed. and trans. W. D. Ross (London: Oxford University Press, 1950), Vol. I.

135. *Ibid.,* c. 6, p. 438.
136. *Ibid.,* p. 482.
137. Aristotle, *Categ.,* c. 5, 2b19-21. Cf. *The Works Of Aristotle,* ed. and trans. W. D. Ross.
138. Porphyry, *op. cit.,* c. 2, p. 616.
139. *Ibid.,* p. 617.
140. *Ibid.,* c. 7, p. 625.
141. *Ibid.*
142. *Ibid.,* c. 8, p. 626.
143. Consult p. 104 of this treatise.
144. Porphyry, *op. cit.,* c. 3, p. 621.
145. *Ibid.,* c. 2, p. 616.
146. Aristotle, *Top.,* IV, c. 1, p. 420.
147. Aristotle, *Categ.,* c. 3, 3b21-23. The meaning of this passage is paraphrased on p. 119 of this study.

FOOTNOTES TO EPILOGUE

1. Cf. among others: Kenneth F. Dougherty, *op. cit.,* pp. 35-37 (comprehension and extension of the concept), pp. 55-58 (the predicables); Rev. Henri Grenier, *op. cit.,* Vol. I, p. 28 (comprehension and extension of the concept), pp. 163-67 (the predicables); Vincent Edward Smith, *op. cit.,* pp. 35-38 (an entire chapter is devoted to extension and comprehension), pp. 40-52 (the predicables); Andrew H. Bachhuber, *op. cit.,* pp. 17-22. (comprehension, extension, and their inverse relationship), pp. 242-53 (the predicables).
2. W. Stanley Jevons, *Studies In Deductive Logic* (Fourth Edition; Macmillan And Co., 1908), p. 126.
3. Cf. Regis Jolivet, *op. cit.,* p. 60.
4. Cf. Andrew H. Bachhuber, *op. cit.,* p. 17.

FOOTNOTES TO APPENDIX I

1. Sir Richard Steele, *A Grammar Of The English Tongue* (The Fourth Edition, corrected; London: J. Roberts et al, 1721), pp. 64-65.
2. R. A. Sicard, Élémens de grammaire générale appliqués à la langue française (seconde édition; Paris: Chez Deterville, 1801), Vol. I, p. 99: "L'étendue d'un mot est le lieu qu'il occupe, pour l'esprit qui le considère; la compréhension est la totalité des idées partielles qui le constituent. Ainsi, les mots qui l'on appelle articles, et dont je traiterai, dans le chapitre suivant, déterminent l'étendue; et les mots adjectifs, dont il est, ici, question, affectent la compréhension; et ils l'affectent, en ajoutant au nom une ou plusieurs idées accessoires, qui font partie de la nature totale de l'objet énoncé par le nom."
The position of a grammarian such as Solomon Barrett is not worth

analyzing in this appendix because he makes no distinction between 'meaning' and 'extension'. If the reader wishes to consult this grammarian's remarks on 'extension', he should read pp. 24, 85-86, 93-95 of Solomon Barrett's text entitled *The Principles Of Grammar* (Revised edition; Boston: Geo. C. Rand And Avery, 1862).

3. James MacKaye, *The Logic Of Language* (Hanover, N. H.: Dartmouth College Publications, 1939), pp. 29-30.

4. Maurice Grevisse, *Le Bon Usage, Cours de Grammaire Française et de Langage Français* (Cinquième édition; Paris: Librairie Orientaliste Paul Geuthner, 1953), p. 162: "*La compréhension* de l'idée exprimée par le nom est le nombre plus ou moins grand des notes ou éléments que comprend cette idée. Son *extension,* ou *l'étendue* de la signification du nom, est le nombre plus ou moins grand des êtres auxquels l'idée peut s'appliquer."

5. Robert T. Harris and James L. Jarrett, *Language and Informal Logic* (New York: Longmans, Green And Co., 1956), p. 106.